ADVANCE PRAISE

"Today, many parents feel the need to "protect" their children in public school. At the same time, few people understand the inner workings of the public school system. Kelly Himes Brolly has succeeded in writing this excellent book to educate and equip both parents and educators about the laws and rules that govern public school K-12 and about the federal and state constitutional rights of parents and students. This book is written for the layperson and is user-friendly, comprehensive, and succinct – which is not an easy balance to strike. This guide is a must-have tool for parents who need to effectively navigate the complexities of legal issues impacting their children in public school. I recommend this book to you without reservation."

— OLLIE L. GARMON, III, RETIRED JUDGE,
ATLANTA, GEORGIA

"Having spent 43 years as a K-12 public school teacher, coach, middle and high school principal, and 17 years as a school superintendent, I read with great interest *Laws, Rules, and Rights: A Guide to Protecting Children in Public Schools*. My first thought was that I truly wished I had it in my graduate education classes. It summarized everything one needed to know about education in the United States, and how public education operates at the federal, state, and local levels. It also presented these ideas in a simple, yet articulate manner. Second, this book clearly described how parents could successfully advocate for their children in the complex world of education. It explained the rules, and how to advocate, and gave clear examples of how to proceed in a professional manner. I heartily endorse this book to advocate for children and encourage parents and school professionals. It is a trusted guide to support our most precious resource, our children."

— JIM RYAN, ED.D., RETIRED SUPERINTENDENT,
PLYMOUTH-CANTON COMMUNITY SCHOOLS, MICHIGAN

Laws, Rules, and Rights

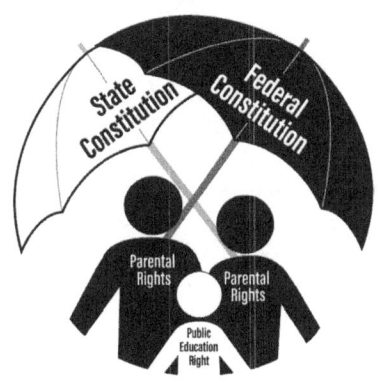

A Guide to Protecting Children in Public Schools

KELLY HIMES BROLLY

Laws, Rules, and Rights: A Guide to Protecting Children in Public Schools
Published by Double Umbrella Publications, LLC
Greensboro, Georgia, U.S.A.

Copyright ©2023, KELLY HIMES BROLLY.

No part of this book may be reproduced in any form or by any mechanical means, including information storage and retrieval systems without permission in writing from the publisher/author. All images, logos, quotes, and trademarks included in this book are subject to use according to trademark and copyright laws of the United States of America.

HIMES BROLLY, KELLY, Author
LAWS, RULES, AND RIGHTS
KELLY HIMES BROLLY

Library of Congress Control Number: 2023901234

ISBN: 979-8-9875832-0-3, 979-8-9875832-3-4 (paperback)
ISBN: 979-8-9875832-2-7 (hardcover)
ISBN: 979-8-9875832-1-0 (digital)

EDUCATION / Parent Participation
EDUCATION / Administration / School Superintendents & Principals
LAW / Educational Law & Legislation

Book Design: Michelle M. White (mmwbooks.com)
Publishing Consultant: Susie Schaefer (finishthebookpublishing.com)

Image Credits:
Cover photo: JenkoAtaman/stock.adobe.com
Author Photo: Haigwood Studios Photography, Roswell, Georgia
Part I photo: andreykr/stock.adobe.com
Part II photo: doganmesut/stock.adobe.com
Part III photo: Natallia/stock.adobe.com
Part III Steps Graphic derived from: Icons-Studio/stock.adobe.com
K-12 Public School Building Image: Fred Stark (Stark Design & Illustration, LLC)
All other artwork and logo design by Michelle M. White

Disclaimer: This book is for educational purposes only. No information contained in this book should be construed as legal advice, nor is it intended to be a substitute for legal counsel on any subject matter. The purchase or use of this book does not create an attorney-client relationship. The information in this book may not reflect the current law in your jurisdiction, particularly where new laws were enacted in the most recent legislative session. The inclusion of links to websites, state bar association websites, and legal groups that provide representation, does not constitute a referral or endorsement of these links, websites, or groups. Readers are encouraged to contact an education law attorney in their jurisdiction with any questions.

All rights reserved by KELLY HIMES BROLLY and
DOUBLE UMBRELLA PUBLICATIONS, LLC.

This book is printed in the United States of America.

*This book is dedicated to
all the hardworking educators and parents
who send their children to public schools.*

CONTENTS

PURPOSE OF THIS BOOK..xi

INTRODUCTION 1

PART I
THE STATE SCHOOL SYSTEM THAT GOVERNS PUBLIC SCHOOLS K-12

A Diagram of Public Schools K-12 8

CHAPTER 1
THE UNITED STATES CONSTITUTION AND THE TENTH AMENDMENT

The States Are in Charge of Education 11
Federal Involvement in Education......................................13

CHAPTER 2
THE STATE CONSTITUTION

The State Constitution's "Education Article" 17

CHAPTER 3
STATE SCHOOL LAWS

The Importance of State School Laws..................................21
Researching State School Laws 45

CHAPTER 4
OTHER STATE LAWS THAT AFFECT PUBLIC SCHOOLS K-12

State Open Meetings Acts 50
State Open Records Acts..54

CONTENTS

State Laws that Give Public Schools and Public Libraries Exemptions
  from State Obscenity Laws 56
Challenging State Obscenity Exemptions 59
New State Mental Health Laws 63

CHAPTER 5

THE STATE BOARD OF EDUCATION AND THE STATE SCHOOL SUPERINTENDENT

The State Board of Education...65
The State School Superintendent..71

CHAPTER 6

THE LOCAL BOARD OF EDUCATION AND THE LOCAL SCHOOL SUPERINTENDENT

The Local Board of Education..75
The Local School Superintendent 84

CHAPTER 7

CHARTER ENTITIES

The Definition and Original Purpose of "Charters" 87
Moving from a Compliance Model to a Testing and Accountability Model 89
The Growing Use of Charter Entities 90
State Laws Governing Charter Entities 91
Key Features of Charter Entities 93
A Caution: Measuring "Improvement" in School Discipline.......................95
Key Provisions of a Charter Document 98

CHAPTER 8

MAGNET SCHOOLS

The Purpose and Characteristics of Magnet Schools 99

CHAPTER 9

CONTROVERSIAL MATERIAL AND CONTENT

Sources of Controversial Material and Content 103
The States' Power Over Curriculum..106

The Public Forum Doctrine: Private Speech in Public Schools......................107
Governmental Tort Immunity and Protecting Students...........................111

PART II
FEDERAL AND STATE CONSTITUTIONAL RIGHTS

The Separation of Powers Doctrine 116
Balancing Government Power and Constitutional Rights........................117
Federal and State Constitutional Protections Are Not Automatic 117
Overview of How Courts Examine Constitutional Rights........................120

CHAPTER 10
STATE CONSTITUTIONAL RIGHTS

The State Constitutional "Right to a Public Education"............................125
The State Constitution's "Bill of Rights" 126

CHAPTER 11
FEDERAL CONSTITUTIONAL RIGHTS

Express and Implied Federal Constitutional Rights 131
The U.S. Constitution's Protection of "Parental Rights"............................134
The Religion Clauses of the First Amendment....................................138
The Free Speech Clause of the First Amendment 147

PART III
APPLYING WHAT YOU HAVE LEARNED

CHAPTER 12
PROTECTING CHILDREN

Submit a Parent Opt-Out of Specific Instructional Materials and Content..........159
Research and Investigate 160
Advocate with Facts Before Your State and Local Boards 162
Connect with Others 164
A Note of Encouragement 164

CONTENTS

ACKNOWLEDGMENTS 167

APPENDIX A:
BLANK SAMPLE PARENT OPT-OUT 169

APPENDIX B:
RELIGION CLAUSES IN THE STATE CONSTITUTIONS 173

APPENDIX C:
STATE AND LOCAL RESOURCES..191

NOTES..235

ABOUT THE AUTHOR...245
How to work with Kelly 246

PURPOSE OF THIS BOOK

The purpose of *Laws, Rules, and Rights: A Guide to Protecting Children in Public Schools* is to teach parents and educators about the structure of the public school system, and more importantly, how to protect children in public schools using state school laws and constitutional rights.

WHY THIS IS IMPORTANT...

Today's Americans lack civic and constitutional literacy, particularly when it comes to public schools and their constitutional rights. This problem permeates all levels of society, including several generations of parents, educators, and even university professors. Beginning in the 1960s, public schools stopped teaching civics and began to teach social studies, which lacked the depth and rigor of previous civics classes. Today, universities and even some law schools teach courses in "education law" that bypass state school laws. Instead, they focus on federal education programs, which make up less than one-tenth of public school funding. As a result, few people know that public schools are governed by state school laws, and state and local board of education rules that have the force of law. Fewer still know that they have constitutional rights that include parental rights, the free exercise of religion, the freedom of speech, and the freedom *not* to speak. These rights are protected under both the federal and state constitutions. The right to a free public education is guaranteed by each state's constitution. This book has clear explanations, illustrations, detailed instructions, and links to state constitutions and laws in all 50 states. It will help you learn the "system" of public education and, more importantly, how to protect children in public schools.

INTRODUCTION

Over the past 34 years, I have viewed the public school system as a teacher, lawyer, parent volunteer, school advocate, and independent contractor with the Georgia State Board of Education's Charter Division. I have also co-authored an *amicus curiae* (friend of the court) brief submitted to the United States Supreme Court on a federal constitutional issue. Along the way, I have learned how to navigate the state school laws, and the state and local board of education rules. All this experience has given me a unique understanding of the public school system. My goal is to share this information with others.

OUR CHILDREN'S EXPERIENCE IN PUBLIC SCHOOLS

When our children were in preschool, I was a litigation attorney in a large law firm. I had taught in public schools for three years and left the teaching profession for law school. My view of public education was and still is that the system has a lot to offer, but you cannot expect it to provide the whole of your children's education. I did not object to *what* the public schools were teaching. Instead, I thought the public schools had grown weak on the basics. I considered it my responsibility to supplement the areas that were important to me.

To give our children a good start, my husband and I chose a Montessori preschool program they attended through kindergarten. I am a fan of accredited Montessori programs because they allow children to discover and enjoy learning with a hands-on approach.[1] They use phonics-based principles to teach reading (including cursive sandpaper letters) and an elaborate bead system to teach math. There are few, if any, worksheets, and no tests. Given the importance of reading, I also helped our children learn to read using a book that was recommended by a friend and college education professor.[2] The scripted lessons only took 10-15 minutes a day. I used the same book for all our children.

Of course, life is full of curve balls, and just as our oldest child was entering grade school, our second child was diagnosed with a chronic medical condition. I temporarily left the practice of law and, with little ones still at home, researched an array of curriculum[3] with a mind toward homeschooling. In the end, I decided to supplement their public school education with classical education materials in history, grammar, vocabulary, and math.

Overall, I emphasized hands-on activities. For history, I made a "timeline" on a 22-foot roll of paper that we hung in our playroom. Using a history series for children, we colored maps and wrote in cuneiform on clay.[4] One night we made an African dinner and read traditional African life lessons from Anansi the Spider. We also read American history with a plethora of materials.[5] For grammar, I taught them a song for the months of the year, poems, traditional short stories, and a list of pronouns to sing and memorize.[6] I thought, "If the kids can sing marketing jingles, they can certainly learn the song for the months of the year." When public school was in session, they rarely had written work from our activities. During the summers, we used inexpensive workbooks for vocabulary and math. Finally, we supplemented public school with lots of books, audio character lessons in the minivan,[7] a stay-at-home mom involved in the schools, music lessons, athletic programs, summer camps, a few tutors, and most importantly, our church. These supplemental materials, which we did from first grade through middle school, made a big difference in their otherwise public education.

As you can see, my focus was on what I considered *missing* or needed to be *reinforced* in our children's education. Twenty-plus years later, the problem is compounded. It is an issue of *what* is being taught. Today, many parents object to public school content on political, moral, or religious grounds. Now parents must: (1) identify what is missing or objectionable, (2) dismantle the objectionable teaching, and (3) add their instruction. This generation of parents has a far more difficult task.

So, I will pose the same questions that I asked myself 20+ years ago: "What do children need to live a fulfilling and productive life?" The things that came to mind were:

- sense of security and love at home with our families;
- a sense of purpose and worth derived from God, who I believe made us and has a plan for our lives;

- faith and hope because life will be difficult at times;
- competence in our skills and work because 40+ hours a week for 40+ years is a long time;
- friendships for fun, encouragement, and to bring out the best in us;
- self-discipline because if you discipline yourself, you can avoid a vast array of difficulties and pain in life; and
- healthy eating and exercise habits because we only get one body, and there are no trade-ins.

These were our thoughts and goals, some of which my husband and I met and some we partially met. But as you consider the critical task of raising children, these are essential ideas to consider, too, not just statistics, curriculum, and test scores.

So, ask yourself, "What is important to your family and reflects your family's values?" Then ask, "Is there a way to accomplish this using your state's public school system?" As I have often said to our children, "If you want to advocate for change or get the most from the system, you need to learn the system."

LEARNING THE PUBLIC SCHOOL "SYSTEM"

Each state has a public school system based upon: (1) the state constitution's "education article;" (2) the state's school laws; (3) the state board of education's rules; and (4) the local boards of education's rules, all of which have the force of law. These components, and the federal constitutional provisions that undergird them, make up the public school system in each state. These laws and rules are enacted by the elected representatives of the state. As a result, they tend to represent the views of the *majority* of voters in the state.

Additionally, we have federal and state constitutional rights. At the federal level, the U.S. Constitution and the Bill of Rights protect our federal constitutional rights. All 50 states also have a state constitution and "bill of rights" or "declaration of rights" that protect our state constitutional rights. Together, these two constitutions give us two layers of protection – one at the federal level and one at the state level. Our federal constitutional rights include the fundamental right of parents to make decisions regarding their children's care, custody, control, and education.[8] Parents also have a right to the free exercise of their religion, which includes how they raise their minor children.[9] The freedom of speech, which includes conduct that constitutes speech, and the freedom not to speak, provide further protections. Using these constitutional rights, parents whose views are not represented in the state's laws and rules may be able to opt out or obtain exemptions. In other words, individual constitutional rights often protect the *minority* of voters in the state.

When these two systems work together, the laws of the *majority* are enforced and the rights of the *minority* are asserted and respected. Like rocks in a rock tumbler, our system of laws and constitutional rights refine one another. The laws become more specific to their purpose, and the rights become more defined and protected. The system operates like a well-oiled machine. But what happens when parents realize their children in public schools are receiving an education that undermines the parents' morals, values, and in some cases, religious beliefs? What happens when people do not understand the public school system and their constitutional rights?

ISSUES

Today, many parents want to "protect" their children in public schools. For example, some of the most common questions parents ask are: "Can the public schools allow books that are considered obscene under state criminal laws? Can the public schools require students to learn raced-based history theories K-12? Can the public schools teach certain sex education topics to young students? Can the public schools require my children to read a book that includes graphic descriptions of child molestation?" Throughout this book, I do not address the merits of these controversial issues nor provide pictures of what is and is not permitted.[10] These are personal decisions for parents and guardians. Instead, this book focuses on the system: the laws and rules that govern public schools K-12 and the constitutional rights of parents and students. Then you will be equipped to answer all these questions and more, including questions regarding high school athletics and everyday school-related concerns.

Another common question today is, "Can I speak at the local board of education meeting?" Each state has "open meetings" laws that give the public access to the local board of education meetings, and in some cases, the right to speak. Most board rules prohibit people from raising personnel matters during the meeting's public comment period to avoid defamation claims. So, if a parent discusses school personnel while complaining about the curriculum, the parent may *not* be able to speak during public comment. However, if the curriculum issue is raised without discussing school personnel, the parent *will* be permitted to speak. Knowing the laws and rules can determine whether you are heard at a local board meeting. So, you need to know the system!

MY PRIMARY GOAL

Since the 1960s, public school students have not received a thorough civics education and scores have continued to drop.[11] Also, few people choose to learn civics on their own.[12] Therefore, my primary goal in writing this book is to teach. I want to teach parents and educators about the public school system and constitutional rights. Then we can protect our children in public schools and respectfully work together to solve many of the controversies brewing nationwide.

> *I want to teach parents and educators about the public school system and constitutional rights. Then we can protect our children in public schools and respectfully work together to solve many of the controversies brewing nationwide.*

The information in this book is not intended as legal advice. Instead, it is a primer on the public school system K-12 and constitutional rights. The focus is on using the system to resolve controversial issues. With some knowledge of the system and a calm and respectful letter or conversation, most problems can be resolved. Fortunately, the system is basically the same in all 50 states. I have provided a comprehensive framework, examples, and links to relevant documents in all 50 states.[13] You will have to do some digging in your state and local school district, but I have provided instructions and tips at the end of each chapter. Most of my experience is in the State of Georgia. So, I will use Georgia as the state example throughout this book. These examples will give you an idea of the types of laws and rules you may find in your state and hints for keyword searches. The code and caselaw citations are for clarity and do not follow the standard legal format with short citations and the use of *"Id."* For conciseness, I use standard abbreviations in case names. Any reference to "parents" includes legal and permanent guardians.

Now, let us start learning the system!

PART I

THE STATE SCHOOL SYSTEM THAT GOVERNS PUBLIC SCHOOLS K-12

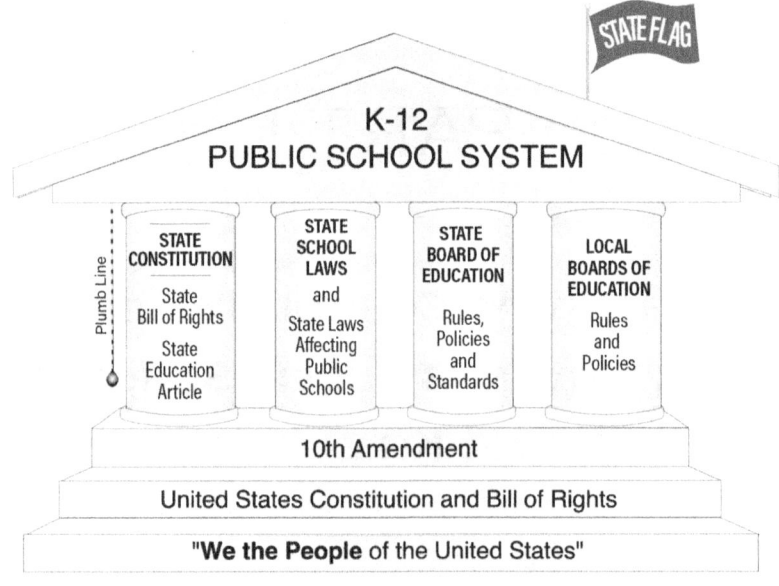

A DIAGRAM OF PUBLIC SCHOOLS K-12

The preceding diagram will help you visualize the public school system. The foundation of "We the People" is at its base, then the "U.S. Constitution and Bill of Rights," and then the "Tenth Amendment," which reserves the power over education to the states or to the people.

The state flag represents each state. Four columns support the building that, in order of importance, represent the following:

1. The **state constitution**, which is the most crucial document governing public education in the state, including the state bill of rights and the state education article;
2. The **state school laws** and several other state laws, which are enacted by the state legislature, signed by the governor, and interpreted by the courts;
3. The **state board of education**, which enacts rules, policies, and standards that govern public education in the state, and the **state school superintendent** who is generally responsible for enforcing the state school laws and the state board of education rules; and

4. The **local boards of education**, which enact rules and policies governing the public schools in their school district, and the **local school superintendents**, who are responsible for enforcing the local board of education rules.

To emphasize that the state constitution is the most crucial document governing public education, a vertical reference line (known as a plumb line) hangs beside the state constitution column. A "plumb line" is a reference line that involves a string, a weight, and gravity, to show the builder what is perfectly vertical. Then the building can be aligned or "trued up" parallel to the plumb line. Similarly, the three columns to the right of the state constitution (state laws; state board rules, policies, and standards; and local board rules and policies) must align with the state constitution and withstand constitutional scrutiny when challenged. You will see this diagram with the pertinent section highlighted throughout this book.

CHAPTER 1

THE UNITED STATES CONSTITUTION AND THE TENTH AMENDMENT

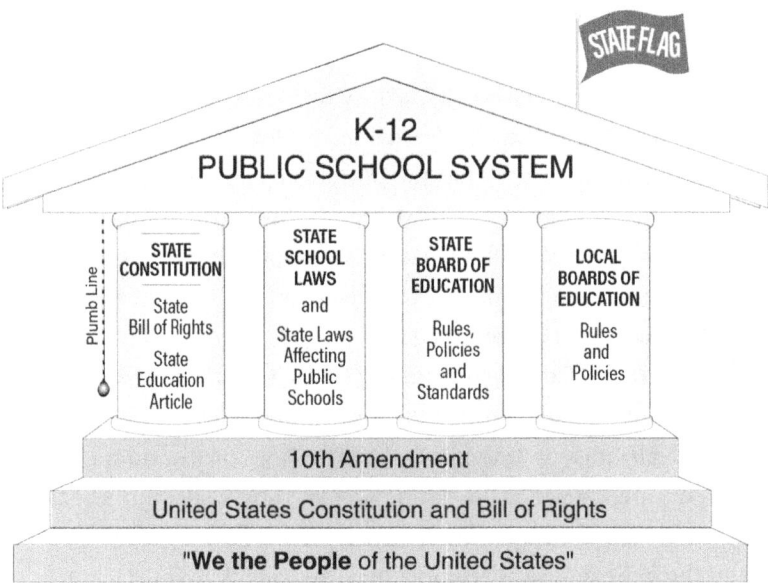

THE STATES ARE IN CHARGE OF EDUCATION

The United States Constitution ("U.S. Constitution" or "federal constitution") does not expressly grant the federal government any power over education. There is also no federal constitutional right to a public education. Instead, each state constitution guarantees the right to a public education.[1] The U.S. Supreme Court has stated that "education is perhaps the most important function of state and local governments."[2] To understand how the power over education was "reserved" to the states, we need to begin with the U.S. Constitution.

The U.S. Constitution begins with three words in large bold type: "**We the People.**" The purpose of the U.S. Constitution is apparent:

> "**We the People** of the United States, in order to form a more perfect union, establish justice, insure domestic tranquility, provide for the common defense, promote the general welfare, and secure the blessings of liberty to ourselves and our posterity, do ordain and establish this Constitution for the United States of America."

U.S. CONST. pmbl. (emphasis original). By the consent of the governed,[3] federal government authority is *established and limited* by the U.S. Constitution.

The U.S. Constitution specifies the powers given to the three branches of the federal government: the executive branch, the legislative branch, and the judicial branch. It also specifies what the states cannot do, such as print their own currency or raise an army. The U.S. Constitution does not specify or enumerate the powers that are reserved to the states. **Instead, all powers that are not delegated to the federal government by the Constitution are reserved to the states or to the people through the Tenth Amendment.**

There are currently 27 amendments to the U.S. Constitution. The first ten amendments are known as the Bill of Rights. The Bill of Rights begins with the First Amendment, which protects the rights of free speech, free association, and the free exercise of religion, to name a few. The Fourth Amendment states that "the right of the people to be secure in their persons, houses, papers, and effects, against unreasonable searches and seizures, shall not be violated." For our purposes, the Tenth Amendment is the most relevant. The Tenth Amendment states:

> "**The powers not delegated to the United States by the Constitution, nor prohibited by it to the States,** *are reserved to the States respectively, or to the people.*"

U.S. CONST. amend. X (emphasis added). The term "reserved" is critical. Some people assume or imply that the federal government granted or gave power to the states, but this is incorrect. The plain language of the Tenth Amendment states that the federal government was given specific enumerated powers. All remaining powers were "reserved" to the states or to the people. ***Therefore, since the U.S. Constitution does not delegate power over education to the federal government nor prohibit the states from governing education, education is left to the states or to the people.*** [4]

There is tremendous strength and wisdom in states having control over education. First and foremost, state control of education prevents the federal government (and the political group in power) from indoctrinating all public school students nationwide. Second, state power over education reduces bureaucracy and promotes local control. Third, state law governance of education highlights the diversity of the states and helps students develop a sense of community as they learn about their state's geography, history, natural resources, customs, and traditions. Differences between state education programs can affect students moving from one state to another, but this is expected given the size and diversity of our nation. Finally, state governance of education has many significant benefits, and most notably, our federal constitution reserves the power over education to the states or the people under the Tenth Amendment.

FEDERAL INVOLVEMENT IN EDUCATION

THE TAXING AND SPENDING CLAUSE

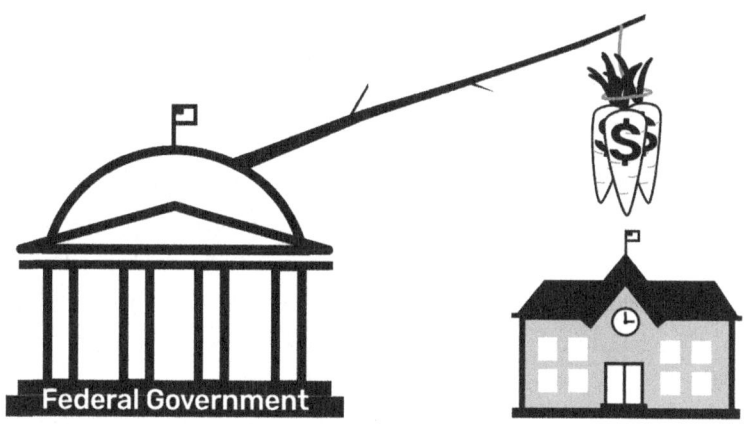

Although the federal government has no express power over education, Congress has been allowed to implement federal education programs under the U.S. Constitution's "Taxing and Spending Clause." U.S. Constitution, Article

I, Section 8. The U.S. Supreme Court described these programs as conditions stating, "Congress has wide latitude to attach conditions to the receipt of federal assistance in order to further its policy objectives. But Congress may not 'induce' the recipient to engage in activities that would themselves be unconstitutional."[5] For example, using the Taxing and Spending Clause, Congress was allowed to withhold a percentage of federal highway funds from states that would not raise the minimum drinking age to 21.[6] Congress was also permitted to enact most of the Patient Protection and Affordable Care Act under the Taxing and Spending Clause.[7]

Congress' extension of its power under the "Taxing and Spending Clause," is also known as the "carrot and stick" method. The carrot and stick method is a farmer's tactic that involves tying a carrot to a stick and dangling it in front of a donkey pulling a cart. The donkey wants to eat the carrot and walks forward to try and get it, thereby pulling the cart in the direction the farmer wants it to go. Similarly, the federal government dangles money in front of the states and school districts to induce them to go in a particular direction using the federal government's education programs. The federal government does this by collecting taxes from the people, and then offering the money to states and school districts if they agree to accept the federal education programs and the accompanying requirements.

Congress' extension of its power under the "Taxing and Spending Clause," is also known as the "carrot and stick" method.

Federal funding of education programs makes up approximately 7.9% of public schools' budgets.[8] These programs benefit many students and include but are not limited to, the "Elementary and Secondary Education Act" (ESEA) (1965 – emphasizing equal access to education), the "Individuals with Disabilities Education Act" (IDEA) (1975 – ensuring students with disabilities are given a "free appropriate public education" that is tailored to their individual needs), the "No Child Left Behind Act" (NCLB) (2001 – emphasizing standards-based education reform), and the "Every Student Succeeds Act" (ESSA) (2015 – replacing the NCLB and modifying the standardized testing).[9] For example, students with learning disabilities may qualify to receive special instruction under the IDEA, which involves the student receiving an Individualized Education Plan (IEP). Because IEP plans are part of a federal program, they are governed by federal law. This book does not address these federal programs and instead, focuses on state school laws and constitutional rights.

It is crucial to understand that the federal government cannot require states and school districts to implement federal education programs. Moreover, as federal education programs expand, it is essential to consider the trade-offs when states and school districts agree to receive money from the federal government and implement a new federal education program. School district officials and parents may not want all the requirements of the federal programs or the responsibility of allocating money and resources to implement, monitor, enforce, test students, and report back to the federal government. If the school district officials do not accept the large amounts of money that accompany these programs, they will be criticized for not getting back the tax dollars that the state residents paid to the federal government. This puts a great deal of pressure on elected and appointed school officials. They must consent and take the money or refuse and pay the price politically (unless the voters are informed and understand the reasoning for such a refusal). Some states and school districts accept the federal programs and find that the funding is insufficient to cover the expenses. Then local school districts must transfer money from their general funds to pay these expenses. In these situations, parents and educators have an opportunity, and some say, the duty, to investigate and carefully consider federal education programs before accepting them.

Additionally, once states and school districts agree to receive money from the federal government, other federal programs are "tacked on." For example, the Family Educational Rights and Privacy Act applies to schools that receive federal money. Its long list of exceptions allows schools to share student data with individuals and government agencies. The Children's Internet Protection Act also applies to schools and public libraries that receive monies from the federal government and requires them to install software that blocks obscene material, pornography, and other materials dangerous to minors. In other words, parents and educators may want some, but not all the federal programs that are "tacked on." Of course, if a federal education program or the tacking-on effect is challenged in the courts, it must be deemed constitutional to continue.

FEDERAL CONSTITUTIONAL RIGHTS

Another aspect of federal involvement in education is the U.S. Constitution, which protects against government infringements (violations) of federal constitutional rights. In the last century, the U.S. Supreme Court has repeatedly held (decided) that the U.S. Constitution gives parents a "fundamental right" to make decisions regarding the care, custody, control, upbringing, and education of their children. For example, in 1923, the U.S. Supreme Court struck down a state law because the state "legislature ha[d] attempted materially to interfere with . . . the power of parents to control the education of their own."[10] In 1925, the U.S. Supreme Court stated that parents have the right "to direct the upbringing and education of children under their control" and struck down a state law requiring all children to attend public schools.[11] In 1972, the U.S. Supreme Court recognized the "liberty of parents . . . to direct the upbringing and education of their children."[12] Then, in 1982, the U.S. Supreme Court recognized the "fundamental liberty interest of natural parents in the care, custody, and management of their child."[13] As recently as 2000, the U.S. Supreme Court stated that the Constitution "protects the fundamental right of parents to make decisions concerning the care, custody, and control of their children."[14] Given that parental rights are "fundamental rights," the courts apply "strict scrutiny," which is the highest level of scrutiny and the most challenging standard for a law or government action to meet. Using the strict scrutiny standard, parental rights prevail unless the government law, rule, or action is "narrowly tailored" to accomplish a "compelling governmental interest."[15]

The U.S. Constitution's Bill of Rights expressly protects the right to free exercise of religion, freedom of speech, and other rights that impact public schools.

Additionally, the U.S. Constitution's Bill of Rights expressly protects the right to free exercise of religion, freedom of speech, and other rights that impact public schools. Again, these rights protect against *government* violations, which include federal, state, and local laws, rules, and actions. Given that public schools are an extension of state and local government, they cannot infringe on constitutional rights either. For more on federal constitutional rights, see Chapter 11.

CHAPTER 2

THE STATE CONSTITUTION

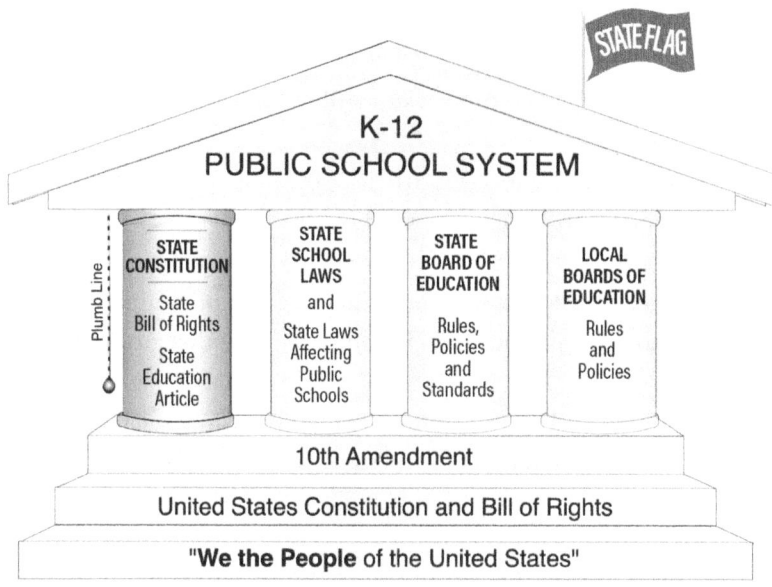

THE STATE CONSTITUTION'S "EDUCATION ARTICLE"

THE STATE CONSTITUTIONAL RIGHT TO A PUBLIC EDUCATION

Every state has a state constitution. All state constitutions also include an "education article" that establishes the state's authority over public education. Using the Constitution of the State of Georgia (Georgia Constitution) as an example, "Education" is under Article VIII. Section I of Article VIII states,

Section I, Public Education

Paragraph I. **Public education, free public education prior to college or postsecondary level; supported by taxation.**

The provision of an *adequate public education* for the citizens shall be the primary obligation of the State of Georgia. Public education for the citizens prior to the college or postsecondary level *shall be free* and shall be provided for by taxation, and the General Assembly may by general law provide for the establishment of education policies for such public education. The expense of other public education shall be provided for in such manner and in such amount as may be provided by law."

G.A. CONST. art. VIII, § I, ¶ 1 (emphasis added).

Each state constitution's education article also establishes and distributes authority to other education-related branches:

- the **state board of education**, which draws representatives from the state to establish rules, policies, and standards that govern the state's public schools;
- the **state school superintendent or commissioner**, who is generally the executive officer of the state board of education and the administrative chief executive officer of the state's department of education;
- the **local boards of education**, which draw representatives from the local school districts to establish rules and policies, hire the local school superintendent, and make budget and strategic planning decisions; and
- the **local school superintendents or commissioners**, who are generally the executive officers of the local boards of education and the administrative chief executive officers of the local school districts.

G.A. CONST. art VIII, §§ II-V. A state constitutional amendment may be needed to change the structure of a state's public education system. To the extent that state legislatures try to change the education structure with laws (i.e., laws that remove local control or give control to another governing body), those laws must be able to pass constitutional muster if challenged in the courts.

Each state legislature has authority over education in its general grant. Sometimes that authority is restated in the education article as well. The authority over public education comes from the U.S. Constitution's Tenth Amendment, then to each state's constitution, and then fans out to the state legislature, the state board of education, the state school superintendent, the local boards of education, and the local school superintendents in this basic format. If you are concerned about a particular school-related issue, you need to examine that issue at each level. To do that, you need to know the basic structure of the state's public school system.

PREEMPTION: THE HIERARCHY OF LAWS, RULES, AND POLICIES

Our system of government has a hierarchy of laws, rules, and policies. Some laws are "higher" and they "preempt" (take precedence over or prevent) the laws, rules, and policies enacted at lower levels of government. For example, the U.S. Constitution and federal laws (that are not in conflict with the U.S. Constitution and its 27 Amendments) are the supreme law of the land.[1] For our purposes, the state constitution is the paramount state document. The next highest is state law. The next highest is state board of education rules and policies, and then the local boards of education rules and policies. Keep this principle in mind if you see a conflict among the various levels. Below is a visual to help you remember the hierarchy.

HOW TO FIND WHAT YOU NEED
Your State's Constitution

- **NOTICE: State constitutions are amended from time to time. It is crucial to check and recheck several sources to confirm that you have the most current version.**
- Go to Appendix C and find your state's information page.
- Find the link to the state constitution.
- Identify the number for the education article.
- Click the link to your state constitution and the education article. The education article will specify the type of education guaranteed in your state. It may use words such as "adequate," "thorough and efficient," "general," "uniform," "general and uniform," a "general diffusion of knowledge" or to "secure the people the advantages and opportunities of education."
- Notice that your state constitution's education article distributes authority to other educated-related branches. Depending on the state, you will see authority granted to the state board of education, the state school superintendent, the local boards of education, and the local school superintendents. Your state constitution may also grant authority to the state legislature either in the education article or another provision. It is essential to find these because the state board of education and the local boards of education are rulemaking bodies. Later, when you want to know the limits of their power, you can refer to the state constitution.

CHAPTER 3

STATE SCHOOL LAWS

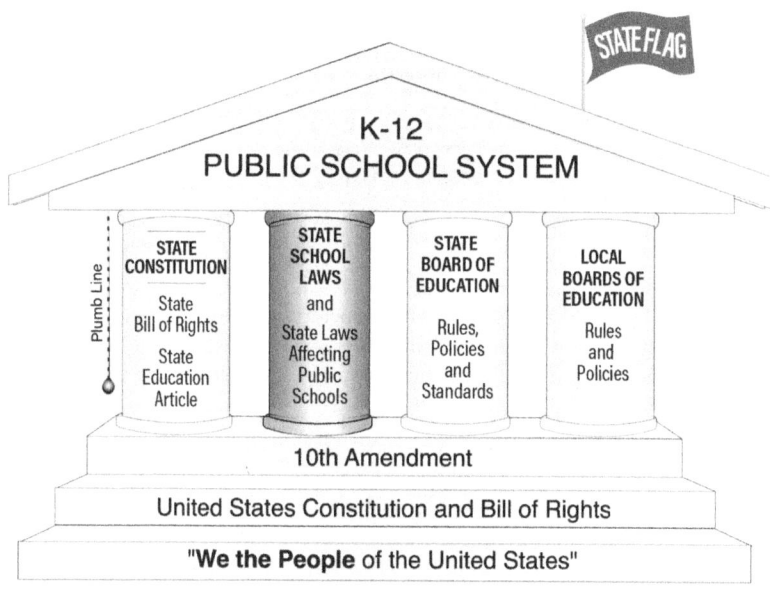

THE IMPORTANCE OF STATE SCHOOL LAWS

FIND YOUR STATE'S "PARENTS' BILLS OF RIGHTS"

If you are concerned about protecting children in public schools, start with your state's Parents' Bill of Rights. Parents' Bills of Rights are one of the best ways to support your right to review all instructional materials and to obtain an opt-out from specific instruction. To help you get accustomed to reviewing state laws, see Georgia's recently enacted Parents' Bill of Rights below:

GEORGIA LAW

O.C.G.A. § 20-2-786   Parents' Bill of Rights

(a) This Code section shall be known and may be cited as the 'Parents' Bill of Rights.'

(b) *The General Assembly finds that it is a fundamental right of parents to direct the upbringing and education of their minor children. The General Assembly further finds that important information relating to a minor child should not be withheld, either inadvertently or purposefully, from his or her parent, including information relating to the minor child's education.*

(c) As used in this Code section, the term:

 (1) *'Governing body' shall have the same meaning as provided in subsection (a) of Code Section 20-2-167.1.*

 (2) *'Instructional material' means instructional materials and content, as defined by the 28 State Board of Education pursuant to Code Section 20-2-1010, and locally approved instructional materials and content, as defined in subsection (a) of Code Section 20-2-1017.*

 (3) *'Minor child' means a person who is less than 18 years of age and who has not been emancipated by operation of law or by court order pursuant to Code Section 15-11-727 or as otherwise provided by law.*

 (4) *'Parent' means a person who has legal authority to act on behalf of a minor child as a natural or adoptive parent or a legal guardian.*

 (5) *'Review period' means the first two weeks of each nine-week grading period of the school year; provided, however, that for schools that do not implement nine-week grading periods, the term 'review period' means the first two weeks of each grading period of the school year.*

(d) **No state or local government entity, governing body, or any officer, employee, or agent thereof may infringe on the fundamental right of a parent to direct the upbringing and education of his or her minor child without demonstrating that such action is reasonable and necessary to achieve a compelling state interest and that such action is narrowly tailored and is not otherwise served by less restrictive means.**

(e) (1) *All parental rights are reserved to the parent of a minor child in this state without obstruction or interference from a state or local government entity, governing body, or any officer, employee, or agent thereof, including, but not limited to:*

 (A) *The right to direct the upbringing and the moral or religious training of his or her minor child;*

 (B) *The right to review all instructional materials intended for use in the classroom of his or her minor child;*

 (C) The right to apply to enroll his or her minor child in a public school or, as an alternative to public education, a private school, including a religious school, a home study program, or other available options, as authorized by law and subject to applicable enrollment requirements;

 (D) The right to access and review all records relating to his or her minor child, including, but not limited to, current grade reports and attendance records, unless otherwise prohibited by law;

(E) The right to access information relating to promotion and retention policies and high school graduation requirements;

(F) The right to provide written notice that photographs or video or voice recordings of his or her child are not permitted, subject to applicable public safety and security exceptions; and

(G) (i) *The right to request, in writing, from the local school superintendent or school principal the information provided for in this Code section. The local school superintendent or school principal shall produce such information for inspection within a reasonable amount of time not to exceed three business days of receipt of a request. In those instances where some, but not all, information requested is available for inspection within three business days....*

(ii) If the local school superintendent or school principal denies a parent's request for information or does not provide existing responsive information within 30 days, the parent may appeal such denial or failure to respond to the governing body.... (iii) A parent aggrieved by the decision of the governing body may appeal such decision to the State Board of Education as provided in subsection (b) of Code Section 20-2-1160.

(2) **Unless such rights have been waived or terminated as provided by law, parents have inalienable rights that are more comprehensive than those listed in paragraph (1) of this subsection. This Code section does not prescribe all rights of parents. Unless otherwise required by law, the rights of a parent of a minor child shall not be limited or denied.**

(f) *Each governing body shall, in consultation with parents, teachers, and administrators, develop and adopt a policy or regulation to promote parental involvement in the public schools. Such policy or regulation shall be posted on each governing body's public website, and a copy of such policy or regulation shall be available for review on site upon request by a parent. Such policy or regulation shall include:*

(1) Procedures for a parent to review records relating to his or her minor child;

(2) (A) *Procedures for a parent to learn about his or her minor child's courses of study, including, but not limited to, parental access to instructional materials intended for use in the classroom.* Instructional materials intended for use in his or her minor child's classroom shall be made available for parental review during the review period. If such instructional materials are not made available by a school or local school system for review online, then they shall be made available for review on site upon a parent's request made during the review period.

>   (B) Procedures for a parent to object to instructional materials intended for use in his or her minor child's classroom or recommended by his or her minor child's teacher;
>
> (3) *Procedures for a parent to withdraw his or her minor child from the school's prescribed course of study in sex education if the parent provides a written objection to his or her minor child's participation. Such procedures must provide for a parent to be notified in advance of such course content so that he or she may withdraw his or her minor child from the course;* and
>
> (4) Procedures for a parent to provide written notice that photographs or video or voice recordings of his or her child are not permitted, subject to applicable public safety and security exceptions....

O.C.G.A. § 20-2-786; or GA H.B. 1178, (Regular Session, 2021-2022) (emphasis added). Georgia's Parents' Bill of Rights cannot be waived by charter entities. O.C.G.A. § 20-2-786(h).

Other states have also enacted a Parents' Bill of Rights. One of the more well-known is Florida's Parents' Bill of Rights (FL Stat §§ 1014.01 – 1014.06). Although these are named "Bills of Rights," both are state *laws*. They are not constitutional *amendments* like our federal Bill of Rights (First through Tenth Amendments). For parental rights in your state, see Protecting Children by Empowering Parents (https://parentalrights.org/), and hit the drop-down for "learn" and "parental rights in every state."

FIND STATE SCHOOL LAWS REGARDING PARENTAL CONSENT ("OPT-IN") AND NON-CONSENT ("OPT-OUT") FOR CURRICULUM, CLASSES, AND ACTIVITIES

Most states *presume* that parents have given their consent to the public schools' curriculum, courses, and activities. The exception to this general rule is when the school is exposed to liability (i.e., field trips, sports participation, and dispensing medication). Then parental consent in writing is required. In the last decade, the term "parental non-consent" has been replaced with the catchy term "opt-out." Likewise, "parental consent" has been replaced with the term "opt-in." Opt-ins require written permission from parents *before* the student can attend the class or participate in the activity. Opt-outs assume that all students will attend the class or participate in the activity *unless* the parents take the initiative to submit a written request or opt-out to the school. Problems with parental opt-outs include: parents are not aware of their right to submit opt-out forms, some schools do not publicize the opt-out forms, students lose or forget to turn in the opt-out forms, the administration overlooks the opt-out forms or does not give them to the teacher, and some teachers fail to enforce opt-outs, particularly if there is a substitute teacher. I know this firsthand because I handed an opt-out form to a school administrator but the school failed to honor the request. As a result, I prefer opt-ins.

State school laws regarding parental consent usually apply to the following:

- Physical examinations;
- Psychiatric and mental health examinations;
- Sex education classes;
- Surveys either generally or regarding specific subjects and family beliefs;
- Joining student clubs and groups at school;
- Data-sharing with third-party vendors; and
- Saying the Pledge of Allegiance and saluting the American flag.

Many states have school laws that give parents "opt-in" or "opt-out" rights for specific courses and activities.

For non-consent or opt-out forms, search online using the terms "parental non-consent form" or "universal opt-out (opt out) letter." Also note that "opt out" is a verb, and "opt-out" is an adjective. When searching for opt-out forms, use both. Also see Appendix A.

Several parental rights groups provide opt-out forms on their websites. Generally, opt-out forms specify: (1) the objectionable subject or activity; (2) the familiar sources of the objectional content (to help schools locate the material); (3) a statement that the opt-out applies to "all curriculum and supplemental instructional materials and content;" (4) a statement about constitutional rights; and (5) the state school law regarding opt-outs (if your state has one). Some groups offer opt-out forms that specify the basis for their religious beliefs (i.e., Truth in Education).[1] **Above all, remember that parents have constitutionally protected parental rights that apply regardless of whether there is a state school law or rule allowing opt-outs.**[2] As parents, it is your decision regarding opt-outs, and you can tailor the forms to your specific needs.

For more on enforcement, see Chapters 5 and 6 regarding superintendents. For more on opt-outs, see Chapter 11 regarding Federal Constitutional Rights.

Hopefully, the school will honor your request and that will be the end of the matter. If local school districts refuse to comply, the state school law permitting the opt-out may be enforced by the local or state school superintendent.

FIND STATE SCHOOL LAWS THAT ADDRESS YOUR CURRICULUM CONCERNS

It is not uncommon to see news outlets featuring parents and educators battling over curriculum in public schools, especially in politics, history, social studies, sex education, and health. Yet, every state has school laws addressing public school curriculum. In fact, many state school laws *support* the curriculum arguments parents are raising against their school boards. Most parents also do not know that the state and local superintendents are responsible for enforcing the state school laws and state and local rules. Most states even require their state and local school superintendents to obtain a bond to secure the faithful discharge of their duties. See Chapter 5. Yet, to enforce the various curriculum laws, you first need to find them.

Here are some of the state school laws regarding public school curriculum in Georgia. You can find similar laws in your state.

State School Laws that Prohibit Partisan Content in Public School Instructional Materials and Content

Surprisingly, several states have laws that prohibit partisan or intensely political instructional material and content. For example, Georgia has a school law that states:

GEORGIA LAW

O.C.G.A. §20-2-1011   Selecting, acquiring, and purchasing instructional materials and content; exclusion of partisan or sectarian material.

The State Board of Education may provide for the selection, acquisition, or purchase of instructional materials and content either by multiple listings or uniform adoption or by any other method that will enable the acquiring of acceptable instructional materials and content at the lowest possible costs, provided such adoption or multiple listings shall in no event constitute a binding contract until ratified in writing by the state board. ***None of the instructional materials and content so purchased shall contain anything of a partisan or sectarian nature.***

O.C.G.A. § 20-2-1011 (emphasis added).[3] To date, there is no published court guidance on what is "partisan" (adherence to a political party)[4] and "sectarian" (religious denomination)[5] as used in this Georgia law. Perhaps this is because no one has challenged public school instructional materials and content based on this law. If someone were to bring a case claiming that certain instructional materials and content violated this law, then the Georgia courts, and ultimately the Supreme Court of Georgia, would provide guidance on the meaning of these terms and whether they are prohibited. This process is how our system operates. The state legislature passes bills, the governor signs the bills into law, and the courts interpret the meaning of the words used in the law. Courts interpret words in a law using their plain meaning, rules of statutory construction, and a credible dictionary from the year when the law was enacted or earlier. Otherwise, people could change the laws by changing the definition of certain words in the dictionary.

State School Laws Regarding Sex Education
Some state school laws require sex education instruction and specify what must be taught. These states usually give parents and guardians the right to either opt out or opt in to sex education classes. Surprisingly, most states do not require parental consent in writing for sex education in public schools K-12. Instead, parents who do not want to sex education must give their non-consent in writing. This can be done with a non-consent or opt-out form. Georgia does not require a reason for the exemption (religious or otherwise), though you should review your state laws on this issue.[6] In my experience, if a parent submits an opt-out form, the public school is not required to offer alternative sex education instruction that the parent might prefer.

> *Some state school laws require sex education instruction and specify what must be taught. These states usually give parents and guardians the right to either opt out or opt in to sex education classes.*

GEORGIA LAW

O.C.G.A. § 20-2-143 Sex education and AIDS prevention instruction; implementation; student exemption.

(a) Each local board of education shall prescribe a course of study in sex education and AIDS prevention instruction for such grades and grade levels in the public school system as shall be determined by the State Board of Education. Each local board of education shall be authorized to supplement and develop the exact approach of content areas of such minimum course of study with such specific curriculum standards as it may deem appropriate. Such standards shall include instruction relating to the handling of peer pressure, the promotion of high self-esteem, local community values, the legal consequences of parenthood, and abstinence from sexual activity as an effective method of prevention of pregnancy, sexually transmitted diseases, and acquired immune deficiency syndrome.

(b) The State Board of Education shall prescribe a minimum course of study in sex education and AIDS prevention instruction which may be included as a part of a course of study in comprehensive health education for such grades and grade levels in the public school system as shall be determined by the state board and shall establish standards for its administration. The course may include instruction concerning human biology, conception, pregnancy, birth, sexually transmitted diseases, and acquired immune deficiency syndrome. The course shall include instruction concerning the legal consequences of parenthood, including, without being limited to, the legal obligation of both parents to support a child and legal penalties or restrictions upon failure to support a child, including, without being limited to, the possible suspension or revocation of a parent's driver's license and occupational or professional licenses. A manual setting out the details of such course of study shall be prepared by or approved by the State School Superintendent in cooperation with the Department of Human Resources, the State Board of Education, and such expert advisers as they may choose.

(c) The minimum course of study to be prescribed by the State Board of Education pursuant to subsection (b) of this Code section shall be ready for implementation not later than July 1, 1988. Each local board shall implement either such minimum course of study or its equivalent no later than July 1, 1989. Any local board of education which fails to comply with this subsection shall not be eligible to receive any state funding under this article until such minimum course of study or its equivalent has been implemented.

(d) *Any parent or legal guardian of a child to whom the course of study set forth in this Code section is to be taught shall have the right to elect, in writing, that such child not receive such course of study.*

O.C.G.A. § 20-2-143 (emphasis added). To see whether your state requires opt-outs or opt-ins for sex education, see the list of states in Chapter 12 under "Submit a Parent Opt-Out of Specific Instructional Materials and Content." For a blank sample opt-out form, see Appendix A. For your state's school laws, see Appendix C. If you and other like-minded parents make similar opt-out requests, no student will be singled out and the group can be given a different assignment in a different location. However, it is *crucial* that you either teach or outsource comprehensive instruction in this area so your children are equipped to function in today's society. There are numerous books and materials available to parents on this topic.

You may be thinking, "What about all the other sexually explicit content intermingled in the curriculum and supplemental materials and content?" Perhaps your child's school has intermingled this subject throughout the day, and it is not limited to a particular class. Some parents are concerned when schools intermingle sexually explicit content throughout many subjects, making exemptions difficult to implement. It is also a concern for legislators, who provide exemptions for sex education in state school laws.

How has this happened? There is compelling evidence that it is the combination of: (1) school laws regarding sex education that "open the door" to a wide range of content; (2) criminal obscenity exemptions for schools and school libraries that would otherwise prohibit much of this content (see Chapter 4); (3) parents who either do not understand their constitutional rights, do not know what their children are learning, or do not oppose the content; and (4) advocacy groups promoting their agendas in public schools. For example, in 2020, the non-profit entity "SIECUS: Sex Ed for Social Change" (https://siecus.org/) published the "National Sex Education Standards" (https://siecus.org/wp-content/uploads/2020/03/NSES-2020-2.pdf). The standards are written in general terms. However, the "Glossary of Sex Education Terms" clarifies what content is being taught (pp. 53-68). The NSES Standards have been adopted by many state and local boards of education. According to public records, SIECUS (Sexuality

> *Some parents are concerned when schools intermingle sexually explicit content throughout many subjects, making exemptions difficult to implement.*

Information and Education Council of the United States) is a national, non-profit organization based in Washington, D.C.[7]

Yet, parents have parental rights, religious freedom, freedom of speech, freedom not to speak, state laws, and board rules permitting opt-outs from sexual content. Some schools may complain that they cannot honor the request because the sexual content is so pervasive throughout the different classes and assignments. In other words, the local school district's curriculum selections have made it *impossible* for parents to truly obtain an opt-out. So, whose problem is this – the local school district or the parents? Even if the school honors the request and the student *is* pulled out numerous times a day, the question becomes: is the local school district denying the child's state constitutional right to an "adequate public education?" The answer is — the courts must decide after a case is brought. Therefore, if the school refuses to honor the opt-out, the parents may want to consult legal counsel. Also, if the school honors the opt-out but the student's day is constantly interrupted by having to leave classes and receive alternative assignments, the parents may want to consult legal counsel. Legal counsel can help parents determine whether there is a reasonable basis in law and fact to claim that the local school district's intermingling of sexual content throughout the instruction and the student's constant need to leave class and receive alternative assignments violates the child's state constitutional right to a "free" and "adequate public education."

> *Yet, parents have parental rights, religious freedom, freedom of speech, freedom not to speak, state laws, and board rules permitting opt-outs from sexual content.*

State School Laws That Require Public Schools to Teach Specific Information Regarding U.S. History and the State's History

Many states have state school laws that require students to be taught patriotism and specific history and social studies information. Moreover, the U.S. Supreme Court has stated that states have the power "reasonably to regulate all schools, to inspect, supervise and examine them, their teachers and pupils; to require that all children of proper age attend some school, that teachers shall be of good moral character and patriotic disposition, that certain studies plainly essential to good citizenship must be taught, and that nothing be taught which is manifestly inimical [harmful, detrimental or hostile] to the public welfare."[8]

To this end, Georgia has five separate state school laws that specify what schools *must* teach, are *strongly encouraged* to teach, and *may* teach in history and social studies. I have included these laws in full for several reasons. First, they show the level of detail in some state school laws. Second, they provide a template for states that want to enact them in their state school laws, state board of education rules, or local board of education rules. Third, they support Georgians who want their children to learn these principles in public schools. Finally, they show that Georgia law prohibits censorship of our nation's historical documents in context.

Georgia public schools *must* teach the following:

GEORGIA LAW

O.C.G.A. §20-2-142   Prescribed courses.

(a) (1) All elementary and secondary schools which receive in any manner funds from the state *shall* provide the following course offerings in the manner and at the grade level prescribed by the State Board of Education:

  (A) *A course of study in the background, history, and development of the federal and state governments and a study of Georgia county and municipal governments; and*

  (B) *A course of study in the history of the United States and in the history of Georgia and in the essentials of the United States and Georgia Constitutions, including the study of American institutions and ideals which shall include a study of the Pledge of Allegiance to the flag of the United States and the Georgia flag in addition to other institutions and ideals.*

(2) **No student shall be eligible to receive a diploma from a high school unless such student has successfully completed the courses in history and government provided for by this subsection, except as provided in paragraphs (3) and (4) of this subsection.** For students moving to Georgia and unable to take the course or courses available to fulfill these requirements in the grade level in which such course or courses are ordinarily offered, the State Board of Education may develop alternative methods, which may include but shall not be limited to an on-line course of study, for such students to learn about and demonstrate an adequate understanding of federal or Georgia history and government.

O.C.G.A. §20-2-142 (emphasis added).

Georgia public schools are *strongly encouraged* to incorporate the philosophies, principles, and materials of the "American History Recognition and Significant Documents Act" into the curriculum. The Act includes three separate laws: (1) the Establishment of Celebrate Freedom Week; (2) the Display of Historically Significant Documents; and (3) the Online Instructional Resources Relating to American History for Educators. This Act became effective in the 2016 to 2017 school year.

GEORGIA LAW

"American History Recognition and Significant Documents Act"

O.C.G.A. § 20-2-1020   Celebrate Freedom Week.

(a) To educate students about the sacrifices made for freedom in the founding of this country and the values, principles, and philosophies on which this country was founded, it is strongly encouraged that the full week in September which includes Constitution Day, September 17, is recognized in public elementary, middle, and high schools in this state as Celebrate Freedom Week. It is strongly encouraged that Celebrate Freedom Week include approximately three hours of appropriate instruction, as determined by each local school system, in each social studies class. It is strongly encouraged that the instruction include an age-appropriate study of the intent, meaning, and importance of the Declaration of Independence and the United States Constitution, including the Bill of Rights, in their historical context including the background of the colonial era along with instruction about the Founding Fathers, such as the signers of the Declaration of Independence and the United States Constitution, the first six Presidents, and particularly George Washington. *The religious references in the writings of the Founding Fathers shall not be censored.* During Celebrate Freedom Week, it is strongly encouraged that local school systems suggest that students in grades three through 12 read at least one book during the school year that focuses on the Founding Era, either the times and events or the people who made significant contributions to independence or toward establishing the new federal or state governments. In addition, local school systems are strongly encouraged to require students in grades three through 12 to recite at least one of the following three excerpts at least once during the week, and local school systems are encouraged to require daily recitations from one or all of these excerpts at the beginning of each school day:

   1. From the Declaration of Independence:

      We hold these Truths to be self-evident, that all Men are created equal, that they are endowed by their Creator with certain unalienable Rights, that among these are Life, Liberty, and the Pursuit of

Happiness — That to secure these Rights, Governments are instituted among Men, deriving their just Powers from the Consent of the Governed ....;

2. From the Preamble of the U.S. Constitution:

We the people of the United States, in Order to form a more perfect Union, establish Justice, insure domestic Tranquility, provide for the common defense, promote the general Welfare, and secure the Blessings of Liberty to ourselves and our Posterity, do ordain and establish this Constitution for the United States of America; or

3. From the First Amendment of the Bill of Rights:

Congress shall make no law respecting an establishment of religion, or prohibiting the free exercise thereof; or abridging the freedom of speech or of the press, or the right of the people peaceably to assemble, and to petition the Government for a redress of grievances.

(b) *Upon written request from a student's parent or guardian, a local school system shall excuse the student from the recitation required by this Code section. This Code section shall not apply to a student who:*

1. *Has a conscientious objection to the recitation; or*

2. *Is the child of a representative of a foreign government to whom the United States government extends diplomatic immunity.*

(c) This Code section shall apply beginning with the 2016-2017 school year.

O.C.G.A. § 20-2-1020 Display of Historically Significant Documents.

(a) To increase student understanding of, and familiarity with, American historical documents, public schools may display historically important excerpts from, or copies of, those documents in school classrooms and common areas as appropriate. Local boards of education and charter schools are strongly encouraged to allow and may encourage any public-school teacher or administrator to read or post in a public-school building, classroom, or event excerpts or portions of writings, documents, records, or images that reflect the history of the United States, including, but not limited to:

1. The Preamble to the Georgia Constitution;

2. The Declaration of Independence;

3. The United States Constitution, with emphasis on the 13th, 14th, and 15th Amendments;

4. The Bill of Rights;

5. The Mayflower Compact;

6. The national motto;

7. The Pledge of Allegiance to the United States flag;

   The Pledge of Allegiance to the Georgia flag;

The National Anthem;

The writings, speeches, documents, and proclamations of the Founding Fathers and Presidents of the United States;

The Emancipation Proclamation;

The Gettysburg Address;

Decisions of the United States Supreme Court; and

Acts of the Congress of the United States, including the published text of the Congressional Record.

(b) *As historical documents, there shall be no content based censorship of American history and heritage documents referred to in this Code section due to their religious or cultural nature.*

O.C.G.A. § 20-2-1022 Online Instructional Resources Relating to American History for Educators.

To increase student understanding of, and familiarity with, American historical documents and to provide curriculum support to classroom teachers of United States history, American government and civics, economics, and social studies, the Department of Education is strongly encouraged to create an online instructional resource page or pages for teachers, which may include, but is not limited to, links to websites, foundational documents, and lesson plan ideas. In order to create shared digital resources available to all students in this state, such online resources may be integrated with the Teacher Resource Link of the Statewide Longitudinal Data System. At a minimum, such resource page or pages may include the items in paragraphs (1) through (11) of subsection (a) of Code Section 20-2-1021 and may focus on the foundational principles of limited constitutional government, federalism, religious liberty, freedom of speech, the right to private property, free enterprise, and the rule of law. *There shall be no content based censorship of American history, writings of the Founding Fathers, or heritage documents referred to in this Code section due to their religious or cultural nature.* It is strongly encouraged that the online teacher resource page be completed and made easily available to teachers no later than July 31, 2016, and support the requirements specified in Code Section 20-2-1020.

O.C.G.A. §§ 20-2-1020, 20-2-1021; 20-2-1022 (emphasis added).

Georgia public schools *may* teach coursework on the founding philosophy and principles of the United States of America, which include:

GEORGIA LAW

O.C.G.A. § 20-2-142.1 Coursework in the founding philosophy and principles of the United States of America.

(a) *The General Assembly finds that the survival of the Republic requires that the nation's children, who are the future guardians of its heritage and participants in its governance, have a clear understanding of the founding philosophy and the founding principles of our government, which are found in the Declaration of Independence, the United States Constitution, the Federalist Papers, and the writings of the founders, and an understanding of the preservation of such founding philosophy, principles, and documents.*

(b) This Code section shall be known and may be cited as the "America's Founding Philosophy and Principles Act."

(c) **Each local board of education may require all students, as a condition of graduation, during their ninth through twelfth grade years to complete and pass a separate semester course covering the following founding philosophy and principles of the United States of America:**

  (1) America's founding philosophy, to include at least the following:

   (A) As articulated in the Declaration of Independence the foundational idea of the Creator-endowed unalienable rights of the people;

   (B) The purpose of limited government, which is to protect the unalienable rights of the people and to protect the people from violence and fraud;

   (C) The structure of government, separation of powers, and checks and balances; and

   (D) The rule of law, with frequent and free elections in a representative government which governs by majority vote within a constitutional framework;

  (2) America's founding principles, to include at least the following:

   (A) Federalism-government as close to the people as possible, limited federal government, and strong state and local government;

   (B) Freedoms of speech, press, religion, and peaceful assembly guaranteed by the Bill of Rights;

   (C) Rights to private property and freedom of individual enterprise;

   (D) The innocence of any crime until proven guilty, with right of habeas corpus, and no unreasonable searches, seizures, or cruel and unusual punishment;

   (E) A virtuous and moral people educated in the philosophy and principles of government for a free people;

   (F) The right to a speedy trial by a jury of peers;

   (G) The principles of economy in spending, constitutional limitations on government power to tax and spend, and prompt payment of public debt;

   (H) Economic system of money with intrinsic value;

   (I) Equality before the law and due process of law with grand jury indictment for capital crimes before holding a person to account;

(J) The right of people to keep and bear arms, strong defense capability, supremacy of civil authority over military;

(K) Peace, commerce, and honest friendship with all nations, entangling alliances with none;

(L) All laws concise and understandable by the people and not ex post facto laws;

(M) Eternal vigilance by "We the People;" and

(N) Founding documents including Declaration of Independence, the United States Constitution, and the Federalist Papers; and

(3) Transformational movements in American history, to include at least the following:

(A) The antislavery movement;

(B) The Civil Rights movement;

(C) Women's suffrage;

(D) The contributions of immigrants to American society; and

(E) The history of the Native American population.

(d) *The Department of Education and local boards of education, as appropriate, may provide, or cause to be provided, curriculum content which reflects the content standards addressed pursuant to subsection (c) of this Code section and teacher training to ensure that the intent and provisions of this Code section are implemented.*

(e) This Code section shall apply beginning in school year 2017-2018.

O.C.G.A. §§ 20-2-142.1 (emphasis added). In total, these five Georgia laws cover a great deal of history and social studies content, leaving little if any time to teach other history theories. You can check your state school laws to see if you have existing social studies and history requirements as well. See Appendix C under your state's school laws.

State School Laws That Prohibit Content-Based Censorship of American History Due to their Religious or Cultural Nature

Several states have school laws that prohibit content-based censorship of historical documents. Georgia has at least two school laws that prohibit this type of censorship. For example:

O.C.G.A. § 20-2-1020   Display of Historically Significant Documents.

(b) *As historical documents, there shall be no content based censorship of American history and heritage documents referred to in this Code section due to their religious or cultural nature.*

> O.C.G.A. § 20-2-1022   Online Instructional Resources Relating to American History for Educators.
>
> ... *There shall be no content based censorship of American history, writings of the Founding Fathers, or heritage documents referred to in this Code section due to their religious or cultural nature.*

O.C.G.A. §§ 20-2-1020 and 20-2-1022 (emphasis added). Arizona, Minnesota, and Utah also have school laws prohibiting censorship. See Appendix C. Similarly, Florida, North Dakota, and Virginia have laws that permit public schools to post historical documents in their original form. See Appendix C. Other states may do the same.

State School Laws That Prevent Racial Discrimination and "Divisive Concepts and Ideologies from Invading the Classroom"

Critical Race Theory ("CRT") is among the more controversial topics being taught in public schools. Some states have enacted laws eliminating CRT, not in name but in concepts. Others are concerned that these laws are too broad and will lead to the elimination of race-related issues that are not part of CRT and are necessary to living in a diverse nation. At the core, defining CRT and its scope is a key issue.

Without addressing the merits of CRT, I would like to question why *any* single "theory" is integrated into the public school curriculum K-12. When schools teach a single theory and integrate it into instruction over a long period of time, the facts are presented in a way that supports that theory. Opposing facts and theories are undermined and excluded. Sometimes the slant is subtle. Sometimes it is evident and forceful. Teaching a single theory through *all* of K-12 tends to make followers, not thinkers. Given the problems associated with teaching theories integrated into instruction over a long period of time, I hope parents and educators will teach all the facts, both the good and the bad, and allow students to develop theories later in their education.

Along those lines, it may be helpful to look at the stages of a classical education, which involves the *trivium*. The *trivium* has three stages: the elementary school or grammar stage, "when the building blocks of information are absorbed through memorization and rules;" the middle school or logic stage, "in which the student begins to think more analytically;" and the high school or rhetoric stage, "where the student learns to write and speak with force and originality."[9] Using the *trivium*, students can be taught all the facts, both the "favorable" and the "unfavorable" history of our nation and the world. Then, when they are more mature, they can learn to make a case for or against various history and social studies theories during the rhetoric stage.

> *Using the trivium, students can be taught all the facts, both the "favorable" and the "unfavorable" history of our nation and the world. Then, when they are more mature, they can learn to make a case for or against various history and social studies theories during the rhetoric stage.*

If you intend to follow the use of CRT in your public schools, the following points may be helpful. First, federal law prohibits racial discrimination. The Civil Rights Act of 1964, Title VI prohibits discrimination based on "race, color, religion, sex, or national origin," and has a process for reporting violations. Second, your state laws may prohibit public schools from teaching racially discriminatory theories. For example, the Georgia legislature recently passed a new law prohibiting "divisive concepts and ideologies from invading the classroom." The new law is too long to include in this book, but one portion states:

GEORGIA LAW

O.C.G.A. § 20-1-11(a) Prohibition Against Divisive Concepts and Ideologies Invading the Classroom.

"Divisive concepts" includes views espousing such concepts:

(A) One race is inherently superior to another race;

(B) The United States of America is fundamentally racist;

(C) An individual, by virtue of his or her race, is inherently or consciously racist or oppressive toward individuals of other races;

(D) An individual should not be discriminated against or receive adverse treatment solely or partly because of his or her race;

(E) An individual's moral character is inherently determined by his or her race;

(F) An individual, solely by virtue of his or her race, bears individual responsibility for actions committed in the past by other individuals of the same race;

(G) An individual, solely by virtue of his or her race, should feel anguish, guilt, or any other form of psychological distress;

(H) Performance-based advancement or the recognition and appreciation of character traits such as a hard work ethic are racist or have been advocated for by individuals of a particular race to oppress individuals of another race; or

(I) Any other form of race scapegoating or race stereotyping.

GA H.B. 1084, (Regular Session, 2021-2022) (General Assembly link at O.C.G.A. § 20-1-11). The new Georgia law requires local boards of education to prohibit their employees from "discriminating against students and other employees based on race" and requires a "complaint resolution process" for violations of the law.[10] If local school districts refuse to comply, the law may be enforced by the local school superintendent or the state school superintendent. For more on enforcement, see Chapters 5 and 6 regarding superintendents.

STATE SCHOOL LAWS REQUIRING EDUCATORS TO TAKE OATHS TO UPHOLD THE U.S. AND STATE CONSTITUTIONS

Some state laws require school officials to take an oath to uphold the U.S. Constitution and the state constitution. States can require teachers to be "of patriotic disposition" because of U.S. Supreme Court decisions that support this requirement."[11] For example:

GEORGIA LAW

O.C.G.A. § 20-2-5   Oaths of members; board meetings.

The members of the State Board of Education shall take an oath of office for the faithful performance of their duties and the *oath of allegiance to the federal and state Constitutions.....*

O.C.G.A. § 20-2-103   Oath of local school superintendent. [Signed and Notarized]

Before entering upon the discharge of his or her official duties, the local school superintendent shall take and subscribe to the following oath of office:

STATE OF GEORGIA

COUNTY OF _____

I, _____, do solemnly swear or affirm that I will truly perform the duties of local school superintendent of the _____ School System to the best of my ability.

I do further swear or affirm:

(1) That I am not the holder of any unaccounted for public money due this state or any political subdivision or authority thereof and that I will manage the finances of the local school system in compliance with all applicable laws and regulations;

(2) That I am not the holder of any office of trust under the government of the United States, any other state, or any foreign state which I am by the laws of the State of Georgia prohibited from holding;

(3) That I am otherwise qualified to hold said office according to the Constitution and the laws of Georgia; and

(4) *That I will support the Constitution of the United States and of this state.*

_____

Signature of local school superintendent

_____

Typed name of local school superintendent

Sworn and subscribed before me this _____ day of _____, _____. (SEAL).

O.C.G.A. §§ 20-2-5 and 20-2-103 (emphasis added). Some states require all school teachers, including university professors, to swear an oath to support the federal and state constitutions. At least one state conditions state funding and tax-exempt status on all teachers having taken the oath either orally or in writing. MI Comp L §§ 388; 388.401; 388.402.

Additionally, the state school superintendent and local school superintendents in Georgia must post an official bond that is "properly conditioned on the faithful discharge of the duties of his or her office." O.C.G.A. §§ 20-2-32 and 20-2-34 (state school superintendent); O.C.G.A. §§ 20-2-104 and 20-2-109 (local school superintendents).[12] Other states do the same.

STATE SCHOOL LAWS THAT ADDRESS HIGH SCHOOL ATHLETICS

State school laws across the nation also address high school athletics. Under the heading of "athletics," state school laws usually define the role of athletic associations in high school athletics, prohibit gender discrimination, and define improper encouragement and rewards for student athletes. O.C.G.A. §§ 20-2-315 through 20-2-318. If you and your children are dealing with controversies in either your high school's athletics program or the athletic associations in your state, the state school laws are a good place to start.

Georgia law provides for a "High School Athletics Overview Committee." O.C.G.A. §§ 20-2-2100 through 20-2-2104. This joint committee includes state legislators from various houses and committees. The Lieutenant Governor and the Department of Education as-

If you and your children are dealing with controversies in either your high school's athletics program or the athletic associations in your state, the state school laws are a good place to start.

sist the committee. The committee also requires cooperation and reporting from all high school athletic associations. The committee's duties include:

GEORGIA LAW

O.C.G.A. § 20-1-2103   Evaluation of Performance of High School Athletic Associations

In the discharge of its duties, the committee shall evaluate the performance of high school athletic associations consistent with the following criteria:

(1) *Fairness and equity in establishing and implementing its standards; and*

(2) *The promotion of academic achievement and good sportsmanship.*

O.C.G.A. §§ 20-1-2103 (emphasis added). If you are having trouble identifying the government entity responsible for your situation, or you are getting the "runaround" on an issue that leaders seem to be avoiding, check to see if your state has a High School Athletics Overview Committee (or a similarly named group). You can begin by looking at your state school laws. There you can search using the table of contents and the key terms above ("athletics," "athletic association," "committee," "joint," etc.).

STATE SCHOOL LAWS THAT ADDRESS STUDENT DISCIPLINE

Student discipline, especially when another student is being bullied, is another common concern for parents. Therefore, parents and educators need to understand that the laws, rules, and policies regarding student discipline start at the *state* level. For example, Georgia law addresses: corporal punishment; improved student learning environment and discipline; public school disciplinary tribunals; chronic disciplinary problem students; and alternative educational systems, to name a few. O.C.G.A. §§ 20-2-730 through 20-2-769.

Then, these state laws are *supported* and *extended* at the state board of education level and at the local board of education level. Student discipline laws can also extend into the state's juvenile code. For more on student discipline, see Chapters 5 and 7.

STATE SCHOOL LAWS THAT PROTECT EDUCATORS

State school laws are replete with protection for educators. Most state school laws address sick leave, personal leave, maternity leave, the right to leave for jury duty, health insurance, and retirement plans. State school laws also protect educators in the classroom. For example, Georgia has a school law protecting duty-free lunch for certain classroom teachers, and setting maximum class sizes for grades K-12. O.C.G.A. § 20-2-182. School laws protect educators for disciplining students within specific boundaries. O.C.G.A. § 20-2-1000. Georgia even has a law protecting grade integrity, which states, "No classroom teacher shall be required, coerced, intimidated, or disciplined in any manner by the local board of education, superintendent, or any local school administrator to change the grade of a student." O.C.G.A. § 20-2-989.20. These laws are a source of protection for educators.

HIDDEN GEMS IN STATE SCHOOL LAWS

If you spend a little time looking at your state's school laws, you may find some hidden gems. You may be reassured about an issue or decide to do more research. In Georgia, you may discover protections you were not aware of previously, such as:

- Limits on collecting student data, O.C.G.A. § 20-2-665;
- Parental consent for participation in school clubs and organizations, O.C.G.A. § 20-2-705;
- Student health, including vaccine-related school laws, O.C.G.A. §§ 20-2-770 through 20-2-779.1 and religious exemptions, O.C.G.A. § 20-2-771(e) and (f); and
- Benefits for homeschool students that include the right to participate in your resident school system's extracurricular and interscholastic activities if you take one class at the public school and meet other conditions, O.C.G.A. § 20-2-319.6.

Other states have similar laws and hidden gems.

"SCHOOL CHOICE" LAWS

"School Choice" is the term used for state government programs that allow public school funds to *follow* students to the school they choose to attend whether public, private, parochial, or, in some cases, homeschools. School Choice programs vary from state to state and have different funding mechanisms such as vouchers, tax credits, or education savings accounts. Some states give their school choice programs names designed to draw support, such as Arizona's Empowerment Scholarship Account program. Regardless of the name, their primary function is to allow a portion of public school funding to *follow* the student.

Despite their benefits, school choice laws face several hurdles. First, they must be permitted under the state constitution, which may recognize the right to a "public" education but not a "private" one. Second, school choice laws must not violate the federal constitution's Establishment Clause. This is less of a concern today because the U.S. Supreme Court abandoned the analysis that may have prohibited school choice programs.[13] Third, school choice programs must avoid violations of the state constitution's religion clause, which may prohibit state funds from passing to religious institutions. See Appendix B. Finally, there are groups on both sides of the political spectrum that oppose school choice laws: those who want to protect public schools and those who want to protect religious freedom. The latter is concerned with any government program that offers money or tax credits to religious institutions (i.e., churches, synagogues, and schools). The concern is that government funding will come with "strings" and accountability measures (either now or later) that will compromise doctrine and erode religious instruction. As a result, tax credits may be needed to avoid these issues in some states.

> "School Choice" is the term used for state government programs that allow public school funds to follow students to the school they choose to attend whether public, private, parochial, or, in some cases, homeschools.

STRENGTHEN YOUR ADVOCACY EFFORTS

If you are concerned about your public school's curriculum, athletics or disciplinary policies, you can use your state's existing school laws to strengthen your advocacy efforts. You may find that the school laws you hoped to implement are already there. You may also want to amend or extend them. For example, parents and educators in Georgia could advocate that the General Assembly (the state legislature) amend some of the above laws regarding history instruction that are currently optional (the "may" and the "strongly encouraged" language) and make it required instruction. These amendments are a much easier solution given that the General Assembly has already strongly encouraged the local boards of education to adopt this curriculum. Alternatively, parents and educators in Georgia could ask their local boards to "restate" the state's school laws regarding history in local board rules. Restating state school laws in local board rules is common, especially when the state's legislature strongly encourages that they become part of the curriculum requirements. It is much easier to amend, extend, or restate an existing law than to create an entirely new one.

ADVOCATE THROUGH PARENT TEACHER ASSOCIATIONS OR ORGANIZATIONS

The national and state chapters of the Parent Teacher Association ("PTA") do many positive things for students and schools. Yet, if your local school PTA intends to advocate for or against state legislation, it is essential to first look at your state PTA's legislative priorities. Why? Because state PTAs generally set the legislative priorities for that state. In other words, state PTAs decide which bills (proposed laws) they do and do not support. Local PTA representatives, while acting as PTA representatives, are generally not permitted to take a conflicting position. You can, of course, speak in your individual capacity, but not while you are representing the PTA. *Therefore, it is crucial to look carefully at your state PTA's legislative priorities before your local PTA advocates for or against a particular legislative bill.*

> *It is crucial to look carefully at your state PTA's legislative priorities before your local PTA advocates for or against a particular legislative bill.*

I learned this firsthand when I served as the legislation chair for several PTAs from 2006 – 2017. In that role, I reported to the schools on state legislation affecting students, as well as state and local board issues. I also went to the state capitol several times a year to attend presentations by legislators on the education committee, and to attend "PTA Day at the Capitol." After several trips to the state capitol, I began to see that the legislative priorities of Georgia PTA were not necessarily in line with our local schools' PTAs. In our situation, many members of our local school PTA favored a bill allowing school vouchers, but our state PTA was against the bill. Our local PTAs were not permitted to take a position that conflicted with Georgia PTA, at least when we were acting as PTA representatives. More importantly, we were sending several dollars of each PTA member's dues to support Georgia and National PTAs. In other words, we were funding legislative priorities and positions that, in some cases, our community opposed.

In 2017, several of our local school PTAs voted to become a Parent Teacher Organization (PTO). PTOs are independent non-profit entities. Unlike PTAs, PTOs are not required to pay a portion of each member's dues to a state and national group. Certainly, there are trade-offs. PTAs offer the strength of state and national advocacy (on issues our community did support) and leadership training. Our school was prepared for those issues and we moved to a PTO. If you choose this option, you will need to see a lawyer and one of the many online PTO programs that can assist you in making the change. Also, governance training for your PTO is an *essential* aspect of successful leadership.

RESEARCHING STATE SCHOOL LAWS

Each state legislature is responsible for passing laws. As you may recall, laws begin with draft legislation called a "bill." The bill is proposed, revised, and passed by members of the state's house and senate (the state legislative branch). The bill is then signed into law by the governor (the state executive branch). The courts (the state judicial branch) interpret the law when it is challenged in the courts. All three branches of state government are involved in enacting and interpreting state law.

State laws are organized in a code (or statute), usually designated by "Title" and followed by a number. For example, Georgia school laws are published in the Official Code of Georgia Annotated "O.C.G.A Title 20." Georgia school laws include approximately 734 separate active school laws, not including their parts and subparts. State school laws address class size maximums, teacher certification requirements, school buses, ethics requirements, teacher pay schedules, limits on administrator and superintendent pay, athletics, student discipline, and curriculum requirements, to name a few.

Sometimes, a new law affects several areas of the law or "Titles." For example, Georgia's new mental health law amends Titles 15 (Courts), 20 (Education), 31 (Health), 33 (Insurance), 35 (Law Enforcement Officers and Agencies), 37 (Mental Health), 45 (Public Officers and Employees), and 49 (Social Services).[14]

"Articles" are groupings of laws passed together. Unfortunately, the law's citation does not necessarily correspond to the article, which can be confusing. Georgia's "American History Recognition and Significant Documents" are organized under Article 19A, which includes three separate laws (O.C.G.A. §§ 20-2-1020 through 20-2-1022). Note that Article 19A is not reflected in the citation. In these situations, a table of contents is helpful because it may specify the location of the article.

As you dive into research, note that states vary in their use of title, chapter, section, paragraph, part, and subpart in citations. Some states separate the numbers in the citations with dashes (-) or periods (.). Some use "c" or "ch" for chapter and "§" for section. The symbols "§§" mean "more than one section." Sometimes the § is left out. The symbol "¶" means paragraph. The symbol "¶¶" means more than one paragraph. The words "et seq.," after the citation means "and what follows." In that case, the citation is to the law cited *and* the related laws that follow it. The date that the law was enacted and amended is listed at the end of the law.

HOW TO FIND WHAT YOU NEED

Your State's School Laws

- Go to Appendix C and find your state's information page.
- Click the link to your state's laws using:
  1. the Justia.com link;
  2. the state legislature's official link; and
  3. Findlaw.com, which is not linked but is another good resource.
- School laws can be hard to find on the state legislature's website because some focus on current legislation. Justia and FindLaw offer free online searches and have a nice table of contents, making it easy to find the title for the state's school laws.
- Once you find the state's school laws, look for "curriculum or curricula," "required courses," or "quality-based education." Rather than a keyword search, I prefer to use [control] [f] because it allows me to search within the state's education title or statute.
- One difficulty with online searches is that curriculum requirements are not necessarily consolidated in one area. For example, most of Georgia's curriculum requirements are in Article 6 under "Quality Based Education," encompassing O.C.G.A. §§ 20-2-130 through 20-2-329.1. However, the state school law preventing partisan instruction is at § 20-2-1011, and the "American History Recognition and Significant

Documents Act," which includes three separate laws, is found at O.C.G.A. §§ 20-2-1020 through 20-2-1022. Because relevant school laws can be virtually anywhere in the title or statute containing the state's school laws, I prefer a book to flip through page by page and scan for laws regarding curriculum and content.

- *Suppose you are serious about having one hands-on source for your state's school laws. In that case, LexisNexis annually publishes a book for many states, which includes the state constitution's education article, the state's school laws, and a few additional sections relevant to education.* Plus, it is annotated, which means it has short, 1-2-sentence summaries of cases and commentaries involving that school law. Georgia's book is titled "Georgia School Laws." See http://store.lexisnexis.com and search for "[Your State's Name] School Laws [Year]." Please note that LexisNexis only carries this book for some states.

- **NOTICE: State laws are continually changing. It is crucial to check and recheck several sources to confirm that you have the most current version of the law.**

CHAPTER 4

OTHER STATE LAWS THAT AFFECT PUBLIC SCHOOLS K-12

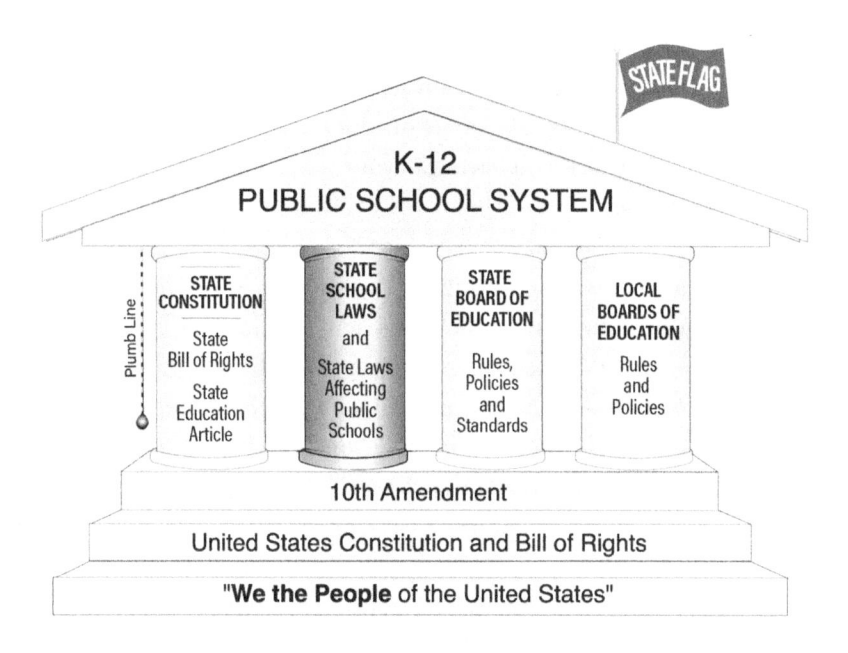

[Illustration: K-12 Public School System depicted as a building with a state flag, supported by four pillars — State Constitution (State Bill of Rights, State Education Article); State School Laws and State Laws Affecting Public Schools; State Board of Education (Rules, Policies and Standards); Local Boards of Education (Rules and Policies) — with a Plumb Line at left, resting on steps labeled "10th Amendment," "United States Constitution and Bill of Rights," and "**We the People** of the United States"]

In addition to state school laws in the "education" section, each state also has laws that affect public schools. For our purposes, I have included four laws that are common or are becoming more common in the states. They include: (1) State Open Meetings Acts, which provide public access to state and local board of education meetings; (2) State Open Records Acts, which provide public access to public school documents; (3) exemptions to the state's criminal obscenity laws for public schools and public libraries, which exist in some, but not all states; and (4) new state mental health laws that allow public schools to have a more significant role in students' mental health care, which exist in some, but not all states.

STATE OPEN MEETINGS ACTS

Each state has an Open Meetings Act (or a similar version) that guarantees public access to specific government agency meetings, including state and local board of education meetings. It is essential to find and understand your state's Open Meetings Act. Why? Because if you intend to speak at a state or local board of education meeting, your voice is more likely to be heard if you understand you state's Open Meetings Act.

As a Georgia hypothetical, assume that the local board of education limited the meeting to matters specifically listed on the board's agenda, which is a relatively easy way for the local board of education to control the discussion on controversial issues. If you have read your state's Open Meetings Act, you may see that it states:

> "Prior to any meeting, the agency or committee holding such meeting shall make available an agenda of all matters expected to come before the agency or committee at such meeting.... ***Failure to include on the agenda an item which becomes necessary to address during the course of a meeting shall not preclude considering and acting upon such item.***"

O.C.G.A. § 50-14-1(e)(1) (emphasis added). If you are aware of this law before the meeting, you and others can call it to the local board of education's attention and raise issues at the meeting that are not on the agenda. This scenario is just one example of why parents and educators need to understand school laws that affect public schools. If you rely on your state's Open Meetings Act, read it entirely! Also, read any education cross-references in the law. The cross-referenced laws may give you additional rights.

Using Georgia's Open Meetings Act as an example, some common provisions state: the Open Meeting Act applies to "school district" meetings; the meetings "shall be open to the public;" "visual and sound recording during open meetings shall be permitted;" and if the meeting is required to be open to the public, but is not, any official action taken by the board during the meeting is "not binding." O.C.G.A. §§ 50-14-1(a) through (c).

School boards and other government agencies that are subject to the state's Open Meetings Act must publicize the time, place, and dates of regular meetings. O.C.G.A. § 50-14-1(d)(1). The state's Open Meetings Act also specifies who can enforce the law and stop the meeting (with an injunction). O.C.G.A. § 50-14-5(a).

A DISTINCTION: ATTENDING VERSUS SPEAKING AT THE LOCAL BOARD MEETING

There is a distinction between the *right to attend* a local board of education meeting and the *right to speak* at a local board of education meeting. In Georgia, the Open Meetings Act provides the right to attend the board meeting in Title 50, but the law that provides the right to speak at board meeting is in Title 20. If you are planning to attend a school board meeting and want to speak during public comment, be sure to look at the laws that govern the meeting. For example, Georgia's school law regarding meetings states that local boards of education:

- Must hold regular monthly meetings;
- Must provide a public comment period during every regular monthly meeting; and
- Must not require notice by an individual more than 24 hours prior to the meeting as a condition of addressing the local board during such public comment period.

O.C.G.A. § 20-2-58.[1] There are time limits on public comment. The local board chairperson can limit the number of people speaking for or against a specific issue. Of course, check the laws in your state that address public comment and seek local legal counsel if you have questions.

CHECK YOUR LOCAL SCHOOL DISTRICT RULES: NO PERSONNEL MATTERS DURING PUBLIC COMMENT

In Georgia, many local school district rules prohibit public comment regarding personnel matters, usually for fear of defamation claims by educators. Suppose you raise a concern about instructional material or content in a way that is critical of specific school officials or teachers. In that case, you are arguably walking into a personnel matter, which cannot be discussed during public comment. If you are asked to stop talking and you do not, the school board may have legal grounds to remove you from the meeting. So, ask yourself, "How can I frame my issue so that it is not a personnel matter?"

LOCAL BOARD MEETINGS: CONSIDER SENDING LETTERS TO THE SCHOOL, SCHOOL BOARD, AND LOCAL SCHOOL SUPERINTENDENT

A respectful, calm, and well-articulated letter to the school principal, the local board of education, and your local school superintendent can often resolve a problem. If you write to your school officials and local board, outline the facts, express your concerns, describe your situation, attach pertinent documents, and requests that the teacher and school administrators address your issue. In other words, ask for what you want. You can reference the state laws, rules, and policies that apply to your situation. You can also reference your constitutional rights, if applicable.

A respectful, calm, and well-articulated letter to the school principal, the local board of education, and your local school superintendent can often resolve a problem.

LOCAL BOARD MEETINGS: IT IS A MATTER OF HOW YOU FRAME YOUR CONCERNS

After sending the letter, you may raise your concerns at a local board of education meeting during public comment. You and other parents who have written similar letters can then speak respectfully and calmly in more general terms. For example, you may raise the issue that schools (generally) within the district are permitting teachers (generally) to use controversial materials and content that do not comply with the state school laws, and state and local board rules and policies. Rather than name the teachers and schools at the meeting, you can reference your letter. This way, the underlying personnel issues are not made public at the meeting.

HOW TO FIND WHAT YOU NEED

Your State's Open Meetings Act

- See Appendix C and the page for your state.
- Click the link to your state's Open Meetings Act.
- Read your state's Open Meetings Act and other laws cross-referenced in it.
- If you have general questions, try to find an annotated version of your state's Open Meetings Act with the cases and commentaries that discuss the provisions. The cases and commentaries may answer your questions.
- Look at your state laws, state board of education rules, and local board of education rules to see if they address public meetings or your state's Open Meetings Act.
- When I speak at a meeting, I often bring a written letter to the board to back-up my speaking points. I bring copies for each board member, plus one extra. I also ask that that the public comment records include my written letter.
- If you plan to use the media and a group of like-minded parents at a local board meeting, be aware that some Open Meetings Acts give local boards the power to reschedule meetings. In fact, the local board may reschedule the meeting *even* after business hours the night before the meeting (i.e., moving the meeting to an earlier time than scheduled). Be prepared. Monitor your phones and email into the late-night hours and have a backup plan if this happens.
- **NOTICE: State laws are continually changing. It is crucial to check and recheck several sources to confirm that you have the most current version of the law.**

STATE OPEN RECORDS ACTS

Each state has an open records law (or a similar version) that guarantees public access to public records, including school district records. Some states refer to these laws as "sunshine laws" or "freedom of information laws." There is a similar law at the federal level known as the Freedom of Information Act (FOIA). 5 U.S.C. § 552. Because education is a matter of state law, we are interested in the state's Open Records Act. Georgia's Open Records Act has provisions that are common in most states:

- Defines "public records" to include "all documents, papers, letters, maps, books, tapes, photographs, computer-based or -generated information, or similar material prepared and maintained or received in the course of the operation of a public office or agency," O.C.G.A. § 50-18-70(a);
- "All public records shall be open for personal inspection and copying, except those which by order of a court of this state or by law are specifically exempted from disclosure," O.C.G.A. § 50-18-71(a);
- Gives the agency three days to determine whether the records are subject to public access, O.C.G.A. § 50-18-71(b); and
- Charges for production and copying of public records shall be reasonable, O.C.G.A. § 50-18-71(c).

Open records requests are a great way to get essential documents on the issue you are researching or investigating. Before you make an open records request regarding curriculum, ask your school administration for a list of your child's textbooks, supplemental resources, online resources, and required reading. Your local school district may have a rule allowing parents to review curriculum and other instructional material and content. To learn how to search your local state and local school rules on their websites, see Chapters 5 and 6. If you do make an open records request, here are a few basics:

1. Locate an open records request form for your state or write your own in letter format. See Appendix C.

2. Identify the government entity that will provide the records you want. You can send the open records request to your child's school if you want textbook and curriculum information. If you are going to identify the third-party contractors for the school district, you can send the request to the school district's "Records Custodian." The government entity's "Records Custodian" usually receives open records requests.
3. The scope of your request is crucial. Records Custodians read them *very* literally. Write your request so that you receive everything you intend to encompass but not so broadly that you receive documents you do not want or need. For example, include [your topic] and request a list of assigned textbooks, course outlines, lesson plans, teacher handouts, Power Points, online resources, and emails between teachers and administrators on [your topic]. Suppose you have concerns about the district-wide adoption of a controversial topic. In that case, your request might include: agreements, budget records, contracts, emails, invoices, policy documents, purchase orders, and payments to third-party contractors for services regarding [your topic]. This list is not exhaustive, but it should give you an idea of what you want to request. If you have questions, contact legal counsel.

> *Each state has an open records law (or a similar version) that guarantees public access to public records, including school district records.*

4. Reference the state's open records law you are using as the basis for your request.
5. Provide your contact information.
6. Request that if they withhold some or all the public records, they respond to you in writing and identify the statutory basis for withholding them.
7. Confirm receipt of your open records request by email with an "email read" receipt and by sending the request via certified mail with a return receipt.

HOW TO FIND WHAT YOU NEED

Your State's Open Records Act

- See Appendix C and the page for your state.
- Click the link to your state's Open Records Act or go to the "National Freedom of Information Coalition" link and click on your state. (https://www.nfoic.org/state-freedom-of-information-laws/)
- Read your state's entire Open Records Act and cross-referenced laws.
- If you have general questions, look for an annotated version of your state's Open Records Act with cases and commentaries that discuss the laws. The cases and commentaries may answer your questions.
- Look at your state laws, state board of education rules, and local board of education rules to see if they address your state's Open Records Act. These rules may expand your rights and provide additional support for your request.
- Your state may offer an online form for requests that are made under the state's Open Records Act. If not, there are many forms available online.
- **NOTICE: State laws are continually changing. It is crucial to check and recheck several sources to confirm that you have the most current version of the law.**

STATE LAWS THAT GIVE PUBLIC SCHOOLS AND PUBLIC LIBRARIES EXEMPTIONS FROM STATE OBSCENITY LAWS

In recent years, there has been controversy over public schools exposing students to sexually explicit instructional materials and content. Our family encountered this when one of our children was required to read a book with several vivid descriptions of child molestation. These types of books are permitted because many states have "exemptions" and "materials that cannot be sold to children [under state criminal laws] can be checked out of the public library or school library and/or be presented as part of school assignments."[2] As this situation becomes more well-known, some people have asked their state legislatures to remove or limit their state's criminal obscenity exemptions. Below is an overview of this controversial issue and some essential arguments to help parents and educators protect children. I will try to make this complex issue easy to understand.

Most states have criminal laws that define "obscene material" or "materials harmful to minors" *and* make it a crime to give this material to minors (generally under 18 years old). Georgia's law currently states in part:

GEORGIA LAW

O.C.G.A. § 16-12-101   **Sale or Distribution of Harmful Materials to Minors; Legislative Purpose**

The General Assembly finds that the sale, loan, and exhibition of harmful materials to minors has become a matter of increasingly grave concern to the people of this state. The elimination of such sales, loans, and exhibition and the consequent protection of minors from harmful materials are in the best interest of the morals and general welfare of the citizens of this state in general and of minors in this state in particular. *The accomplishment of these ends can best be achieved by providing public prosecutors with an effective power to commence criminal proceedings against persons who engage in the sale, loan, or exhibition of harmful materials to minors.*

GEORGIA LAW

O.C.G.A. § 16-12-103   **Sale or Distribution of Harmful Materials to Minors; Selling, Loaning, Distributing, or Exhibiting; . . .**

(a) *It shall be unlawful for any person knowingly to sell or loan for monetary consideration or otherwise furnish or disseminate to a minor:*

    (1) Any picture, photograph, drawing, sculpture, motion picture film, or similar visual representation or image of a person or portion of the human body which depicts sexually explicit nudity, sexual conduct, or sadomasochistic abuse and which is harmful to minors; or

    (2) Any book, pamphlet, magazine, printed matter however reproduced, or sound recording which contains any matter enumerated in paragraph (1) of this subsection, or explicit and detailed verbal descriptions or narrative accounts of sexual excitement, sexual conduct, or sadomasochistic abuse and which, taken as a whole, is harmful to minors.

> (b) (1) It shall be unlawful for any person knowingly to sell or furnish to a minor an admission ticket or pass or knowingly to admit a minor to premises whereon there is exhibited a motion picture, show, or other presentation which, in whole or in part, depicts sexually explicit nudity, sexual conduct, or sadomasochistic abuse and which is harmful to minors or exhibit any such motion picture at any such premises which are not designed to prevent viewing from any public way of such motion picture by minors not admitted to any such premises....

O.C.G.A. §§ 16-12-101 and 16-12-103 (emphasis added). Surprisingly, many states exempt public schools, public school libraries, and public libraries from criminal obscenity laws. In other words, they can show or give students access to these materials without criminal liability.[3]

Some state obscenity exemptions are broad and protect employees, boards of directors, and trustees of schools and libraries from criminal liability,[4] and with no restrictions on the time, place, or manner of the exposure. Other states have more limited exemptions, such as the State of Florida.[5] Although the exemption language varies from state to state, the arguments for challenging exemptions are essentially the same. Georgia's exemption states:

GEORGIA LAW

O.C.G.A. § 16-12-104   Sale or Distribution of Harmful Materials to Minors; Library Exception

The provisions of Code Section 16-12-103 **shall not apply to any public library operated by the state or any of its political subdivisions nor to** *any library operated as a part of any school,* **college, or university.**

O.C.G.A. § 16-12-104 (emphasis added). As you can see, Georgia's current exemption applies to school libraries.

In 1995, the Opinion of the Attorney General was that libraries may be required by legislation to protect minors from harmful material.

OPINION OF THE ATTORNEY GENERAL

O.C.G.A. § 16-12-102; and Op. Att'y Gen. No. U95-24.

Public libraries may be required by legislation to take appropriate action to protect minors from exposure to materials which fall within the definition of harmful to minors.

O.C.G.A. § 16-12-102; and Op. Att'y Gen. No. U95-24 (below the law) (emphasis added).

That did not happen. Rather, in 2022 the General Assembly placed the burden on *parents* and *legal guardians* to find harmful material in libraries *after* students have access to it. See GA S.B. 226, (Regular Session, 2021-2022).

In April 2022, the Georgia General Assembly enacted a new law that requires all local boards of education to adopt a "complaint resolution policy." When parents or permanent guardians allege that material harmful to minors has been provided or is currently available to students in that local school system, they must file a complaint. O.C.G.A. § 20-2-324.6. The school principal (or designated person) will determine whether the material is harmful to minors and whether it will be removed or restricted. O.C.G.A. §§ 20-2-324.6(b)(4) and (5). Librarians are *not* required to find or call attention to harmful materials before they are available to minors. Georgia's law places the burden on parents and legal guardians to find and file a complaint about the allegedly harmful material in public school libraries — after students have access to it.

In April 2022, the Georgia General Assembly enacted a new law that requires all local boards of education to adopt a "complaint resolution policy."

If you are searching for new legislation in your state on this issue, see Appendix C or search using similar terms such as "obscenity," "exempt," "school," "harmful material," "minors," and "complaint resolution." ***As obscenity exemptions become well-known, people are learning how this material is permitted in public schools and libraries.***

CHALLENGING STATE OBSCENITY EXEMPTIONS

1. Curriculum Requirements Support Removal of Obscenity Exemptions

A few state obscenity exemptions have been removed or revised using the state legislative process. Some revisions are so watered down that they still do not protect students from what some parents consider pornography. Suppose you want to advocate for removing or revising your state's obscenity exemption. In that case, you can focus on the state's curriculum requirements for health and sex education to determine if the exemption is even necessary. Some people *assume* that the school *needs* the exemption to teach sex education, when that may not be accurate. The point is: if teachers are following the state's health and sex education curriculum requirements, then an exemption from the state's criminal obscenity law is unnecessary. Suppose teachers are *not* following the state's health and sex education curriculum requirements. In that case, the law serves its purpose and protects students from teachers who want to venture into matters that may be considered obscenity under state criminal laws. In other words, the state's health and sex education curriculum requirements *must* be considered in any discussion regarding criminal obscenity exemptions.

2. Existing Protections for School Officials Support Removal of Obscenity Exemptions

You can also urge state legislatures to consider other existing protections for school personnel. For example, Georgia school laws give board members, school administrators, and teachers a variety of protections such as governmental immunity (O.C.G.A. §§ 20-2-992 and 20-2-2020); defenses in civil and criminal actions (O.C.G.A. § 20-2-993); insurance (O.C.G.A. § 20-2-991); and training for alleged sexual misconduct by school personnel (O.C.G.A. § 20-2-751.7). There may be even more protections at the state and local board of education level. In other words, they are *already* protected. You can use key terms to find similar laws in your state. Another persuasive argument is weighing risks. On the one hand, there is the risk of exposing students to instructional materials considered obscene or harmful under state criminal laws. On the other hand, there is the risk of teachers being held liable despite specific curriculum requirements and existing protections under state law. There are compelling arguments that this is an easy choice in favor of protecting students.

3. There Is a Strong Argument That State Obscenity Exemptions Cannot Withstand Constitutional Scrutiny

Parental rights, including the right to control the raising of one's children, are considered fundamental constitutional rights. When parental rights are affected, the U.S. Supreme Court has applied "strict scrutiny," which requires the government to have a "compelling actual purpose" in enacting the law and the law must be "narrowly tailored" to meet that purpose. The courts are responsible for analyzing the law and making the determination. In other words, why did the government *need* to pass the law? What was the purpose behind the law? How crucial is the government's interest in this issue? Then the courts look to see if the law is narrowly tailored to meet that purpose. Broad and sweeping laws do not tend to fare well in the courts. Courts want laws written narrowly so they do not violate people's constitutional rights.

If a court applied "strict scrutiny" to an obscenity exemption, it would likely ask some of the following questions: What is the purpose of the exemption? Was it to protect health and sex education teachers in public schools? Can public school teachers follow the state's health and sex education curriculum requirements without violating the state's obscenity law? Is the health and sex education curriculum "obscene" under the state's law? Is the law even necessary when school personnel already have governmental immunity, defenses in civil and criminal actions, insurance, training for alleged sexual misconduct by school personnel, and other protections in school law and at the state and local board of education level as well? Is there a "compelling" reason for the exemption?

> *Courts want laws written narrowly so they do not violate people's constitutional rights.*

Additionally, the courts would likely consider whether the exemption is narrowly tailored to meet the government's interest or purpose. Is the exemption limited to instructional time? Is the exemption limited to sex education teachers? Do coaches, bus drivers, cafeteria workers, and the maintenance staff need the exemption? One can argue that some obscenity exemptions permit any school personnel on any day and at any time to expose children to an array of obscene materials under the state's criminal laws and still be exempt from prosecution.

In other words, state obscenity exemptions can be challenged based on constitutionally protected parental rights that are recognized as "fundamental rights" under the federal and state constitutions.[6] If challenged, there are compelling arguments that the courts would apply "strict scrutiny" and the obscenity exemptions would be deemed unconstitutional — nationwide.

So, how would such a case arise? Generally, when someone violates a criminal law, the victim reports the crime to the police, preferably with legal counsel. The police and victim then prepare a report of the crime. The police may refuse to accept, prepare, or follow-up on the report based on an exemption in the law. The prosecutor may do the same. Nonetheless, the victim(s) and legal counsel may decide to bring a "case" against the state government challenging the constitutionality of the obscenity exemption based on parental rights, the right to free exercise, and the state right to a public education, etc. This could be done by a parent or group of parents. Legal counsel is necessary. For more on constitutional rights, see Chapters 10 and 11.

Additionally, Parents and Educators Can File a Complaint with the Federal Communications Commission under the Children's Internet Protection Act

If you are concerned about the online materials in your school, school library, or public library, it is essential to know that Congress passed the Children's Internet Protection Act (CIPA) in 2000. (https://www.fcc.gov/consumers/guides/childrens-internet-protection-act). CIPA applies to schools, school libraries, and public libraries that receive monies from the federal government. CIPA requires them to install software that blocks obscene material, pornography, and other materials dangerous to minors. To file a complaint, see the instructions on the Federal Communications Commission (FCC) Consumer Guide (https://www.fcc.gov/sites/default/files/childrens_internet_protection_act_cipa.pdf).

HOW TO FIND WHAT YOU NEED

Your State's Obscenity Exemption

- See Appendix C and find your state's information page.
- If applicable, click the link to your state's obscenity law and exemption.
- You can also look under your state's criminal laws.
- **NOTICE: State laws are continually changing. It is crucial to check and recheck several sources to confirm that you have the most current version of the law.**

NEW STATE MENTAL HEALTH LAWS

Given nationwide concerns regarding mental health, several states are considering or enacting new mental health laws, some of which will affect children in public schools. Georgia's new mental health law titled the "Mental Health Parity Act," amends several titles or areas of the law: Titles 15 (Courts), 20 (Education), 31 (Health), 33 (Insurance), 35 (Law Enforcement Officers and Agencies), 37 (Mental Health), 45 (Public Officers and Employees), and 49 (Social Services). To see the changes to these Titles in one document, you can look at the signed bill through the governor's website.[7]

Georgia's new mental health law is based on the Georgia Behavioral Health Reform and Innovation Commission Report, which recommends "school-based health centers" and "state-wide telehealth for schools." (https://www.house.ga.gov/Documents/Committeedocuments/2020/behavioralhealth/BH_commission_report.pdf).[8] As parents debate the new mental health law, some want and need their children to have access to these services. Others are concerned that teachers and administrators will have too much power over their children's healthcare decisions and personal information. My goal is to teach parents and educators about new laws that affect public schools. Parents can decide whether to submit an opt-out form.

Regarding children, the law designates the *State School Superintendent* as a member of the Behavioral Health Coordinating Council.[9] It also states that the Department of Behavioral Health and Developmental Disabilities shall: "Establish the Multi-Agency Treatment for *Children* (MATCH) team within the department. *The state MATCH team shall be composed of representatives from* the Division of Family and Children Services of the Department of Human Services; the Department of Juvenile Justice; the Department of Early Care and Learning; the Department of Public Health; the Department of Community Health; the *Department of Education*; the Office of the Child Advocate; and the Department of Corrections . . . . The state MATCH team shall facilitate collaboration across state agencies to explore resources and solutions or complex and unmet treatment needs for children in this state and to provide for solutions, including both public and private providers, as necessary. **The state MATCH team will accept referrals from local interagency children's committees throughout Georgia for children with complex treatment needs not** *met through the resources of their local community and custodians."*[10] Of concern, the word "custodians" is not clearly defined.[11]

Using this example, you can see that there is *coordination* among the various agencies. So, in your state, you might search within your state's new mental health law for the terms "coordinating" (or a variation), "children," "State School Superintendent," "Department of Education," and "data sharing." You may also search terms such as "school," "students," and "infants."[12] I prefer to use [control][f] for these types of searches within a document.

The General Assembly just passed the new mental health law. So, it is unclear how schools will create "school-based health centers," provide "statewide telehealth for schools," and whether it will include more extensive counseling and psychiatric services.[13] It is also unclear how student data will be shared among the various agencies, presumably under one of the Family Educational Rights and Privacy Act ("FERPA") exceptions.

HOW TO FIND WHAT YOU NEED

Your State's Mental Health Laws

- See Appendix C and find your state's information page.
- Click the link to your state's laws through one of the three links:
  1. the state legislature's official link;
  2. the Justia.com link; and
  3. Findlaw.com.
- Look for your state's mental health laws.
- Look at your state legislature and governor's websites for new laws that are either pending or recently signed into law by the governor.
- Use the terms above to search for key issues related to children and schools.
- **NOTICE: State laws are continually changing. It is crucial to check and recheck several sources to confirm that you have the most current version of the law.**

CHAPTER 5

THE STATE BOARD OF EDUCATION AND THE STATE SCHOOL SUPERINTENDENT

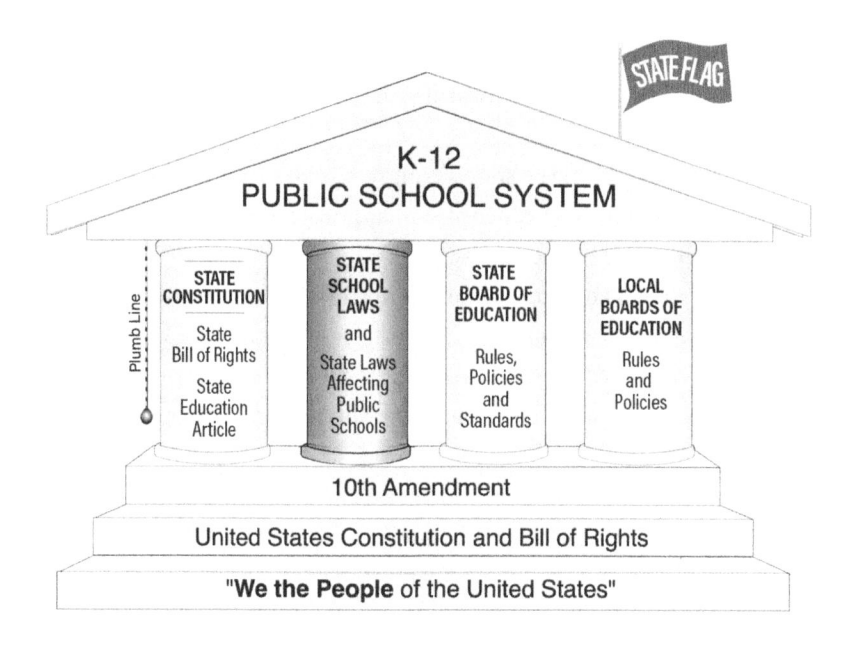

THE STATE BOARD OF EDUCATION

ESTABLISHING WHAT STUDENTS LEARN AT EACH GRADE LEVEL

The state board of education's most crucial functions includes setting curriculum standards for the state's public schools. Generally, the state board of education does not write curriculum; instead, it identifies what students should learn at each grade level. The state board of education also approves textbooks that will be funded if chosen by local school boards.

On one occasion, I attended a Georgia State Board of Education meeting with several other parents and our local board of education member. Our goal was to advocate for a particular mathematics curriculum to be accepted and, more importantly, funded by the Georgia State Board of Education. Our local board member, who recognized the importance of a strong mathematics program, explained the need for approval and the process of appearing. You can do the same to obtain funding for curriculum you support.

REQUIREMENTS OF THE STATE BOARD OF EDUCATION

The rules that your state board of education must follow will be listed in your state constitution, state school laws, and state board of education rules. In most states, the state board of education members are:

- Representatives of the state's congressional districts;
- Either elected by the people or appointed by the state governor and confirmed by the state senate;
- Required to take an oath of office for the faithful performance of their duties and an oath of allegiance to the federal and state constitutions;
- Required to elect a chairperson to preside at board meetings, set the agenda, and perform other duties;
- Required to meet as a board at least quarterly;
- *Required to give adequate notice to the public of the upcoming public meetings, which should be posted on the state board of education's website;*
- **Required to hold one or more annual public meetings in their district to listen to performance issues and problems in the public schools within their district;**
- Required to prepare and submit to the governor and state legislature an estimate of the funds necessary to operate the state's public school system;
- May be required to post a bond conditioned on the faithful discharge of their duties; and

The rules that your state board of education must follow will be listed in your state constitution, state school laws, and state board of education rules.

- May have additional fiduciary duties (i.e., duties of care, loyalty, good faith, confidentiality, not engaging in conflicts of interest, etc.)

KEY RESPONSIBILITIES OF THE STATE BOARD OF EDUCATION

The state board of education is also a rulemaking body that passes rules, policies, and standards that local school districts must follow. Although the state board of education is responsible for a plethora of areas involving the state's education system, for our purposes, their most essential functions are:

> *The state board of education is also a rulemaking body that passes rules, policies, and standards that local school districts must follow.*

- **Establishing Rules, Policies, and Standards Regarding Local Boards of Education:** including local board member requirements, ethical standards, compensation, sanctions (including the power to withhold funding to the local school district), appellate review of local board of education decisions and actions; and rules stating that gatherings of local board of education members are subject to the state's Open Meetings Act;
- **Establishing Rules, Policies, and Standards Regarding Curriculum and Virtually Every Other Aspect of Public Schools K-12:** including graduation requirements, vocational education requirements, career education, online programs, curriculum standards, determinations of which curriculum are funded for local boards of education, instructional materials selection and recommendation, student testing, student data collection, athletics, school counselors, buses, and even the construction guidelines for educational facilities (i.e., square footage, bidding, etc.); and
- **Establishing Rules, Policies, and Standards Regarding Charter Entities:** including petitions for start-up charter schools, conversion charter schools, charter and hybrid charter systems, and charter renewals.

THE EXTENSION OF STATE SCHOOL LAWS THROUGH STATE BOARD OF EDUCATION RULES, POLICIES, AND STANDARDS.

In each state, school laws are *supported* and *extended* through state board of education rules, policies, and standards.

State Constitution
(Education Article)

|

State Legislature
(State School Laws)

|

State Board of Education
(State Board Rules, Policies, and Standards)

|

Local Board of Education
(Local Board Rules and Policies)

Once you understand the structure, it is a matter of knowing that these laws and rules exist and having a little guidance on where to find them. Then, you will be able to find your issue in school laws and then follow it into the state board of education rules, policies, and standards. These are usually organized under the state's "Administrative Code," "Administrative Rules," or "Administrative Regulations." To help you, I have linked these citations on your state's page in Appendix C. In Georgia, they are found in the "Compilation of the Rules and Regulations of the State of Georgia," under "Rules of Georgia Department of Education."

STATE BOARD OF EDUCATION RULES, POLICIES, AND STANDARDS: CURRICULUM

Earlier, you looked at Georgia's school laws regarding social studies and history curriculum. You also saw that the Georgia State Board of Education expanded those laws with rules, policies, and standards. For example, the

Georgia State Board of Education rule regarding "Instruction in United States and Georgia History and Government" reiterates the state law and specifies *when* public schools must teach various parts of the history curriculum. It also states that, "Local boards of education shall exempt students who enter a Georgia public school after the eighth-grade year from the required course of study in Georgia history and government." GA Rules and Regs 160-4-2-.07. In other words, the state board of education gives additional guidance on the state school law and cites the law at the bottom of the rule.

STATE BOARD OF EDUCATION RULES AND POLICIES: STUDENT DISCIPLINE

State board of education rules also specify student discipline requirements that are an extension of state school laws. For example, GA Rules and Regs 160-4-8-.15 (2)(a)(1)-(4) states:

> (2) REQUIREMENTS. (a) Each local board of education shall adopt policies designed to improve the student learning environment by improving student behavior and discipline. These policies shall provide for the development of age-appropriate student codes of conduct that contain the following, at a minimum:
>
> 1. Standards for student behavior during school hours, at school-related functions, on school buses, and at school bus stops designed to create the expectation that students will behave themselves in such a way so as to facilitate a learning environment for themselves and other students, respect each other and school district employees, obey student behavior policies adopted by the local board of education, and obey student behavior rules established by individual schools;
>
> 2. Verbal assault, including threatening violence, of teachers, administrators, and other school personnel;
>
> 3. Physical assault or battery of teachers, administrators, or other school personnel;

> 4. Disrespectful conduct toward teachers, administrators, other school personnel, persons attending school-related functions or other students, including use of vulgar or profane language; ...
>
> Authority: O.C.G.A §§ 16-11-127.1; 20-2-152; 20-2-240; 20-2-735; 20-2-736; 20-2- 737; 20-2-738(b); 20-2-742; 20-2-751.1; 20-2-751.2; 20-2-751.4; 20-2-751.5; 20-2- 751.6; 20-2-752; 20-2-753; 20-2-754; 20-2-755; 20-2-756; 20-2-758; 20-2-759; 20-2- 1181.

GA Rules and Regs 160-4-8-.15 (2)(a)(1) – (4). This particular rule continues and includes numerous other offenses, including, but not limited to, verbal assault of other students, willful or malicious damage to real or personal property of the school or to personal property of any person legitimately at the school; unlawful use or possession of illegal drugs or alcohol; bullying, and "any off-campus behavior of a student which could result in the student being criminally charged with a felony and which makes the student's continued presence at school a potential danger to persons or property at the school or which disrupts the educational process." GA Rules and Regs 160-4-8-.15(2)(a)(5) – (15). It also cites to the provisions of Title 20 that pertain to student discipline. Therefore, if your child is being bullied, you can look at the state law, the state board of education rule, and then the local board of education rule on this issue.

STATE BOARD OF EDUCATION RULES: APPEALS

State school laws usually give state boards of education appellate authority over decisions by the local boards of education. For example, GA Rules and Regs 160-1-3-.04 allows appeals from local boards of education to the state board of education on "issues respecting the administration or construction of school law." GA Rules and Regs 160-1-3-.04(1). Regarding appeals, GA Rules and Regs 160-1-3-.04(4) states:

> (4) APPEALS TO THE STATE BOARD OF EDUCATION. (a) After a hearing by the [local board of education] when held in accordance with state law and/or state board policies, regulations, or

rules, any party aggrieved by a decision of the [local board of education] rendered on an issue respecting the administration or construction of school law may appeal to the state board by filing the appeal in writing with the local school superintendent. The appeal shall set forth:

1. The question in dispute;
2. The decision of the local board; and
3. A concise statement of the reasons why the decision is being appealed...

Authority: O.C.G.A. §§ 20-2-240; 20-2-940; 20-2-1160.

GA Rules and Regs 160-1-3-.04(1). As you can see, this authority comes from state school law, which is cited at the end of the full rule. Just knowing that this appeal process exists is important information that can help resolve disputes.

To find the state board of education rules in your state, follow the instructions in the section titled, HOW TO FIND WHAT YOU NEED: Your Local Board of Education and Your Local School Superintendent.

THE STATE SCHOOL SUPERINTENDENT

REQUIREMENTS OF THE STATE SCHOOL SUPERINTENDENT

In some states, the "superintendent" is called a "commissioner." To find the rules and requirements that the state school superintendent must follow, look at your state constitution and state school laws. In most states, the state school superintendent:

- Is either elected by the people or appointed by the state governor and confirmed by the state senate;
- Is required to take an oath to discharge the duties of their office diligently and faithfully, and support the state and federal constitutions;
- Is required to post a bond[1] conditioned on the faithful discharge of their duties; and

- May have additional fiduciary duties (i.e., duties of care, loyalty, good faith, confidentiality, not engaging in conflicts of interest, etc.)

KEY RESPONSIBILITIES OF THE STATE SCHOOL SUPERINTENDENT: ENFORCEMENT

Generally, the state school superintendent is the executive officer of the state board of education and the administrative chief executive officer of the state's department of education. For our purposes, the state school superintendent's most crucial power is:

- *The responsibility to faithfully and efficiently execute the school laws and the state board of education's rules and regulations.*

If you have a problem and need assistance enforcing school laws or the state board of education rules and regulations, it is best to begin with a spirit of cooperation. The state school superintendent may not be aware of the issue and would appreciate a calm letter or discussion of your concerns. You can contact the state school superintendent through the official email listed on the website. It is best to look at the state board of education website for details. If necessary, obtain legal counsel to assist you with enforcement of the laws and rules. O.C.G.A. §§ 20-2-32 and 20-2-34.[2]

HOW TO FIND WHAT YOU NEED

Your State Board of Education's Rules and Policies

- Go to Appendix C and find your state's information page.
- To find the laws and rules that your state board of education must follow, see your state's constitution and your state's school laws. Look for the section regarding "state board of education."
- To find the laws and rules that your state school superintendent must follow, see your state's constitution and your state's school laws

under the heading "state school superintendent." This section will also indicate whether the state school superintendent has the power of enforcement.
- Generally, state board of education rules are compiled in the state's "Administrative Code," "Administrative Rules," or "Administrative Regulations." To help you, I have linked these cites on your state's page in Appendix C.
- You can also look on your state board of education website. Many states combine their state department of education and state board of education on a single website. Links to both are under your state's information page in Appendix C.
- Click the drop-down for state board of education "rules" or "policies" or "standards" and select. You will find a table of contents or a keyword search.
- If you are researching whether the state board of education has rules that follow a state school law, search for the law in the keyword search by its citation.
- Do not rely on keyword searches alone. Scroll through the table of contents and look for related topics also.
- Look for state board of education curriculum review periods and public input.
- If you have specific concerns, look for public meetings held by the state board of education member representing your area. You may also contact your area representative and state superintendent through their official emails, which are generally listed on the state board of education website.
- If you need help locating the information on the website, you can email or call your state department of education or state board of education for assistance.
- **NOTICE: State board of education rules and policies are continually changing. It is crucial to check and recheck several sources to confirm that you have the most current version of the rule or policy.**

CHAPTER 6

THE LOCAL BOARD OF EDUCATION AND THE LOCAL SCHOOL SUPERINTENDENT

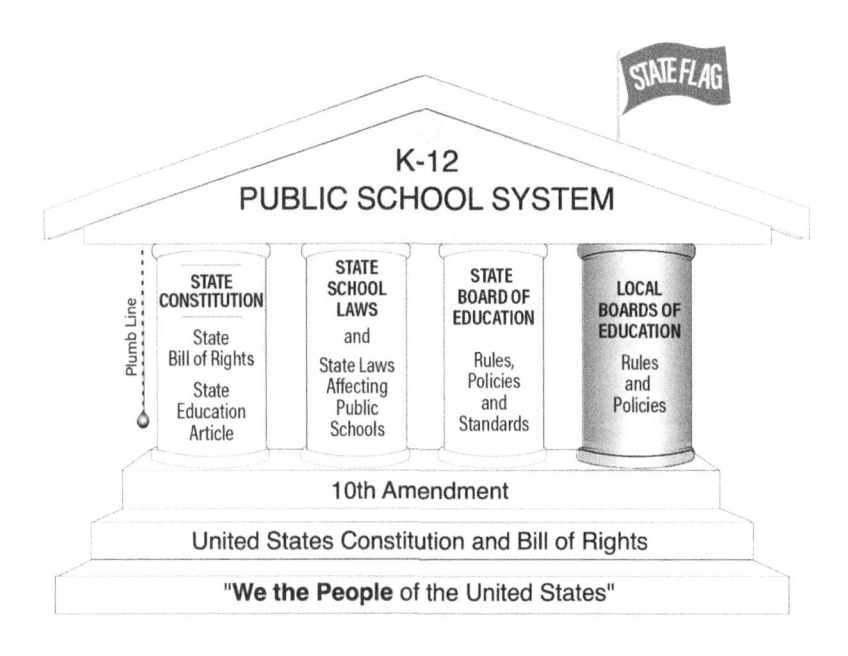

THE LOCAL BOARD OF EDUCATION

The local board of education is the perfect forum to get involved at the ground level. You can have a significant impact, particularly if you approach the system in a cooperative manner. The strength of a parent, or better yet, a group of parents who understand the system and are advocating to protect children, can be transformative. If your local board member is among the few who offer monthly "community meetings," attend. If your local board member does not offer community meetings, suggest that he or she meet with a group of parents at a local school library or public library to address your concerns. You may be surprised to learn that your local school leadership agrees with you but needs your knowledge and support.

REQUIREMENTS OF THE LOCAL BOARD OF EDUCATION

Generally, the local board of education members are:

- Elected by the people within their school district, which may be organized by borough, city, county, parish, or township;
- Subject to qualification requirements, election requirements, term limits (if applicable), staggered terms, insurance requirements, salary limits, codes of ethics, and standards for removal, all of which are established by state law and state board of education rules and policies;
- Required to hold a regular monthly meeting and provide a public comment period during every monthly meeting;
- May be required to post a bond conditioned on the faithful discharge of their duties; and
- May have additional fiduciary duties (i.e., duties of care, loyalty, good faith, confidentiality, not engaging in conflicts of interest, etc.)

KEY RESPONSIBILITIES OF THE LOCAL BOARD OF EDUCATION

Local boards of education have broad powers, including:

- Establishing the school district's budget;
- Hiring the local school superintendent;
- Establishing the goals in the school district's strategic plan, which the local school superintendent then implements;
- Deciding upon educational programs, curriculum, course offerings, and general educational opportunities (subject to the standards set by the state board of education); and
- Establishing rules and policies regarding curriculum requirements, attendance requirements, grading requirements, class withdrawals, discipline procedures, and graduation requirements.

THE LOCAL BOARD OF EDUCATION'S RULES AND POLICIES

Your local board of education must pass rules and policies governing the schools within its district. The local rules and policies address curriculum, class assignments, class withdrawals, schedules and schedule changes, class exemptions, attendance, grading requirements, clubs and organizations, on-line instruction, discipline, graduation, booster clubs, and public comment during the local board of education meetings. You will find the rules on their website. If you have a school-level concern, check your local board's rules and policies to see if they address the issue before you contact the teacher or school administration. On several occasions, I researched something before speaking with the school administration and was able to share nuances in the rules with the school administration.

THE LOCAL BOARD OF EDUCATION: CURRICULUM

Your local board's rules and policies regarding curriculum should be consistent with the state school laws and state board rules regarding curriculum. You can compare them. Additionally, you can look at the general heading of "instructional materials and content" to see your local school district's processes. For example, your local board may give parents a right to review the curriculum and be involved in the decision-making process. Here is an example:

> **Forsyth County School District**
> **Board Policy IFA: Instructional Material and Content**
>
> All instructional materials (print and electronic) used by the Forsyth County Schools that constitute the principal source of study for a course shall be selected through a process that is thoroughly planned and well documented. The selection process shall be guided by state board regulations and any procedures implemented by the Superintendent. A committee appointed by the Superintendent and/or his or her designee shall select the instructional resources best aligned to state content standards, as well as those that contribute most to the philosophy, aims, and objectives of the school system and the needs of students. As part of the process, the district will:

- *Provide notice to parents and guardians by the most practical means, which may be accomplished in the same manner as other notices to parents and guardians.*
- ***Provide the opportunity for public comment and parental input prior to the adoption or use of any proposed instructional material and content that constitutes the principal source of study for a course.***
- Post in a prominent location on its website and make available for review in print form upon request, a list of proposed instructional materials and content for public review, including
- The version or edition number, if applicable.
  - The state funded course number for which the instructional resource will be used, if applicable.
  - The identification number, in accordance with any guidelines established by the state board of education.

Once materials are approved:
- The district will make available all approved instructional materials and
- content for review on site upon request.
- The district and each school will maintain a website and post in a prominent location a list of the locally approved instructional materials and content that constitute the principal source of study for a course used by the school system or school.

The district will also:
- Designate at least one employee to serve as the contact person for any inquiries related to or requests for review of locally approved instructional materials and content, supplementary or ancillary material, and to coordinate its efforts to comply with and carry out its responsibilities.

- Make available any supplementary or ancillary materials for review upon request by any parent of a student in the school or who will be matriculating to such school.

Use of all instructional materials in Forsyth County Schools shall be in accordance with applicable federal copyright law, as well as its most current guidelines and interpretations.

Special consideration may be given to requests for adoption of instructional resources for programs that may affect a small number of schools.

In order to remain current with the great expansion of knowledge and changes that occur in the world today, the selection of instructional resources shall be an ongoing process based on areas of greatest need.

Original Adoption 12/31/1995 | Last Revised 12/15/2020 | Last Reviewed 12/15/2020 (emphasis added).

If parents are aware of their right to review and provide input on the local school district's instructional materials and content, they can review the materials and object if necessary. This can make all the difference in local controversies over curriculum.

THE LOCAL BOARD OF EDUCATION: STUDENT DATA PRIVACY COMPLAINTS

You may also find information that is valuable to you, such as the protection of student data. This local board of education rule clarifies some of the guidelines for student data as follows:

DeKalb County School District
Board Policy JRA: Student Data Privacy Complaints

It is the policy of the DeKalb County Board of Education that the DeKalb County School District shall comply with the Family

Educational Rights and Privacy Act ("FERPA") and the Student Data Privacy, Accessibility, and Transparency Act, which are designed to ensure that education records and student data are kept confidential and secure from unauthorized access and disclosure.

For the purposes of this policy, a "parent" is defined as a natural parent, a guardian, or an individual acting as a parent in the absence of a parent or guardian. An "eligible student" is defined as a student who has reached 18 years of age or is attending a postsecondary institution.

Any parent or eligible student "Complainant" may file a complaint with the District if that individual believes or alleges that a possible violation of rights under the above laws has occurred not more than one (1) year prior to the date the complaint is received by the District.

Complaints shall be handled in accordance with the following procedures:

1. The Superintendent shall designate at least one individual ("Designee") to respond to student data privacy complaints.
2. Upon receipt of a request from a Complainant, the Designee shall provide within 3 business days of complaint form, which may also be made available on the District's website.
3. A written response shall be provided to the Complainant within 10 business days of the Designee's receipt of the completed form.
4. The Complainant may file an appeal with the Superintendent within 10 business days of receipt of Designee's response.
5. The Superintendent shall provide a written response to Complainant within 10 business days of receipt of appeal.
6. The Complainant may file an appeal to the Board of Education within 10 business days of receipt of the Superintendent's response.

7. The Board of Education shall render a final decision within 10 business days of receipt of an appeal....

State Authority: O.C.G.A. §§ 20-2-0661 through 20-2-0668; 38-3-0022.2

Federal Authority: 15 U.S.C. §6503; 18 U.S.C. § 1513; 34 C.F.R. § 98.7; 34 C.F.R. § 98.7; 34 C.F.R. § 99.7

THE LOCAL BOARD OF EDUCATION: HIGH SCHOOL COURSE WITHDRAWALS

The local board of education even establishes rules and policies regarding high school course withdrawals. If you ask about the process of high school course withdrawals, you may only receive half of the information included in the rule. For example, you might see that the rule accounts for "exceptions":

Cobb County School District
Administrative Rule IHA-R Grading Systems 7/1/19

5. **Withdrawing:**
   a. **From a Course:** If a student withdraws from a course after the first ten days of the semester, the withdrawing student will receive the grade of 10 in the course, and the course and grade shall be recorded on the cumulative record. *The Superintendent or designee may make exceptions to this paragraph if a different action is appropriate.* In the event the Superintendent or designee elects to change a withdrawing student's grade of 10, the grade change and identity of the party responsible for the grade change must be clearly indicated in the withdrawing student's record.
   b. **From School:** If a student withdraws from school prior to the completion of a semester, the courses taken, grades earned, or attendance shall not be recorded on the cumulative record. This information shall be recorded on the withdrawal form and the decision

concerning grades and credits shall be the responsibility of the school to which the student transfers....

Legal Reference: O.C.G.A. § 20-2-989.20 Grade Integrity; O.C.G.A. § 20-2-157 Uniform reporting system (post-secondary op, HOPE, other financial aid eligibility); Rule 160-4-2-.13 Statewide Passing Score; Rule 160-5-1-.15 Awarding Units of Credit and Acceptance of Transfer Credits and/or Grades; Rule 160-5-1-.18 Competitive Interscholastic Activities in Grades 6-12. (emphasis added).

If you read the rule before requesting a withdrawal, then you or, better yet, your high school student can ask for the "exception" in the rule. This scenario is an excellent opportunity for high school students to learn first-hand that life is made up of systems, and that they can advocate for themselves using the system.

Additionally, see the legal reference at the bottom of local board of education rules. These references show you the specific state school laws and state board of education rules that are "above" the local board of education rule on course withdrawals. In other words, you can begin researching your issue at the local board level and then move "up" the hierarchy as well.

To find the local board of education rules in your state, follow the instructions in the section titled, "HOW TO FIND WHAT YOU NEED: Your Local Board of Education and Your Local School Superintendent."

START AT THE SCHOOL LEVEL TO AVOID PROBLEMS

Usually, I try to solve problems at the school level by talking with the teachers. For example, suppose you are concerned about inappropriate content in supplemental reading assignments, such as books glamorizing suicide, particularly if your child is depressed. In that case, it is a good idea to talk to the teachers at the beginning of the year. Ask if they assign reading from books other than the textbook. If so, ask if they select the books from a list of books already approved by the state board of education or the local board of education. If they answer yes, ask for copies of the lists and follow up until you receive them. Also, ask if they allow students to choose alternative books, just in case. It is helpful for the teachers to know you are sensitive to an issue such as suicide. Be polite and kind. This will let them know you are concerned. Plus, I suspect the teachers will think more carefully before assigning books to avoid potential problems.

If you object to a particular assigned book, ask for an alternative one. This approach works particularly well when the teacher is warned at the beginning of the school year. There is no guarantee that the teacher will not retaliate, but if you are kind and go to the teacher first, it is less likely.

If the state board of education's or local board of education's approved list includes a book that you think is inappropriate for students, let them know. One approach is to calmly and respectfully call or email the teacher or school official about the book. You can also include the objectionable sections in your message. We experienced this when one of our children was given a summer reading assignment before the teacher was assigned for the upcoming year. Another parent alerted me that the book had detailed descriptions of a young girl being molested by her uncle. I purchased and read the entire book. Then I left several messages for the head of the school district's language arts department (because no teacher had been assigned yet). When I did not receive a return call, I calmly read a section of an assigned summer reading (describing the child molestation) to the individual's administrative assistant. I wanted her to know why a call-back was important to me. I did get a return call. Ultimately, our child received another book to read during the summer.

If you object to a particular assigned book, ask for an alternative one.

WORKING WITH YOUR LOCAL BOARD MEMBER

If you have concerns at the local level, you can also contact the local board member representing your area through his or her official email. Hopefully, your elected local board member shares your values and vision for your school and will listen to your concerns. Here are some tips:

- Attend your local board member's community meetings or meet with your local board member separately.
- Learn your school district's practices and system.

- If you oppose your board member on an issue, first try to understand the board member's reasoning. You may only see part of the picture.
- Ask questions and share your ideas.
- If you are fortunate, as I was, your local board member will be firm but able to be persuaded with appropriate facts and reasoning.
- Try to persuade and offer support if the board member embraces your position. Your board member may agree with your position, but feels outnumbered on the board or thinks he or she lacks support in the community.
- Once you agree with your board member on an issue, encourage friends and neighbors to show support at the upcoming local board of education meeting. Board members appreciate public support, particularly when an important vote is presented. You may even want to speak before the local board to support their vote. This can strengthen the board member's commitment, and change the tide on matters of local concern.
- Always be respectful and even-tempered.
- If your local board members do not represent the concerns of your community, vote them out at the next election. In my experience, very little is accomplished with over-the-top yelling. As I have said to our children, "You must *think* your way out of this one."

THE LOCAL SCHOOL SUPERINTENDENT

REQUIREMENTS OF THE LOCAL SCHOOL SUPERINTENDENT

The local school superintendent is also empowered by the state's constitution, state school laws, and the state and local board of education rules and policies. Generally, the local school superintendent is:

The local school superintendent is also empowered by the state's constitution, state school laws, and the state and local board of education rules and policies.

- Selected by the local board of education;
- Responsible for implementing the school district's strategic plan (how the students learn

the material);
- Required to take an oath to discharge the duties of office diligently and faithfully, and support the federal and state constitutions;
- Required to post a bond conditioned on the faithful discharge of duties; and
- May have additional fiduciary duties (i.e., duties of care, loyalty, good faith, confidentiality, not engaging in conflicts of interest, etc.).

KEY RESPONSIBILITIES, INCLUDING ENFORCEMENT POWERS

Generally, the local school superintendent is the executive officer of the local board of education. For our purposes, the local school superintendent's most essential powers include:

- Responsibility for the faithful and efficient execution of the local board of education rules and policies that are not in conflict with state school laws; and
- **Responsibility for enforcing the state laws and the state board of education's rules and policies.**

If you have a problem and need assistance at this level, it is best to contact the local school superintendent through his or her official email. Given that the local school superintendent is responsible for enforcement of the state school laws and state and local rules, you can request in writing that he or she enforce them. Sometimes, the local school superintendent is unaware of the issue, and this method can resolve the issue quickly. If the local school superintendent refuses to enforce the laws and rules, you may have a basis to move "up" the chain of command to the state school superintendent for enforcement. O.C.G.A. §§ 20-2-104 and 20-2-109. You may also choose to hire local legal counsel to pursue the matter.

The local school superintendent is responsible for the enforcement of the state school laws and the state and local rules.

HOW TO FIND WHAT YOU NEED

Your Local Board of Education's Rules and Policies

- Go to the website for your local school district and find the drop-down for the local board of education.
- Click on the link for rules and policies.
- If you are researching a particular topic, do not rely on a keyword search alone. Scroll through the table of contents as well.
- If you have specific concerns, look for public meetings held by the local board of education member representing your area. You may also contact your area board member through his or her official email listed on the local board of education website.
- If you need help locating the information on the website, you can email or call your local board of education for assistance.

CHAPTER 7

CHARTER ENTITIES

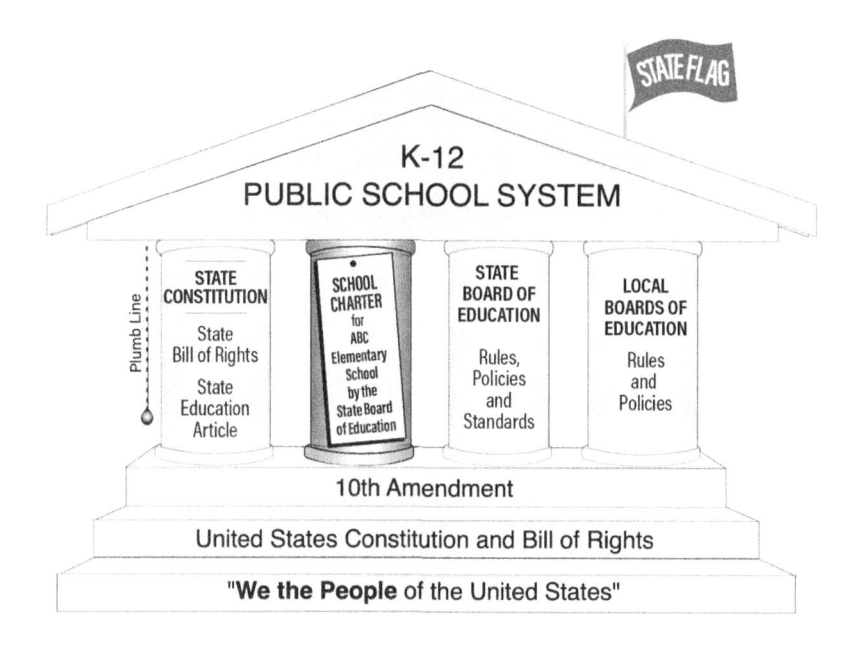

```
                    K-12
          PUBLIC SCHOOL SYSTEM        [STATE FLAG]

  STATE          SCHOOL        STATE          LOCAL
CONSTITUTION    CHARTER       BOARD OF       BOARDS OF
                  for        EDUCATION       EDUCATION
   State         ABC
Bill of Rights  Elementary    Rules,          Rules
                 School      Policies          and
   State         by the        and           Policies
 Education    State Board   Standards
  Article    of Education

              10th Amendment
    United States Constitution and Bill of Rights
       "We the People of the United States"
```

THE DEFINITION AND ORIGINAL PURPOSE OF "CHARTERS"

"Charters" are documents that grant power from a government entity (traditionally a sovereign such as a king or queen) to an individual or group of people. The earliest known charters date back to the 670s. The most famous charter, the Magna Carta (Latin for the Great Charter), was signed by King John in 1215. In fact, many colonies were set-up using charters from the kings and queens of England, Spain, and France. A charter is different than a contract because the charter is granted by a sovereign or government authority. In essence, it is the transfer of *governmental* power to others that creates a public or private institution within specific guidelines.

The original purpose of charter schools was to give a few schools freedom from state laws to apply new and innovative teaching techniques and, if successful, apply those techniques in traditional public schools. For several reasons beyond this book's scope, charter schools have expanded nationwide in both their number and type. Today, there are charter schools, charter school systems, and hybrid charter school systems ("charter entities" for simplicity). Charter entities vary depending upon the state's school laws that are "waived" as part of their freedom to experiment with new methods.

WAIVERS OF SCHOOL LAWS AND STATE BOARD RULES AND POLICIES

The central feature of charter entities is the "waiver" of the state's school laws and some of the state board of education's rules and policies. A waiver is intentionally giving up a known claim, right, or privilege. The state *waives* its right to enforce the state's school laws and the charter entity *receives* the waiver. Although it is a bit corny, think of a waiver as a hand "waving" goodbye to something.

The central feature of charter entities is the "waiver" of the state's school laws and some of the state board of education's rules and policies.

In exchange for the waiver, the charter entity clarifies how it will operate and be accountable using improved test scores, school discipline reports, community satisfaction, and other conditions. The state's school laws are not "gone." The state's school laws are still part of state law and are applicable to traditional schools. Depending upon which waivers the charter entity chooses, some state school laws also continue to apply to these charter entities.

"Charter schools" usually have a blanket waiver of almost all school laws. An independent board governs charter schools. "Charter school systems" have a blanket waiver of nearly all school laws but the local board of education holds the waivers and passes them to individual schools using a system of flexibility requests. "Hybrid charter school systems" receive a limited number of waivers of specific school laws. These waivers are also held by the local board of education and given to the individual schools. Hybrid charter school systems have a variety of names, such as Investing in Educational Excellence (IE²) or Strategic Waiver School Systems (SWSS).

MOVING FROM A COMPLIANCE MODEL TO A TESTING AND ACCOUNTABILITY MODEL

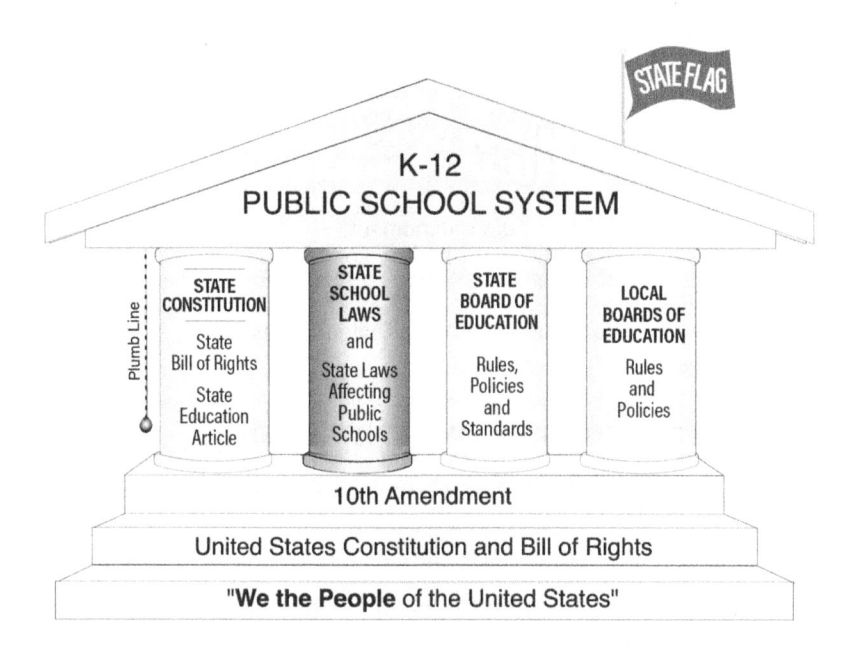

![Diagram of a building representing the K-12 Public School System. The roof is labeled "K-12 PUBLIC SCHOOL SYSTEM" with a State Flag. Four pillars support the roof: STATE CONSTITUTION (State Bill of Rights, State Education Article) with a Plumb Line; STATE SCHOOL LAWS and State Laws Affecting Public Schools; STATE BOARD OF EDUCATION Rules, Policies and Standards; LOCAL BOARDS OF EDUCATION Rules and Policies. The foundation steps read: "10th Amendment", "United States Constitution and Bill of Rights", and "**We the People** of the United States".]

TRADITIONAL PUBLIC SCHOOLS OPERATE ON A COMPLIANCE MODEL.

Traditional public schools "must comply" with the state's school laws and the state board of education rules and policies. Since the inception of public schools, state legislatures have been passing and amending school laws (i.e., approx. 743 in Georgia). Likewise, state boards have been developing rules, policies, and standards. Absent extenuating circumstances (i.e., a recession), there are no waivers of these laws, rules, and policies. Testing occurs but it is not as important as with charter entities. To use a driving analogy, traditional public schools must stay in their lanes and obey the traffic signs.

K-12 PUBLIC SCHOOL SYSTEM

STATE FLAG

Plumb Line

STATE CONSTITUTION	SCHOOL CHARTER	STATE BOARD OF EDUCATION	LOCAL BOARDS OF EDUCATION
State Bill of Rights	for ABC Elementary School	Rules, Policies	Rules and Policies
State Education Article	by the State Board of Education	and Standards	

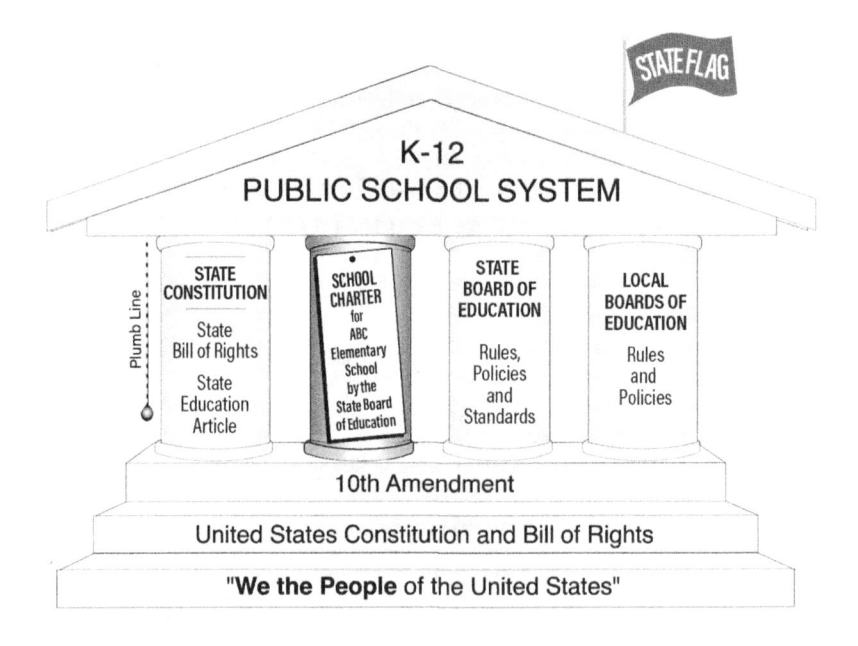

10th Amendment

United States Constitution and Bill of Rights

"**We the People** of the United States"

CHARTER ENTITIES OPERATE ON A TESTING AND ACCOUNTABILITY MODEL.

Charter entities receive a waiver of the state's school laws and state board of education's rules in exchange for improved test results and accountability. Moreover, the charter entities' continued existence depends on accountability reports, improved test results, and other conditions in the charter document. When the charter entity's term is about to expire, its charter "renewal" is, by and large, based upon the results of the student's test scores and the other accountability measures. Discipline reports and graduation rates are considered during the charter renewals. Subjects such as cursive handwriting are not taught in many charter entities because they are not easily tested. To use the driving analogy: charter schools can drive outside their lanes and there are few road signs to obey. The focus is on whether they reach the destination (the accountability measures) in the required period of time.

THE GROWING USE OF CHARTER ENTITIES

The Georgia map below shows the pervasiveness of charter entities in this state. There are 180 school districts in Georgia. Only two school districts,

Webster County School District and Buford City School District (the tiny black dot in the Gwinnett County School District), are traditional school systems that operate under all the state's school laws in Title 20. They are called "Title 20/No Waiver School Systems." The white and light gray school districts are either charter school systems or hybrid charter school systems.

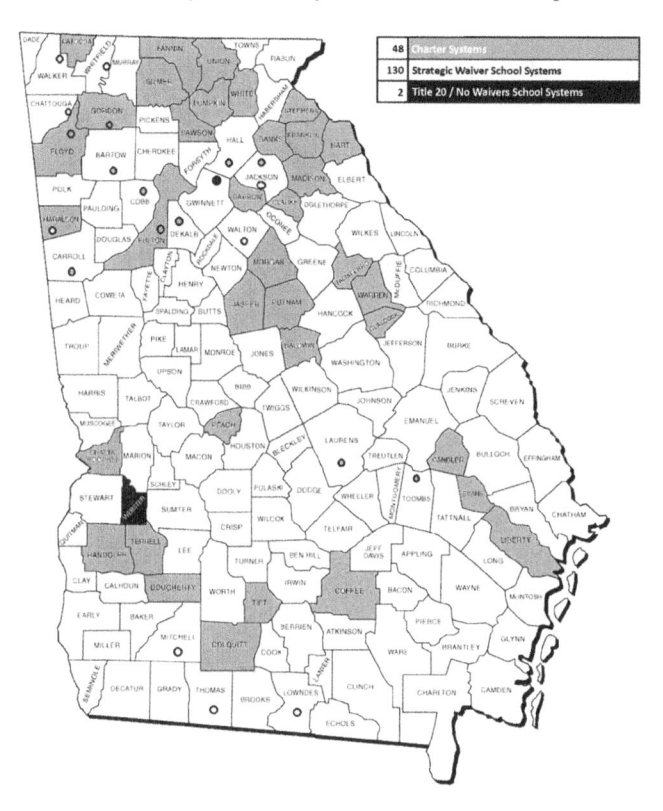

STATE LAWS GOVERNING CHARTER ENTITIES

AUTHORIZED BY THE STATE LEGISLATURE

For charter entities to exist in a state, the state constitution and state laws must authorize them. Otherwise, they would not be allowed. You can search your state laws using the terms "charter" and "authorize." In Georgia:

- *Charter schools* are allowed under the Charter School Act of 1998. O.C.G.A. §§ 20-2-2060 et seq.

- *Charter systems* and *hybrid charter systems* (in Georgia called "Investing in Education Excellence" (IE2 Systems) or "Strategic Waiver School Systems" (SWSS) are permitted under "Increased Flexibility for Local School Systems." O.C.G.A. §§ 20-2-80 et seq.

Suppose your children attend a traditional public school that is not a charter school, a charter school system, or a hybrid charter school system. In that case, their school must operate under *all* the school laws enacted by the state legislature. If not, your public school has waived some or all of state school laws.

BLANKET WAIVERS, BROADEST POSSIBLE WAIVERS, AND LIMITED WAIVERS

The charter document defines what laws and rules are waived and not waived. These laws and rules are identified by their citations in the charter document. This makes it easy to identify which school laws have been waived and which school laws still apply. However, if the charter document refers to a "blanket waiver" or "the broadest possible waiver," then it has waived all state school laws permitted by the state legislature. In other words, the charter document does not specify what is and is not waived. A parent or educator who wants to know what is waived cannot tell from the charter document itself. In that case, the parent or educator must look at the state school laws. If the state school laws specify what can and cannot be waived, then it is likely that all the laws specified by the legislature are waived. If the state legislature has not specified what can and cannot be waived, and it becomes an issue, the courts must decide.[1] This conundrum is a problem with charter entities that have an unspecified "blanket waiver" or "the broadest possible waiver." The public does not have notice of the state school laws that apply to their public schools.[2] Hopefully, state legislatures and school officials will draft charter documents that clearly identify the laws, rules, and policies that will be waived **before** the community is asked to accept the charter entity.

KEY FEATURES OF CHARTER ENTITIES

A PERSONAL NOTE ON COMMUNITY ACCEPTANCE OF CHARTERS

In 2011, our county school district was considering the switch from a traditional to a charter school system. They wanted parent acceptance and offered information on the benefits of becoming a charter system. I was a parent advocate and understood the strengths and weaknesses of moving to such a model. My biggest concern was the lack of specificity on what was being included in the "blanket waiver" of school laws. I did not want things that are important to most parents (i.e., class size, teacher pay, and teacher certification) to be waived. I addressed the waivers, and to its credit, our school system made some changes.

In my experience, community acceptance of charter entities faces several obstacles. First, most parents do not have a legal background *and* the time to understand the complexities and ramifications of waiving most school laws. Second, the school and school system officials who propose the idea of charters to the community have a vast budget, many lawyers, and a vested interest in being free from school laws that limit their power and, in some cases, limit their pay.[3] Hopefully, this book will remedy some of these problems and teach you, the parents, and educators, about the system so that you can make well-crafted arguments for and against various aspects of the charter entity being proposed in your community. For example, what will schools do with the large amount of money saved by waiving class size maximums?[4] Will it be spent on more administrators? Will they waive protections for teachers regarding grade integrity[5] and duty-free lunch?[6] These are crucial questions to ask, particularly to state legislators who are elected to protect the interests of parents and students. The legislatures also determine which state school laws are waivable.

CHARTER ENTITIES PROVIDE "FLEXIBILITY"
Schools Tailored to the Community

One feature of charter entities is that they can tailor the waiver of state school laws and state board of education rules to the needs of the community. This works particularly well when parents have a long-term commitment to public schools and are willing to serve on the independent board that governs the charter school. For example, a group of parents supported by their community may choose to start a "classical" charter school as a start-up (a new school) or a conversion charter (convert an existing school into a classical charter school). The school may adopt a classical curriculum and offer Latin as the foreign language, primarily because it is helpful in law, medicine, and science. The charter school may choose to have uniforms as well. There are many classical charter schools throughout the nation and this model is among my favorites.[7] Charter schools can also focus on STEM (Science, Technology, Engineering, and Math) and the arts, to name a few.

Flexibility: Replacing Waived School Laws with Rules
Another feature of charter entities is that the waived school laws can be replaced with rules. For example, schools and school districts can waive teacher certification requirements and replace them with rules that requires a PhD plus work experience. Then a high school principal can hire a retired NASA engineer who does not have a teaching certificate to teach physics. Freedom from state school laws can also allow more flexibility in scheduling classes, allow schools to require uniforms, allow participation in sports to count for physical education credit, and provide more online learning options. The crux is that parents and communities need to understand the protections they have in their state's school laws and rules, and that rules can manage the waived provisions.

Using Waivers to Manage School Controversies
Additionally, charter entities can use waivers to manage local controversies. For example, the state legislature allows charter entities to exist and limits what state school laws can and cannot be waived. If a state legislature begins to see the importance of a particular school law that it does not want to be waived by *any* charter entity, it can make the school law "non-waivable." For example, Georgia's Parents' Bill of Rights cannot be waived by charter entities. O.C.G.A. § 20-2-786(h). Additionally, the charter entity has the power to "give up" the waiver of the school law by amending its charter or removing it from its charter document at the next charter renewal. Suppose your children attend a charter entity and your community is upset because a particular school law has been waived. In that case, the community can request that the state

legislature make it non-waivable (which would apply to everyone in the state) or the charter entity can amend the charter and give up the waiver either now or at the charter renewal (which would only apply to that charter entity). This is one way to manage controversies in communities with charter entities.

A CAUTION: MEASURING "IMPROVEMENT" IN SCHOOL DISCIPLINE

Nationwide, public schools measure academic improvement in one way or another. At the federal level, there is the "Every Student Succeeds Act," and each state has its standardized test. Many programs also measure "improvement" in school discipline. While these tests and measurements have benefits, there has been recent concern in how programs measure "improved" school discipline. Some public schools (both charter entities and traditional schools) are required or encouraged to provide quantitative data showing a reduction in these discipline incidents as a measure of "improvement." For example, Georgia's Charter School Renewal Application requires schools to provide data on student suspensions.[8] Why is this a potential problem? Because it can lead to the under-reporting of discipline problems, as teachers or administrators feel the pressure to "lower the numbers." Underreporting can lead to troubled students "slipping through the cracks" and not getting the help they desperately need.

Some public schools (both charter entities and traditional schools) are required or encouraged to provide quantitative data showing a reduction in these discipline incidents as a measure of "improvement."

The book, *Why Meadow Died, The People and Policies that Created the Parkland Shooter and Endanger America's Students*, provides an example. In *Why Meadow Died*, the authors explain that between 2008 and 2016, the Department of Education promoted the PROMISE program, which was intended to dramatically decrease student arrests and close the school to prison "pipeline." The authors argue that rather than maintaining high standards of behavior, the local school board lowered behavioral standards and became so lenient with school discipline that few, if any, arrests were made. As a result, the juvenile prison population was reduced but not the juvenile crime rate. In other words, the schools "improved" statistically, but were not improved.

The book outlines that, as a result of this systemic issue, the Parkland shooter was overlooked and was not placed in the programs that could have helped him. Despite numerous warning signs listed in the book, he did not get the help he needed. The authors conclude that if these warning signs had been put in the shooter's record, the background check would have "flagged" him, and he would not have been permitted to purchase a firearm.

I am not suggesting that there is a problem with every program that measures school discipline. I am suggesting closer examination of any federal or state program that *only* emphasizes quantitative discipline reporting or any program that incentivizes under-reporting disciplinary actions.

Considering this concern, *"Should we be using a different measure that encourages schools to identify and help troubled students before they hurt themselves or others?"* Should we measure the number of students identified and given help because of discipline incidents? Can we accept measures that show an *increase* in the number of students identified? Should we make it easier for teachers and administrators to report school discipline incidents in students' records? Can we require less paperwork for teachers and administrators who report discipline incidents? If you are concerned about this issue, you can ask your school administrators and local board of education whether they are required or encouraged to measure improvements in school discipline with only fewer incidents. You can ask whether they are able to explain their results, how much paperwork is required to report a discipline incident, and whether they see any potential problems with the measurement process at the school. Hopefully, in the schools where it is needed, the well-meaning individuals who chose these measurements can improve the process and reach all the students who need help.

Again, this concern was identified as part of a federal program. Yet, if we only examine the more extensive federal program, then local programs and charter entities (which measure many aspects of school improvement), may not be aware of the potential problem. I hope to alert parents and educators of this issue so that more troubled students can be reached.

HOW TO FIND WHAT YOU NEED

Your Charter School or Charter System Document

To see if your state authorizes charter entities:
- See Appendix C and your state's information page with links to the state school laws.
- Look at the table of contents and use a keyword search to see if the state school laws permit charter entities.
- Some states refer to the charter document as a "charter contract." Technically, this term is redundant because a charter is a contract with a sovereign. Using this term is like calling a lease a "lease contract." However, the word "charter document" is an excellent way to specify the nature of the relationship and distinguish between the school (sometimes called a "charter") and the charter document itself.

To find your charter school or charter system's charter document:
- First, determine which part of the government issued the charter.
- If you have a charter system, then the charter was likely granted by the state board of education. Begin at the state board of education website and look for departments. Click the link for charter schools and charter systems. Then click on the link for the list of charter and hybrid charter system contracts. Click on your charter system document.
- If you have a charter school, the authorizer could be either the state or local board of education. Many charter schools make their charter documents available on the school website. If it is unavailable, look on the state board of education and the local board of education websites under the drop-down for departments and charter schools. Scroll through to find your charter school's document.
- Sometimes, it is easiest to do an online search for "ABC School Charter." However, this may not be the most recent charter document. To verify that it is current, check with your state or local board that authorized the charter.

- Always read the entire charter document, not just an exhibit page with a list of waivers. If you need help finding your charter document, call the state board of education's charter schools division or the local board of education's charter schools division for assistance.

KEY PROVISIONS OF A CHARTER DOCUMENT

THE KEY PROVISIONS OF A CHARTER DOCUMENT INCLUDE:

1. The government entity that granted the charter (usually the state board of education or the local board of education);
2. The individuals who signed the charter (to verify that it is the final signed version);
3. The term of the charter (usually five years);
4. The renewal period (usually two to five years, depending upon the school or school system's performance);
5. A statement that the school or school system will provide testing and accountability results *in exchange for* freedom from school laws and rules;
6. Waivers of the state's school laws, the state board of education rules or policies, and possibly local board of education rules and policies; and
7. Non-waived provisions (the school laws and rules that are specifically not being waived are sometimes referenced by their citations but tend to include school insurance requirements, federal programs, criminal laws, and governmental immunity for schools).
8. If your school community does not want the charter entity to continue (you want to revert back to being under state school laws and state board of education rules) you can seek "non-renewal" under the terms of the charter document. **Complaints should be made in writing to the charter authorizer.** If you are a charter system or SWSS, the authorizer is the state board of education.

CHAPTER 8

MAGNET SCHOOLS

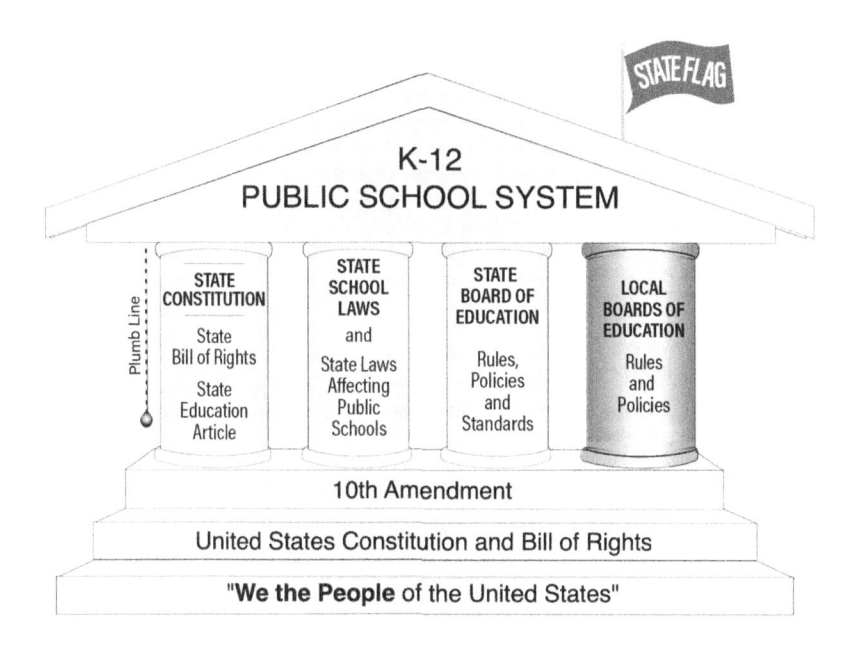

THE PURPOSE AND CHARACTERISTICS OF MAGNET SCHOOLS

In the 1960's and early 1970's, educators began looking for ways to desegregate. The event that prompted desegregation was the U.S. Supreme Court decision overturning the "separate but equal" doctrine and a second decision requiring desegregation of public schools "with all deliberate speed."[1] One effective and voluntary means of desegregation was "magnet schools."

The original purpose of magnet schools was to have *voluntary* desegregation by "attracting" students (like a magnet) from different attendance zones within the same local school district. Using magnet schools to attract students was considered a much better alternative than *forced* desegregation through busing. For magnet schools to be successful, local school districts had to permit enrollment outside their established school zones and provide a learning environment that would attract students and their families.

States vary in what they require of magnet schools in terms of: the state school laws and the state and local rules. Since magnet schools function within local school district attendance zones and are publicly funded and publicly run, many of the nuances specific to magnet schools are decided and approved by the local board of education. Although they vary from one local school district to another, magnet schools have several defining characteristics.

The original purpose of magnet schools was to have voluntary desegregation by "attracting" students (like a magnet) from different attendance zones within the same local school district.

1. Diversity is an explicitly stated purpose;
2. Magnet schools attract students across attendance zones within a local school district;
3. Magnet schools accept students based on an application (test scores, teacher recommendations, and grades) and a lottery system;
4. Magnet schools are publicly funded and publicly run (whereas charter schools can be privately run); and
5. Magnet schools offer a distinct curriculum or instructional method to attract students and parents, such as:

    - STEM (Science, Technology, Engineering, and Math) Curriculum;
    - Fine or Performing Arts Curriculum;
    - International Baccalaureate or International Studies Curriculum;
    - World Languages Curriculum (i.e., immersion programs that teach all or most subjects in another language);
    - Classical Curriculum;
    - Career and Technical Education (CTE) Curriculum;
    - Montessori Style of Learning; and
    - Gardner's Learning Style.

Magnet schools continue to flourish in the United States. In some communities, magnet schools have been so successful that there is fierce competition to be accepted. See below if you are interested in sending your child to a magnet school.

HOW TO FIND WHAT YOU NEED

Magnet Schools in Your Area

- Go to the website for your local school district and find the drop-down that lists the schools within the district. Many magnet schools have the word "magnet" within their name. You can also look through the local school district departments to see if there is a magnet schools oversight department.
- Alternatively, go to the website for your local school district and find the drop-down for the local board of education.
- Click on the link for rules and policies.
- Type the word "magnet" in the keyword search and look for rules and information regarding magnet schools.
- If you need help locating the information on the website, email or call your local school district for assistance.

CHAPTER 9

CONTROVERSIAL MATERIAL AND CONTENT

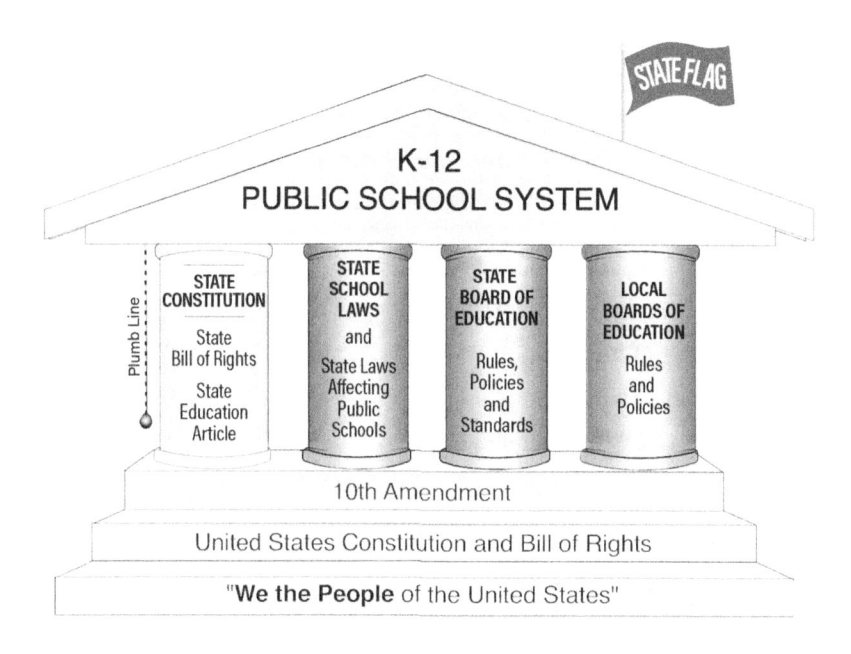

SOURCES OF CONTROVERSIAL MATERIAL AND CONTENT

You may be thinking, "If we have state school laws and state and local board of education rules and policies that set curriculum, how does all this controversial material and content come into the classroom?" The answer is, "It depends." There is evidence that it comes in primarily through all three "columns" in the diagram, and the most common sources are:

ADVOCACY GROUPS

In recent years, public schools have been treated like a "public forum" for advocacy groups to advance their agendas. This has happened even though some courts have held that these groups do not have "standing" or a "position" in public education. Those with standing generally include: (1) legislators and state and local board members who are elected to pass school laws that are constitutional and in keeping with the views of the majority that voted them into office; (2) educators who are hired by state and local school systems to carry out the laws and rules governing education and to teach the students; (3) parents who send their children to public schools and have legal standing on behalf of their minor children; and (4) students who attend public schools but are no longer minors (over the age of 18). Nonetheless, many advocacy groups have been allowed to promote controversial ideas and agendas in public school.

TEXTBOOK PROVIDERS, THIRD-PARTY VENDORS, AND SCHOOL BOOKFAIRS

Textbook providers, third-party vendors, and school bookfairs are another potential source of controversial instructional materials and content. Generally, the state board of education approves and funds the textbooks of its choosing. Local boards of education then choose the textbooks they want to use from among this larger group. Third-party vendors are the outside entities that supply instructional materials for students in the form of tablets, online tutorials, textbooks, workbooks, assessments, surveys, etc. School bookfair providers are usually chosen at the school level. Suppose you and your children are seeing controversial materials and content among these materials. In that case, you can bring it to the attention of your principal, local board, and local superintendent. Yet, principals and local board members cannot address problems they are not aware of. If you are not successful at that level, you can

Third-party vendors are the outside entities that supply instructional materials for students in the form of tablets, online tutorials, textbooks, workbooks, assessments, surveys, etc.

follow the chain of command and raise the issue before your state board of education member, the state board of education, and the state school superintendent as needed. Your state school laws and state and local board rules may also allow for parent comment before these materials are approved and funded. So, you can get involved in the approval process.

"SUPPLEMENTAL" INSTRUCTIONAL MATERIAL AND CONTENT

Sometimes the "curriculum" does not include all the instructional materials and content taught to students. As a result, parents reviewing the "curriculum" may not see the supplemental instruction. To avoid this problem, parents can request to see "supplemental instructional material and content" specifically.

Some supplemental materials fall under the broad catch-all headings: "Social Emotional Learning" (SEL), and "Diversity Equity and Inclusion" (DEI). *To be clear, I am not suggesting that everything that falls under SEL and DEI is controversial.* For example, SEL can include character education programs. Plus, we are a diverse nation and need to get along with one another. Nonetheless, these broad categories are a good place to look if you are concerned about supplemental materials and content.

TEACHER SUPPLEMENTS

Many teachers enhance learning with supplements, even at their own expense, such as reading and math flashcards, games, worksheets, and materials for bulletin boards. Usually, these materials and content are neither controversial nor outside the curriculum standards. Until now, there has not been a reason to monitor or place limits on them. However, as educational philosophies change, new teachers are entering the profession with new ideas that are sometimes "outside" the curriculum requirements and not in keeping with state school laws and state and local board rules and policies. Teachers are professionals and should be treated like professionals. A local school board policy on supplementing (without overly burdening teachers with additional reporting requirements) is a reasonable course of action. If teachers do not comply, parents can follow the chain of command and raise the issue at the local and state board levels as needed.

STATE UNIVERSITY SCHOOLS OF EDUCATION AND CONTINUING EDUCATION PROGRAMS

State university schools of education and continuing education programs for educators are another source of controversial materials and content.[1] On the one hand, state governments adopt school laws and rules that require teachers to teach A, B, and C. The state government also funds state university schools of education and continuing education for educators to teach A, B, and C. However, if state universities and continuing education programs teach D, E, and F, there is a problem. The state is funding both sides of a controversy.

While I appreciate the intellectual freedom associated with state universities generally, schools of education have a unique duty: to prepare future teachers to teach students in a public school system governed by our democratic process. Moreover, our democratic process requires that changes in public school should begin with state laws and work their way down through state and local boards of education rules, not by infiltrating the public schools with private speakers.

THE STATES' POWER OVER CURRICULUM

States have broad powers to enact laws and rules that are "reasonably related to legitimate pedagogical [educational] concerns."[2] In fact, annotated versions of state school laws have case summaries that elaborate on the state's power over curriculum. State school laws giving local boards control of curriculum do the same. The conflicting personal views of advocacy groups, third-party vendors, and authors of supplemental materials and content have no standing in the public school curriculum.

Educators and *classroom teachers*, on the other hand, have constitutional rights, including the Freedom of Speech and the Freedom *not* to Speak. Their situation is different. For these individuals, the question is: "Where is the boundary between a classroom teacher's constitutional rights and the state's right to (a) control public school curriculum, and (b) limit government employees' private speech? Yet, this issue becomes irrelevant if parents exercise their constitutional rights to *give* non-consent or opt out of certain curriculum, courses, and content.

THE PUBLIC FORUM DOCTRINE: PRIVATE SPEECH IN PUBLIC SCHOOLS

In recent years, public schools have been bombarded by "private speakers" who want access to students. Whether it is to advance their ideas and agendas or gather data to increase outcomes and sales, they all want access to the hearts and minds of students. Yet, who decides what private speech makes its way to students? Are public schools the proper place for these groups to advance their ideas and agendas? The Establishment Clause restricts religion but what about other groups and agendas that do not qualify as a "religion"? Does the right to freedom of speech allow *anyone* to "speak" in public schools with words and written materials? More importantly, have legislators, public school officials, and state and local board members considered using the "public forum doctrine" to limit private speech?

Does the right to freedom of speech allow anyone to "speak" in public schools with words and written materials?

FREEDOM OF SPEECH ON GOVERNMENT PROPERTY

The Free Speech Clause restricts *government regulation of speech*. It states, "Congress shall make no law ... abridging the freedom of speech." U.S. CONST. amend. I. The Free Speech Clause also restricts *state* and *local* governments from "abridging the freedom of speech" through caselaw.[3] Yet, the government has been allowed to regulate speech and speech-related conduct on government property (i.e., public schools, public libraries, school board meeting in a municipal building, etc.). In other words, the Free Speech Clause does not give *everyone* the right to speak in public schools. For example, suppose a state government regulation limits a private individual or group's right to free speech in public schools, and the regulation is challenged. In that case, the courts may analyze the regulation using the "public forum doctrine."

The U.S. Supreme Court established the public forum doctrine to analyze speech on government property. The public forum doctrine allows the government to place regulations on speech depending on the type of government property involved: public forums (public parks and streets), designated or limited public forums (school auditoriums opened for private organizations when school is not in session and municipal buildings opened for school board meetings), and nonpublic forums (public schools, military bases, and postal service properties). Depending on the forum, the courts apply a different test or analysis to determine what private speech the government can prohibit.

PUBLIC SCHOOLS ARE NONPUBLIC FORUMS

The U.S. Supreme Court has held that public schools are nonpublic forums.[4] Using the nonpublic forum analysis, state government can limit private speech in public schools if the laws and rules they enact are viewpoint neutral and rationally related to a legitimate governmental objective."[5] A legitimate objective includes "educating students"[6] and arguably increasing scores in core academic subjects. In other words, there are compelling reasons for state legislators and school officials to enact laws and rules that put more stringent limits on *private speakers* in public schools. This may be done using the nonpublic forum analysis.

In 2000, Congress enacted the Children's Internet Protection Act (CIPA). CIPA requires public schools and libraries that receive federal monies to install internet software that blocks obscenity, pornography, and materials considered dangerous to minors. CIPA also has a process for reporting violations.

State government can limit private speech in public schools if the laws and rules they enact are viewpoint neutral and rationally related to a legitimate governmental objective.

The American Library Association sued the federal government claiming that the internet software was an unconstitutional restriction of library patrons' First Amendment rights. The U.S. Supreme Court disagreed and upheld CIPA. Although the U.S. Supreme Court did not decide the case using the public forum doctrine, it stated the following regarding the views of "private speakers":

> A public library does not acquire Internet terminals in order to create a public forum for Web publishers to express themselves, any more than it collects books in order to provide a public

forum for the authors of books to speak. *It provides Internet access, not to encourage a diversity of views from private speakers, but for the same reasons it offers other library resources: to facilitate research, learning, and recreational pursuits by furnishing materials of requisite and appropriate quality.* As Congress recognized, [t]he Internet is simply another method for making information available in a school or library. It is no more than a technological extension of the book stack.

U.S. v. Am. Library Ass'n, 539 U.S. 194, 206-207 (2003) (emphasis added) (internal citations omitted). To read the entire case, go to https://supreme.justia.com/cases/federal/us/539/194/#tab-opinion-1961285.

There is also a practical problem with private speakers in public schools: they take up precious time needed for instruction in core subjects. Whether it is a non-profit organization raising awareness for an important cause, a legal or judicial group advancing advocacy skills, or a graduate program implementing a new theory, they all take up precious time needed for instruction in the core subjects. I am not suggesting that these issues are not good ideas. Rather, "good" ideas, may not be the "best" use of students' time. The issue is one of priority. Also, some private speakers use public school students like guinea pigs for surveys and gathering data. All this private speech takes up time, which is among the most valued commodities of public schools.

I experienced this problem in 2019 when I volunteered to tutor troubled high school students in reading. One student was a 16-year-old girl. I was told she read at the 2nd to 3rd-grade level, but after our first session, I realized she was far below that level and needed help with basic vowel sounds, vowel combinations, and even the sounds of some consonants. This placed her near the kindergarten to 1st-grade level. My time with her increased from once a week to virtually every day, barring conflicts with some nonessential school activities. Certainly, these were "good" activities, but not necessarily what she needed to function in society – the ability to read. In the end, she made headway, but there was not enough time to get her above a 2nd-grade reading level.

The bottom line is that learning core academic subjects such as reading and mathematics are critical to functioning in society. *Although some instruction may be a "good" idea, public schools are not capable of nor responsible for teaching everything that students need to know in life.* They have limited responsibilities and a limited amount of time. They should not be expected nor required to do everything. Plus, they should be empowered and given tools to protect students from all the outside voices clamoring for their attention. The public forum doctrine is just that – a tool to protect students. How does it work? Legislators and public school officials can enact legislation and rules to prevent the plethora of private speech that is infiltrating the public schools and speaking to the impressionable and captive audience of students, preferably using the nonpublic forum analysis.

> *Although some instruction may be a "good" idea, public schools are not capable of nor responsible for teaching everything that students need to know in life.*

THE REASONING BEHIND LEGISLATION AND RULES IS CRITICAL

Sometimes the courts examine the reasoning behind the legislation and rules when deciding whether they are constitutional. As a hypothetical, assume that parents across the state begin submitting "opt-out" forms at their public schools based on their parental rights, religious freedoms, and freedom not to speak. Then assume that it becomes so pervasive that one-fourth of the students from classes across the state do this. After a while, the legislators and school officials get together and decide to change to the curriculum and focus on core academic subjects. They begin to debate and clarify the reason for the curriculum changes. Is the reason for the changes the opt-outs based on religion, or is it something larger – too much private speech that is not focused on educating students in the core academic subjects? There are compelling arguments that it is the latter.

The nonpublic forum doctrine provides a rationale for state legislators and school officials to limit private speech in public schools. *First, educating students and increasing scores in core academic subjects is a legitimate governmental interest.* Limiting private speakers (advocacy groups, third-party vendors, supplemental instructional materials and content, teacher supplements, and personal agendas) in public school classrooms is also rationally related to educating students and increasing scores in core academic subjects. By virtually any measure, student test scores are down nationwide, partly due to the COVID-19 closures. Core academic subjects are a priority and increasing scores in core academic subjects is a legitimate governmental concern. *Second, laws and rules that prevent private speakers in public schools are viewpoint neutral.* The private speech is not being removed because of its viewpoint. Instead, it is removed because it takes time out of the school day that needs to be focused elsewhere. Of course, it would genuinely have to be "viewpoint neutral." Then challenges to the laws and rules based on viewpoint would likely fail. As you can see, the public forum doctrine is far more efficient and a fairer method to use as the rationale for changes in state school laws and board rules. For more on the public forum doctrine, see Chapter 11, Freedom of Speech Clause.

GOVERNMENTAL TORT IMMUNITY AND PROTECTING STUDENTS

In this section, I am not suggesting that parents and students bring legal action against teachers, administrators, or schools. None of us want our public schools to be involved in civil actions that undermine our schools and communities. On the other hand, there are times when parents and educators can leverage governmental tort immunity to protect students from potential harm – without litigation. I will try to make this complex issue understandable.

Traditionally, federal and state governments have "sovereign immunity" and cannot be sued for tort actions (i.e., negligence) unless they consent to be sued.[7] You may be thinking, "why would government consent to be sued?" One answer is that the threat or possibility of litigation can operate as a deterrent to negligent behavior, and the government does not want its employees to be negligent, especially when dealing with the public.

Today, the federal and some state governments have consented to certain tort actions with laws that "waive" their immunity and allow them to be sued.[8] Other state governments have not "waived" their immunity, but state court decisions make the standard of proof "higher" and require "notice" to the government of the potential harm *before* it occurs. The goal is for government employees to be more careful but not overly burdened by the threat of litigation. Hence, some states require notice to the government (or school) of potential harm.

For example, in Georgia, there was caselaw in 2010 that allowed parents and students to bring tort claims against schools *if the school had "notice" of the potential harm*. At that time, our children's school district was deciding whether principals would be allowed to have part-time rather than full-time clinic aides because of funding deficits. As the mother of a child with a chronic medical condition that needed a full-time clinic aide, I was concerned. Although I advocated before our school district, and hoped they would provide full-time clinic coverage, this was a matter of life and death. So, I went the next step. I requested and gathered letters from pediatricians, medical specialists, emergency room doctors, and the medical advisor of our community fire department. The letters stated that children with our child's condition and other life-threatening conditions needed full-time clinic coverage. I prepared a cover letter and sent (via certified mail return receipt requested and email) copies to the local school board and superintendent. Additionally, I used our local school advisory council process to recommend full-time clinic coverage. The school district was "on notice." I hoped they would realize the potential harm (and their potential liability) and act prudently, despite the recession. I do not know if my letter made a difference. We had many good board members at the time. Nonetheless, the school board made full-time clinic coverage mandatory the upcoming year, protecting *all* K-12 students in the school district.

This scenario is an example of how parents, with the assistance of legal counsel, can use their state school laws, waivers of immunity, caselaw, and "notice" of potential harm to protect children in public schools. The goal is to avoid potential injuries and litigation using legal notice to the school. This process can be beneficial when the potential injury to students is supported by written expert opinion. Local legal counsel is necessary for these situations.

HOW TO FIND WHAT YOU NEED

Determine the Source

- The first step is determining the source of the controversial material and content. Is the content permitted under state school laws, state board rules, and local board rules? This is where researching the laws/rules and submitting an open records request can be helpful. If only your school or teacher permits the content, you can inquire at the lowest level and work your way up the chain of authority for resolution.
- The next step is to determine whether the content impacts your federal and state constitutional rights. Ultimately, this is a fact-sensitive decision that you must make with your legal counsel.
- If you are a parent looking for local legal counsel, see Appendix C for your state and the link to your state's bar association. Also, see the end of Chapter 11, which has a list of legal groups that work to protect federal and state constitutional rights (including parental rights, religious freedom, and freedom of speech), sometimes at a free or reduced cost.
- Contact your school and school district's legal counsel if you are an educator.
- If you are looking for legal assistance, please act immediately because time limitations called statutes of limitations may apply to your situation.

EQUAL JUSTICE UNDER LAW

PART II

FEDERAL AND STATE CONSTITUTIONAL RIGHTS

"Every banana republic has a Bill of Rights. What's more important is the separation of powers and independent courts to enforce the rights of individuals." [1]
— U.S. Supreme Court Justice Antonin Scalia

THE SEPARATION OF POWERS DOCTRINE

The separation of powers doctrine refers to the division of government responsibilities into several distinct branches of government. The purpose of the separation of powers doctrine is to prevent the concentration of power in any one branch and to provide for checks and balances.[2] In the United States, the separation of powers has several structural components. First, there is the separation of powers at the federal level to check and balance power among the federal branches – the executive, the legislative, and the judicial. Second, there is federalism and the separation of powers between the federal and state governments using the Tenth Amendment. The Tenth Amendment empowers the state governments to prevent the federal government from abusing its power. Third, there is the separation of powers at the state level to check and balance power between the executive, the legislative, and the judicial branches. The purpose of our constitutional design is to prevent the abuse or concentration of power, and protect individual liberty through constitutional rights.

> *The purpose of our constitutional design is to prevent the abuse or concentration of power, and protect individual liberty through constitutional rights.*

BALANCING GOVERNMENT POWER AND CONSTITUTIONAL RIGHTS

The federal and state constitutions operate as "power" and "rights" documents. On the one hand, they distribute power to the three branches of federal and state government. On the other hand, power goes to the people by way of their rights, which are guaranteed under the "Bill of Rights" in the federal constitution and the bill of rights or declaration of rights in the state constitution. This balance of power is brilliant because it establishes an equilibrium and operates as a check between the government's power and the people's power. When the people's rights are violated, and government's power unduly altered, the balance is out of equilibrium. Action may be taken to bring it back into balance. However, for the rights of the people to be expressed and government laws and acts declared unconstitutional, people must assert their constitutional rights, beginning at the local level and preferably in a calm and respectful manner.

FEDERAL AND STATE CONSTITUTIONAL PROTECTIONS ARE NOT AUTOMATIC

There may be hundreds if not thousands of laws being enforced and government actions taking place that, if challenged, the courts would deem them "unconstitutional." However, courts do not, as a matter of course, review newly enacted laws and rules to determine whether they are constitutional. Likewise, courts do not monitor state and government officials' actions and determine whether they are constitutional. In fact, courts specifically *avoid* and *refuse* to hear hypothetical cases. In legal terms, these cases are not justiciable (cannot be heard by the court). As a result, individuals and their legal counsel must examine state and federal laws and government actions, and if they are "justiciable" (see general requirements below), the individuals may challenge the laws and government actions under their federal and state constitutions. Then the courts can determine whether they are constitutional.

Generally, for a constitutional case to be justiciable (heard by the court), all of the following conditions must be met: (1) there must be an actual "case or controversy" (rights must be threatened); (2) the case must be "ripe" (the court cannot review a state law until it is enforced or a government action until there is harm or immediate threat of harm); (3) the case must not be "moot" (a real live controversy must exist at all stages of review, with some exceptions for class actions and things that are capable of repetition but end before the court can decide the case); and (4) the parties must have "standing" (the person can demonstrate a concrete stake in the outcome).

Applying the principles of justiciability, you may want to challenge portions of your school's curriculum and request an exemption based on your federal and state constitutional parental rights, which include the right to make decisions regarding your child's education. Asserting your rights could involve a simple and respectful letter requesting an exemption and stating the basis for your request. If the school grants your request for an exemption, then you have successfully used the system to protect your child from instruction that you oppose. On the other hand, if the school denies your request, you can decide whether to assert your constitutional rights further up the chain of command, i.e., at the local board of education level. This process is how constitutional rights are recognized. People assert their rights, the schools either recognize or disregard their rights, and if the matter is not resolved, then it has the potential to go to court with the assistance of legal counsel.

Asserting your rights could involve a simple and respectful letter requesting an exemption and stating the basis for your request.

Challenges to the constitutionality of laws and government actions are nothing new. For example, in the 1970s, the State of Wisconsin had a law requiring all children to attend school until they were 16 years old, including the Amish who at that time attended public schools.[3] If they did not stay in school, they were subject to truancy laws. *The State of Wisconsin could have carved out an exemption in the truancy law for the Amish but it did not.* The Amish challenged the truancy law and brought their case in court, asserting that the government had violated their constitutional rights (the right to the free exercise of their religious beliefs and their parental rights). *This interaction between the state truancy law and the assertion of rights formed the basis of the Amish's "case."* The case went to the U.S. Supreme Court, which recognized the Amish's constitutional rights and decided in their favor. This process is how our system works regarding our federal and state constitutional rights.

> So, why aren't people asserting their constitutional rights today? First, there is evidence that asserting one's rights is no longer fashionable.

Additionally, courts only rule on (or decide) the legal questions presented to them. They will not answer questions that are not presented. In fact, legal briefs have a specific section called "questions presented." Suppose you submitted a written parent opt-form and opted out of all school surveys but your child's teacher requires him or her to take all surveys anyway. Then suppose you are unable to resolve the issue, and in the end, you challenge the school district based on your constitutionally protected *parental rights*. In that situation, the courts will only examine the question of *parental rights*. The courts will not consider your child's right to freedom of speech and his or her *freedom not to speak* (writing is a recognized form of speech). The point is, the courts' role is very circumscribed; they only answer the legal questions presented. As a result, it is essential to know and be prepared to assert all your constitutional rights, if necessary.

So, why aren't people asserting their constitutional rights today? First, there is evidence that asserting one's rights is no longer fashionable. In the past, people who adhered to personal convictions were admired, considered to be of good character, and often placed on a pedestal for honoring beliefs

Second, civics education in the public schools has been weakening since the 1960's and, according to the National Education Association, "only 25% of students reach the 'proficient' standard on the NAEO Civics Assessment."

over temporal matters. While growing up, I heard the phrase, "If you don't stand for something, you will fall for anything." Today, however, there is an emphasis on acceptance and tolerance. These concepts, while essential to living in a diverse society, can run counter to asserting one's personal convictions and constitutional rights. Second, civics education in the public schools has been weakening since the 1960's and, according to the National Education Association, "only 25% of students reach the 'proficient' standard on the NAEO Civics Assessment."[4] In other words, people do not *know* their rights or *how* to assert their rights.

OVERVIEW OF HOW COURTS EXAMINE CONSTITUTIONAL RIGHTS

As an overview, federal constitutional cases go through several levels of courts before reaching the U.S. Supreme Court. In the federal system, there are three basic levels: (1) the Federal District Courts in each state, which are the federal trial courts; (2) the 13 Circuit Courts of Appeals that take appeals from the Federal District Courts from several states; and (3) the U.S. Supreme Court that takes appeals from the Circuit Courts of Appeals. Of course, this path has exceptions and nuances, but this is the general course for constitutional cases brought before the U.S. Supreme Court.

At the Federal District Court level, which is the trial court level, constitutional cases (like other cases) begin with "pleadings" that outline the positions of both "parties" to the case. Then both sides take "discovery," which includes written questions and answers, an exchange of documents that are relevant to the case, and depositions. Then they file "motions" asking to court to decide the case based on the "law" and without a trial. If there is a trial, the court considers the applicable "law" and the "facts" are put in evidence. The trial court decides the case with a written opinion that includes its "findings of fact" and "conclusions of law." The court's written decision becomes part of caselaw.

If either party thinks the court "erred," they can appeal the case to the next level, the Circuit Court of Appeals. Then, if either party chooses, they can appeal to the U.S. Supreme Court. Some cases work their way through the state court system, and if a federal constitutional issue is involved, the case is potentially appealable to the U.S. Supreme Court. The U.S. Supreme Court can accept or reject the appeal (the legal term is granting or denying "certiorari"). Suppose the U.S. Supreme Court rejects the appeal (denies certiorari). In that case, the decision by the Circuit Court of Appeals "stands" as precedent for that circuit, which may be different from the precedent in other circuits. As you can see, the state and circuit that you live in influence your constitutional rights.

When federal (and state) courts decide cases involving constitutional rights, they go through three steps outlined in simple terms below.

1. COURTS IDENTIFY THE LAW OR GOVERNMENT ACTION

First, courts identify the specific government action at issue. Remember, constitutional rights protect individuals from government infringement. Depending upon the facts, the government infringement may be:

- a school rule or policy;
- a local or state board of education rule or policy;
- a local, state, or federal law, rule, or policy;
- an exemption or waiver of a local, state, or federal law, rule, or policy;
- an action by a federal official;
- an action by a local or state government official (including public schools, which are an extension of the state government); or
- enforcement of an anti-discrimination law or rule by a local, state, or federal government official.[5]

Remember, constitutional rights protect individuals from government infringement.

There may be other government actions not listed. Obviously, the government is involved in *public school* laws, rules, and policies. However, when *private schools* make rules and policies, they are not government or state actions.

2. COURTS IDENTIFY THE CONSTITUTIONAL RIGHT

Next, courts identify the federal or state constitutional right that may have been violated. Some constitutional rights are explicitly stated in the constitutions. Some are implied, such as the right of privacy. For our purposes, the rights at issue will likely include:

- the child's right to a public education under the state constitution;
- the parent's parental rights (the right to control their children's education) under the federal and state constitutions;
- the child's and parents' rights to free exercise of religion, freedom of speech, and the freedom not to speak under the federal and state constitutions; and
- unrecognized (new) constitutional rights that you and your legal counsel decide to bring before the courts.

3. COURTS APPLY THE APPROPRIATE LEVEL OF "SCRUTINY" TO THE LAW OR GOVERNMENT ACTION

Courts apply different standards to laws and government actions depending upon the constitutional rights at issue. Some constitutional rights are deemed more important than others. Laws and government actions that infringe on more important constitutional rights receive more "scrutiny" by the courts. Higher scrutiny means that it is harder for the law or rule to be deemed constitutional. Court scrutiny involves two components: (1) examining the purpose of the law or government action; and (2) examining the precision of the law or government action that meets that purpose.

> *Laws and government actions that infringe on more important constitutional rights receive more "scrutiny" by the courts.*

a. The Purpose of the Law

Courts first examine the "government's interest" in passing the law. In practical terms, the courts examine the purpose or need for the law or government action. What was the purpose or intent of the law? Why did the government need to enact the law? How critical is the problem that the government tried to solve by enacting the law? Really important constitutional rights require that the government have a "compelling actual purpose" for the law. The intermediate level of constitutional rights requires that the government have an "important actual purpose" for the law. Less important constitutional rights require that the government have a "legitimate conceivable purpose" for the law.

b. The Precision of the Law

Courts then examine the law to see if it is "narrowly tailored" or the least restrictive alternative to solving the problem. In other words, courts want legislatures to enact laws that are written narrowly to address specific problems so that they do not inadvertently violate people's constitutional rights. Broad and sweeping laws do not tend to fare well in the courts. That is why laws are written with such detail. Legislators must draft laws that pinpoint the conduct that should be prohibited but not violate the constitutional rights of others. If there is a compelling actual purpose, the law must be "narrowly tailored" to the government's purpose. If there is an important actual purpose, the law must be "substantially related" to the government's purpose. If there is a legitimate conceivable purpose, the law only needs to be "rationally related" to the government's purpose. To summarize:

- **Strict Scrutiny**: The law must be "narrowly tailored" to achieve a "compelling actual government purpose."
- **Intermediate Scrutiny**: The law must be "substantially related" to achieve an "important actual government purpose."
- **Rational Basis Test**: The law must be "rationally related" to achieve a "legitimate conceivable government purpose."

For the rational basis test, notice that there is a difference between an "actual" purpose and a "conceivable" purpose, which may or may not be the *real* reason the government passed the law or rule.

Out of deference to the people's constitutional rights, legislators at the federal, state, and local level, as well as state and local boards of education, are expected to pass laws and rules that, if challenged, would be deemed constitutional. In addition, the laws should be written clearly (not vaguely) so that people have "notice" of what is and is not prohibited; otherwise, the law may violate the Due Process Clause. However, if the people stop asserting their constitutional rights and challenging the laws, legislators may be less careful protecting constitutional rights. Then, there is likely to be more and more encroachment on constitutional rights – both federal and state.[6]

> *Out of deference to the people's constitutional rights, legislators at the federal, state, and local level, as well as state and local boards of education, are expected to pass laws and rules that, if challenged, would be deemed constitutional.*

CHAPTER 10

STATE CONSTITUTIONAL RIGHTS

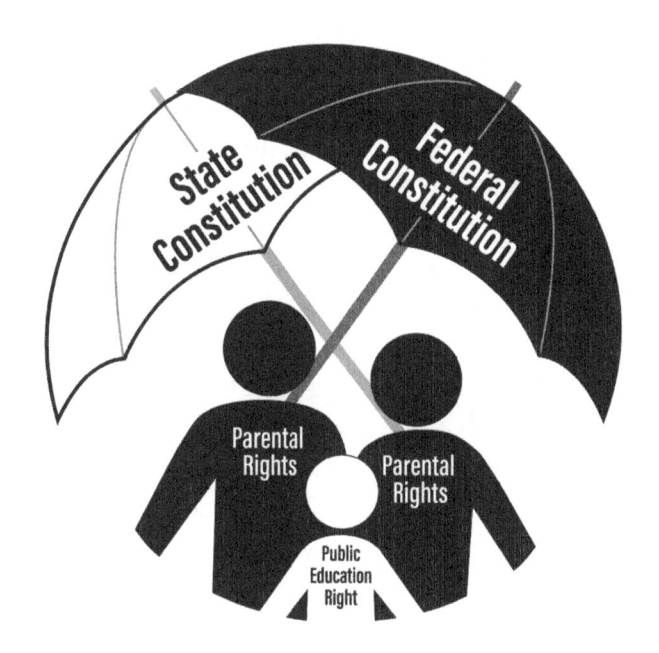

THE STATE CONSTITUTIONAL "RIGHT TO A PUBLIC EDUCATION"

As mentioned in Chapter 1, there is no federal constitutional right to a public education. Instead, each state constitution guarantees the right to a public education.[1] Each state constitution also has an "education article" which establishes the state's authority over public education and the people's right to a public education. To learn more about this right, let us re-examine the Georgia Constitution in Article VIII, Section I, which states:

> The provision of an ***adequate public education*** for the citizens shall be the primary obligation of the State of Georgia. Public

education for the citizens prior to the college or postsecondary level ***shall be free*** and shall be provided for by taxation, and the General Assembly may by general law provide for the establishment of education policies for such public education. The expense of other public education shall be provided for in such manner and in such amount as may be provided by law."

Georgia Constitution, Article VIII, Section I, Paragraph 1 (emphasis added).

The state right to a public education and the meaning of the terms used in the state constitution are interpreted by the courts, and ultimately by the state's highest court. For example, in 1979, the Supreme Court of Georgia considered a case involving summer school.[2] The issue before the Court was whether the right to a free public education included the right to attend summer school for free. The Court held that the right to a free public education was presently limited to 180 days. In other words, a "free" and "adequate education" in Georgia does not include free summer school. This case demonstrates how each state constitution recognizes a state right to a public education and each state's highest court decides on the meaning of the words used in the state's constitution.

THE STATE CONSTITUTION'S "BILL OF RIGHTS"

All 50 state constitutions also include a bill of rights or a declaration of rights like the U.S. Constitution's Bill of Rights. For example, the Georgia Constitution's Bill of Rights protects: life, liberty, property, freedom of conscience and religion, freedom of speech and the press, the right to keep and bear arms, the right to assemble and petition the government, the right to a trial by jury, and protections against illegal searches and seizures, to name a few. Each state also recognizes parental rights. In other words, you have parental rights under *both* your state constitution and its bill of rights, and the U.S. Constitution and its Bill of Rights (the First through Tenth Amendments).

One of the benefits of pursuing your rights under your state constitution is: the state can grant *greater* rights to individuals. The Supremacy Clause establishes a "floor" or "backstop" for constitutional rights. U.S. CONST. art. VI, § 2. State constitutions, legislatures, and courts cannot go **below** the federal floor and grant fewer rights. However, the states can grant **more** rights. For example, the U.S. Constitution protects the free exercise of religion. Yet, many state constitutions protect religion and matters of "conscience."[3] This gives the states more latitude to address belief systems that are not traditionally viewed as religions.[4] See Appendix B.

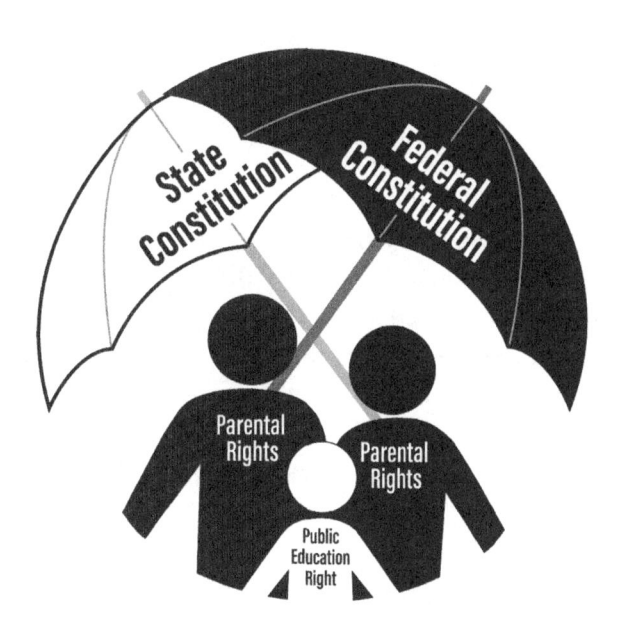

To visualize the two layers of protections provided by the federal and state constitutions, meet the Rights family: Bill, Belinda, and Billy. The Rights are standing under two umbrellas representing the federal and state constitutions. This double-umbrella analogy works well because the courts refer to people having rights guaranteed "under" a constitution. In this context, "under" means "within the authority of" or "with the authorization of." The top umbrella represents the rights guaranteed under the federal constitution. The lower umbrella represents the rights guaranteed under the state constitution. The laws, rules, and government actions that infringe upon or violate our rights can be challenged as "unconstitutional" under *both* the state and federal constitutions. The two umbrellas mostly overlap and provide two layers of protection, but only in some places. Some rights are guaranteed only under the state constitution, such as the right to an education.

The two umbrellas mostly overlap and provide two layers of protection, but only in some places. Some rights are guaranteed only under the state constitution, such as the right to an education.

To help you remember the rights commonly asserted in the school setting, Bill and Belinda have "parental rights" written on their shirts. Billy's "public education right" is written on his shirt. Each state constitution describes the right to an education differently, using words such as "adequate," "thorough and efficient," "general," "uniform," "general and uniform," a "general diffusion of knowledge," and to "secure the people the advantages and opportunities of education." Many also include the words "public" and "free." If the Rights family lives in Georgia, Billy's right to a public education would be defined as a "right to a free and adequate public education." If the Rights family moves to Pennsylvania, Billy will have a "right to a thorough and efficient system of public education." Bill, Belinda, and Billy Rights have many other shirts representing their other rights under their federal and state constitutions.

HOW TO FIND WHAT YOU NEED:

Your State Constitution's Education Article

1. Go to Appendix C and find your state's information page.
2. Click the link to your state constitution and look for the bill of rights or declaration of rights similar to the rights in the U.S. Constitution. Each state constitution provides an additional layer of rights to the people.
3. Also, look at your state constitution's education article, which specifies the type of education guaranteed in your state. It may use words such

as "adequate," "thorough and efficient," "general," "uniform," "general and uniform," a "general diffusion of knowledge," or to "secure the people the advantages and opportunities of education."
4. Remember that there is no *federal* constitutional right to a public education; rather, that right is guaranteed under the *state* constitutions.

CHAPTER 11

FEDERAL CONSTITUTIONAL RIGHTS

EXPRESS AND IMPLIED
FEDERAL CONSTITUTIONAL RIGHTS

The U.S. Supreme Court has recognized express and implied federal constitutional rights. The express rights are listed in the U.S. Constitution's Bill of Rights (First through Tenth Amendments).

The U.S. Supreme Court has the final say on the meaning of the words used in the U.S. Constitution. As a result, the *express rights* are *explained* in "caselaw," which are the written decisions by the courts, and for our purposes, the U.S. Supreme Court. The *implied rights* are both *recognized* and *explained* in caselaw. So, this chapter includes many quotes from U.S. Supreme Court decisions. The cases are cited in footnotes if you want to read them.

EXPRESS RIGHTS: THE U.S. CONSTITUTION'S BILL OF RIGHTS (FIRST THROUGH TENTH AMENDMENTS)

First — ***Right to Free Exercise of Religion, Freedom of Speech***, Freedom of the Press, Freedom of Assembly, and the Freedom to Petition Government
Second — Right to Keep and Bear Arms, and Maintain a Well-Regulated Militia
Third — No Quartering of Soldiers
Fourth — Freedom from Unreasonable Searches and Seizures
Fifth — Right to Due Process of Law, Freedom from Self-Incrimination, and Freedom from Double Jeopardy
Sixth — Rights of Accused Persons to a Speedy Trial, Counsel, Impartial Jury, and to Confront Accusers
Seventh — Right to a Trial by Jury in Civil Cases
Eighth — Freedom from Excessive Bail or Fines, and Freedom from Cruel and Unusual Punishments
Ninth — Non-Enumerated Rights
Tenth — Rights Reserved to the States or to the People

There are additional express rights, such as the right to vote, which is guaranteed in the Fifteenth, Nineteenth, and Twenty-Sixth Amendments. These amendments state that the voting rights of U.S. citizens cannot be abridged on account of race, color, previous condition of servitude, sex, or age (18 and older). The Fourteenth Amendment provides that no state shall "deprive any person of life, liberty, or property without due process of law."[1] The Free Speech Clause includes the "concomitant" negative free speech right, the right not to speak or be required to act in a manner that constitutes speech.[2]

> *The Free Speech Clause includes the "concomitant" negative free speech right, the right not to speak or be required to act in a manner that constitutes speech.*

The U.S. Constitution can be amended to include additional express rights. The first step involves a proposed amendment by either: (1) Congress with a two-thirds majority vote in both the House of Representatives and the Senate; or (2) a constitutional Convention called for by two-thirds of the state legislatures. Then the proposed amendment must be ratified by either: (1) three-fourths of the states' legislatures; or (2) three-fourths of the states in the ratifying Conventions. U.S. CONST. art. V. Unfortunately, Congress and the state legislatures have not been able to agree to amend the U.S. Constitution, particularly on social issues. As a result, people have looked to the U.S. Supreme Court to interpret the Constitution in a way that recognizes additional rights.

IMPLIED RIGHTS: U.S. SUPREME COURT DECISIONS

There are two categories of implied constitutional rights. The first category is "fundamental rights," which are "deeply rooted in [our] history and tradition" and essential to our "scheme of ordered liberty."[3] Some of the implied fundamental rights recognized by the U.S. Supreme Court are listed below:

Implied Fundamental Rights include, but are not limited to...

- Right to Interstate Travel[4]
- Right of Privacy, including:
  - **_Parental Rights (including the right to make decisions regarding the care, custody, control, and education of one's children)_**[5]
  - Right to Marry[6]
  - Right to Procreate[7]
  - Right to Purchase and Use Contraceptives[8]
  - Right to Read Obscene Material in the Home, except child pornography[9]
  - Right to Keep Extended Family Together[10]

As you consider the implied Right of Privacy and all it includes, bear in mind that none of these rights are explicitly stated in the U.S. Constitution. They are *implied*. Someone thought these should be a constitutional right. They initiated the case that made it to the U.S. Supreme Court, which recognized the right. The case now stands as precedent for the established implied right. In fact, there is a Federal Rule of Civil Procedure that lists the standards for bringing new cases. This standard permits cases that are "nonfrivolous argument(s) for extending, modifying, or reversing existing law *or for establishing new law.*" Fed. R. Civ. P. 11(b)(2) (emphasis added). More constitutional rights may be recognized and existing constitutional rights may be expanded, but only after people bring cases before the U.S. Supreme Court to assert their constitutional rights and freedoms.

More constitutional rights may be recognized and existing constitutional rights may be expanded, but only after people bring cases before the U.S. Supreme Court to assert their constitutional rights and freedoms.

The second category of implied rights is the first eight amendments, which have been made applicable to the states.[11] Originally, our federal constitutional rights were only protected against *federal* government infringements.[12] State constitutions restricted state and local governments. Later, the U.S. Supreme Court held that the first eight amendments also restricted state and local governments.[13] In other words, the restrictions were implied to the states.[14]

THE U.S. CONSTITUTION'S PROTECTION OF "PARENTAL RIGHTS"

Throughout the last century, the U.S. Supreme Court has championed the fundamental rights of parents by striking down laws that "unreasonably interfere with the liberty of parents and guardians to direct the upbringing and education of their children under their control."[15] In 1972, the U.S. Supreme Court stated:

> **The history and culture of Western civilization reflect a strong tradition of parental concern for the nurture and upbringing of their children. This primary role of the parents in the upbringing of their children is now established beyond debate as an enduring American tradition.** If not the first, perhaps the most significant statements of the Court in this area are found in *Pierce v. Society of Sisters,* in which the Court observed: 'Under

the doctrine of *Meyer v. Nebraska, 262 U.S. 390*, we think it entirely plain that the [Nebraska law] unreasonably interferes with the liberty of parents and guardians to direct the upbringing and education of children under their control."[16]

In *Meyer v. Nebraska*, the U.S. Supreme Court struck down a state law prohibiting modern language instruction other than English.[17] Several years later, in *Pierce v. Society of Sisters*, the U.S. Supreme Court stated that parents have the right "to direct the upbringing and education of children under their control" and struck down a state law requiring all children to attend public schools.[18] In 1972, the U.S. Supreme Court struck down a Wisconsin law recognizing the "liberty of parents . . . to direct the upbringing and education of their children." Since then, the U.S. Supreme Court has continued to recognize parental rights as "fundamental rights." In 1982, the Court reiterated the "fundamental liberty interest of natural parents in the care, custody, and management of their child."[19] As recently as 2000, the U.S. Supreme Court stated that the U.S. Constitution "protects the fundamental right of parents to make decisions concerning the care, custody, and control of their children."[20]

Additionally, parental rights include the power to direct the religious upbringing of one's children. In *Wisconsin v. Yoder*, the U.S. Supreme Court stated, "[h]owever read, the Court's holding in *Pierce* stands as a charter of the rights of parents to direct the religious upbringing of their children."[21] "The values of parental direction of the religious upbringing of their children in their early and formative years have a high place in our society."[22] In other words, parents have *rights* and *standing* regarding the religious education of their minor children.

Given that parental rights are "fundamental rights," any federal, state, or local government law, rule, or action that infringes on parental rights receives the highest level of scrutiny by the Courts – strict scrutiny.[23] To pass "strict scrutiny," the law or rule must be "narrowly tailored" to meet the government's

> Given that parental rights are "fundamental rights," any federal, state, or local government law, rule, or action that infringes on parental rights receives the highest level of scrutiny by the Courts – strict scrutiny.

"compelling actual purpose" for the law or rule. For more information on parental rights in your state, see Appendix C for school laws regarding parental rights. See also, "Protecting Children by Empowering Parents" at (https://parentalrights.org/) and hit the drop-down for "learn" and "parental rights in every state."

THE PROPOSED PARENTAL RIGHTS AMENDMENT

If parental rights are already recognized as "implied rights," why propose a Parental Rights Amendment to the U.S. Constitution? The answer is twofold. First, the U.S. Supreme Court could decide to apply a lower level of scrutiny to parental rights. Second, some members of Congress are concerned that the United States Senate might ratify the United Nations' "Convention on the Rights of the Child." If so, the concern is that the "Convention on the Rights of the Child" would be "incorporated into"[24] the United States Constitution under the "Supremacy Clause." The "Supremacy Clause," which is in Article 6, Section 2 of the U.S. Constitution, states:

> This Constitution, and the Laws of the United States which shall be made in Pursuance thereof; **and all Treaties made, or which shall be made, under the Authority of the United States**, shall be the supreme Law of the Land; and the Judges in every State shall be bound thereby, any Thing in the Constitution or Laws of any State to the Contrary notwithstanding.

U.S. CONST. art. VI, § 2 (emphasis added). The concern is that the "Convention on the Rights of the Child" is a treaty that would supersede state school laws, state laws affecting children, and implied parental rights, among other things. This is a legitimate concern. Legal documents routinely "incorporate" other documents "by reference" (by referring to them). A parental rights amendment to the U.S. Constitution will solve this problem.

As noted earlier, the U.S. Constitution can be amended. The first step involves a proposed amendment by either: (1) Congress with a two-thirds majority vote in both the House of Representatives and the Senate; or (2) a constitutional Convention called for by two-thirds of the state legislatures. Then the proposed amendment must be ratified by either: (1) three-fourths of the states' legislatures; or (2) three-fourths of the states in the ratifying Conventions. U.S. CONST. art. V.

The first Parental Rights Amendment to the U.S. Constitution was proposed in 2008. No action was taken after the first attempt but others continued to propose similar amendments. Representative Jim Banks (R-IN) proposed the amendment below:

SECTION 1 – The liberty of parents to direct the upbringing, education, and care of their children is a fundamental right.

SECTION 2 – *The parental right to direct education includes the right to choose, as an alternative to public education, private, religious, or home schools, and the right to make reasonable choices within public schools for one's child.*

SECTION 3 – Neither the United States nor any State shall infringe these rights without demonstrating that its governmental interest as applied to the person is of the highest order and not otherwise served.

SECTION 4 – The parental rights guaranteed by this article shall not be denied or abridged on account of disability.

SECTION 5 – This article shall not be construed to apply to a parental action or decision that would end life.

H.J. Res. 36. The legislatures of Louisiana, South Dakota, Idaho, Montana, Florida, Wyoming, and Oklahoma have passed resolutions calling on the U.S. Congress to propose the Parental Rights Amendment to the states for ratification. In October 2022, Congresswoman Debbie Lesko (AZ-08) proposed another Parental Rights Amendment to the U.S. Constitution. Please search online for additional details, as a congressional number was not assigned to the proposed amendment as of this writing.

Prior to reading this book, you may have thought, "Why would anyone oppose a state or federal Parents' Bill of Rights?" Now you understand. Parents' Bills of Rights expressly state that parental rights are "fundamental rights" and they require the courts to apply "strict scrutiny" or "the highest order of protection to parental rights." See O.C.G.A. § 20-2-786(d); FL Stat § 1014.03; H.J. Res. 36 §§ 1 and 3 . Now you know that strict scrutiny establishes a high bar.

It requires all laws and government actions that infringe on parental rights (when challenged) to be "narrowly tailored" to achieve a "compelling actual government purpose." **When strict scrutiny is applied, parental rights almost always "win."** More specifically, when strict scrutiny is applied, parental rights will likely "win" over other groups that do not have "fundamental rights." Similarly, if strict scrutiny is applied, parental rights will likely "win" over state and federal laws that infringe on parental rights. Therefore, people who oppose Parents' Bills of Rights tend to fall into two basic groups. One group wants their rights to prevail over parental rights. The other group wants the federal, state, and local governments to have more control over children, perhaps even more control than their parents. The central issue: control over other people's minor children. As Lincoln would say, this is the nub of the matter.

THE RELIGION CLAUSES OF THE FIRST AMENDMENT

Many parents want to "protect" their children in public schools because of their religious beliefs. A complete discussion of the Religion Clauses of the First Amendment and their application in public schools is beyond the scope of this book. However, my goal is to provide a basic understanding of the Religion Clauses and explain the standard of scrutiny that courts apply to the free exercise of religion.

The First Amendment begins with the Religion Clauses and states:

> "**Congress shall make no law respecting an establishment of religion, or prohibiting the free exercise thereof;** or abridging the freedom of speech or of the press, or the right of the people peaceably to assemble, and to petition the Government for a redress of grievances."

The Religion Clauses inform the relationship between government and religion.

U.S. CONST. amend. I (emphasis added). The Religion Clauses explicitly restrict Congress (the federal government). State and local government are restricted by caselaw interpreting the First and Fourteenth Amendments.[25]

The Religion Clauses inform the relationship between government and religion. On the one hand, the government shall not establish a religion. This portion of the Religion Clauses is referred to as the "Establishment Clause." On the other hand, the government shall not prohibit the free exercise of religion. This portion of the Religion Clauses is referred to as the "Free Exercise Clause." The two work together.

DEFINING "RELIGIOUS BELIEFS"

The U.S. Supreme Court has not defined religious beliefs. It has, however, made it clear that religious beliefs are not limited to traditional or organized religion.[26] There is also no requirement of a supreme being.[27] In a case interpreting a statute (not the U.S. Constitution), the U.S. Supreme Court stated that the "belief must occupy a place in the believer's life parallel to that occupied by orthodox religious beliefs."[28] The courts cannot declare a religious belief to be "false," but they can determine whether the belief is being sincerely asserted.[29]

Many state constitutions' bills of rights or declarations of rights use additional language in their protections of the free exercise of religion. For example, many states protect freedom of "religion" and "conscience" or "the right to worship according to the 'dictates of one's conscience'." If you believe that people have a body, a mind, and a spirit, then it is not surprising that our nation's move away from traditional religion has left many people with a void that is being filled with new belief systems and causes. These belief systems may not be deemed "religions" for First Amendment purposes. However, they may qualify for protection as matters of "conscience." See Appendix B.

Whether these textual differences in the state constitutions mean that states will protect religion and conscience differently is for each state's highest court to decide.

THE RIGHT TO FREE EXERCISE OF RELIGION:
THE STANDARD OF SCRUTINY

The First Amendment of the U.S. Constitution expressly recognizes the right to free exercise of religion. In a recent U.S. Supreme Court decision, the Court stated:

> The Free Exercise Clause provides that "Congress shall make no law . . . prohibiting the free exercise" of religion. Amdt. 1. . . . **The Clause protects not only the right to harbor religious beliefs inwardly and secretly. It does perhaps its most important work by protecting the ability of those who hold religious beliefs of all kinds to live out their faiths in daily life through 'the performance of (or abstention from) physical acts.'**[30]

In other words, the Free Exercise Clause protects more than just beliefs. It includes the right "to live out [people's] faiths in daily life through 'the performance of (or abstention from) physical acts.'"[31] This is a powerful statement by the U.S. Supreme Court.

In the sections above, we looked at the standard of "scrutiny" courts apply to constitutional rights. Those standards usually fall into one of the three levels, but not always. With the express right to free exercise of religion, "it depends."

Until 1990, the right to free exercise of religion received the highest level of scrutiny — strict scrutiny.[32] However, in April 1990, the U.S. Supreme Court carved out an exception in the *Smith* case. The U.S. Supreme Court held that strict scrutiny did not apply when the law that infringes on religion is: (1) a law of "general applicability" (applies to everyone); and (2) the law is "neutral" (does not target religion).[33] When these two criteria are met, the rational basis test, which is the lowest level of scrutiny, is applied to the law. As a result, any law or government action that meets these two criteria is analyzed using the rational basis test.

After *Smith*, many people were upset that "strict scrutiny" did not apply to all restrictions on the right to free exercise of religion, which is an express constitutional right. Congress responded to the *Smith* decision with the Religious Freedom Restoration Act ("RFRA"), which is a federal law that "ensures that interests in religious freedom are protected" and requires "strict scrutiny" for all federal claims based on the right to free exercise of religion.[34] The federal RFRA specifically referenced the Smith decision and was aimed at "restoring" the strict scrutiny standard set by prior cases. A unanimous House and nearly unanimous Senate passed the bill that

Many states enacted either state constitutional amendments or state RFRAs requiring "strict scrutiny."

was signed into law by President Clinton.[35] Later, the U.S. Supreme Court held that Congress could require the federal courts to apply strict scrutiny, but not the state courts.[36] In other words, the federal RFRA protects against federal infringements of the right to free exercise of religion with "strict scrutiny," but not state and local infringements on the right to free exercise of religion. In turn, many states enacted either state constitutional amendments or state RFRAs requiring "strict scrutiny." The goal of state RFRAs is to restore the strict scrutiny standard to the express right to free exercise of religion.

THE RIGHT TO FREE EXERCISE OF RELIGION: STRICT SCRUTINY APPLIES IF...

To summarize, there are several situations where strict scrutiny is still applied to federal and state laws and government actions that infringe on the right to free exercise of religion. First, strict scrutiny is applied when "hybrid rights" are involved, such as the right to free exercise of religion *and* parental rights,[37] or the right to free exercise of religion *and* the right to free speech.[38] Second, strict scrutiny applies if the law or government action is facially discriminatory against religion.[39] For example, in *Carson v. Makin*, a Maine law allowed parents and students to apply public funds toward private high school tuition if the private school was "a nonsectarian [not religious] school."[40] On its face, the law discriminated against religious schools when other private schools were permitted to receive funding. As a result, strict scrutiny applied and the U.S. Supreme Court held that the law violated the parents' and students' right to free exercise of religion. Third, strict scrutiny applies if the laws, rules, or facts allow exemptions, accommodations, or opt-outs for secular reasons but not religious reasons.[41] If there is a secular exemption, there should be a religious exemption also. Fourth, strict scrutiny applies under the federal RFRA if a federal law or federal government action infringes on the right to free exercise of religion.[42]

At the state level, if the law or government action is challenged under the state constitution, strict scrutiny applies if: (1) the state courts have interpreted the state constitution to apply strict scrutiny to either the "right to free exercise of religion," the "rights of conscience," or similar phrases; (2) the state has a RFRA or other law requiring state courts to apply strict scrutiny; or (3) the state has a religious freedom constitutional amendment. To see if your state has one of these three applications of strict scrutiny, see the Becket

Religious Freedom Restoration Information Central at (https://www.becketlaw.org/research-central/rfra-info-central/).[43] You must also confirm your research at your state legislature's website for new and pending RFRA laws and religious freedom constitutional amendments. Appendix C lists some state RFRAs. State constitutions may also protect matters of "conscience." See Appendix B. Finally, there are federal and state civil rights laws that prohibit discrimination based on religion.[44]

This raises the question: if there is an issue of religious discrimination against students or educators in a public school (i.e., cases where there is a government "actor"), how do individuals decide whether to: (1) *assert their rights* under the U.S. Constitution; (2) *assert their rights* under the state constitution, which may include protection for matters of "conscience"; and/or (3) *report a violation of their rights* under the federal, state, or local civil rights law? The answer: this is a fact-sensitive decision to be made by legal counsel. Yet, legal counsel will likely consider the fact that all federal and state laws (and acts)[45] are open to constitutional challenges, and at the end of the day, they must not conflict with the constitutional rights and protections under the U.S. Constitution.

THE ESTABLISHMENT CLAUSE: THE U.S. SUPREME COURT'S ANALYTICAL FRAMEWORK

Until 1947, the U.S. Supreme Court did not hold that any government action violated the Establishment Clause.

The Establishment Clause states, "Congress shall make no law respecting an establishment of religion." U.S. CONST. amend. I. Until 1947, the U.S. Supreme Court did not hold that any government action violated the Establishment Clause.[46] Thereafter, the U.S. Supreme Court began forming the elements of what came to be known as the *Lemon* Test.[47] The *Lemon* Test was either ignored or applied in various forms from 1971 to 2014. The U.S. Supreme Court abandoned the *Lemon* Test in 2014 and confirmed its abandonment in 2022.[48]

Today, when federal courts examine whether a law, rule, or government action constitutes an establishment of religion, they "examine historical practices and understandings" and consider: (1) whether the government is coercing religious practices; (2) whether the government is favoring one religion over another; or (3) whether the government is favoring one denomination over another.[49] In the public school context, "coercion" is arguably easier to find because the states have mandatory attendance policies (truancy laws) that make students a captive audience. There is also an argument that young children are more vulnerable and open to suggestion because of their youth. So, if you see some elements of religion in public schools, it may be because the federal courts have recognized a distinction between proselytizing (attempting to convert) versus teaching about a religion, which is permitted.[50]

Additionally, the Equal Access Act in Title VIII of the Education for Economic Security Act of 1984, 20 U.S. Code § 4071, allows public schools to treat religious clubs in the same manner that it treats other groups without violating the Establishment Clause.[51]

RELEASED TIME FOR RELIGIOUS INSTRUCTION PROGRAMS

The U.S. Supreme Court has held that released time for religious instruction ("RTRI") programs are permitted in public schools and do not constitute an establishment of religion. Few people know that specific RTRI programs are constitutional and operate alongside public schools in many states. In 1952, the U.S. Supreme Court upheld a New York City law that allowed students in public schools to be released during school hours for off-premises religious instruction.[52] Parental permission was required, students were not coerced to attend, and public funds were not used to transport students or pay for the program. When challenged, the U.S. Supreme Court upheld the New York City law. In turn, several states passed laws permitting RTRI programs if certain criteria were met (i.e., parental permission, off-premises, no coercion to attend, transportation provided by parents, etc.).[53] Other states permit them based on court decisions. Search using the key terms with and without a hyphen (released time and released-time) to see if your state has a state law or court decision regarding RTRI programs. Also note that several religious groups have national RTRI programs, with some providing guidance on how to establish an RTRI program in your state.[54] If you are interested in starting an RTRI program, consult with legal counsel. It is essential to meet the appropriate criteria established by state law and the U.S. Supreme Court decisions permitting RTRI programs.

THE ESTABLISHMENT CLAUSE AND THE "WALL OF SEPARATION" METAPHOR

To many people's surprise, there is no requirement in the First Amendment nor the U.S. Constitution that there be "a wall of separation between church and state."

To many people's surprise, there is no requirement in the First Amendment nor the U.S. Constitution that there be "a wall of separation between church and state." Rather, the "wall of separation" metaphor is part of our caselaw and has been championed by some who want to remove religion from our public discourse. The origin of this metaphor and how it became known is explained below.

The "wall of separation" language is attributed to Thomas Jefferson, who included it in a letter to the Danbury Baptist Association. The letter was later included in *Writings of Thomas Jefferson*, H. Washington ed. 1861, vol. 8 pp. 113. Thomas Jefferson, who was an ambassador to France, was not in the United States when the Bill of Rights was passed by Congress, nor when it was ratified by the states.

In early U.S. Supreme Court cases, the justices and their law clerks often examined the founding father's writings and included some of their statements in caselaw. By 1878, the *Writings of Thomas Jefferson* was published and available. It was cited by the U.S. Supreme Court, apparently without considering that Thomas Jefferson was a "detached observer" to the drafting of the First Amendment. The U.S. Supreme Court first used the metaphor in 1878, and later in *Everson v. Board of Education* in 1947.[55]

Over the years, the "wall of separation" metaphor has been harshly criticized, even by former U.S. Supreme Court Chief Justice Rehnquist. In 1985, Chief Justice Rehnquist's dissent (the portion of the case where he disagreed with the decision by the majority of the Court) outlined the errors in the Court's historical analysis of the "wall of separation" language.[56] Justice Rehnquist stated:

> *It is impossible to build sound constitutional doctrine upon a mistaken understanding of constitutional history, but unfortunately the Establishment Clause has been expressly freighted*

[burdened] with Jefferson's misleading metaphor for nearly 40 years. Thomas Jefferson was of course in France at the time the constitutional Amendments known as the Bill of Rights were passed by Congress and ratified by the States. His letter to the Danbury Baptist Association was a short note of courtesy, written 14 years after the Amendments were passed by Congress. He would seem to any detached observer as a less than ideal source of contemporary history as to the meaning of the Religion Clauses of the First Amendment.[57]

After harshly criticizing the Court's reliance on Jefferson's metaphor, the Justice stated, "whether due to its lack of historical support or its practical unworkability, the Everson wall has proven to be all but useless as a guide to sound constitutional adjudication. It illustrates all too well the wisdom of Benjamin Cardozo's observation that '[m]etaphors in law are to be narrowly watched, for starting as a device to liberate thought, they end often by enslaving it.'"[58] In conclusion, Justice Rehnquist stated, "The wall of separation between church and state is a metaphor based on bad history, a metaphor which has proved useless as a guide to judging. It should be frankly and explicitly abandoned."[59] However, because Justice Rehnquist's words are part of a dissenting opinion, the Court did not explicitly abandon the metaphor. The metaphor continues to be used in our caselaw.

To be clear, I am not suggesting that this history of the "wall of separation" language should cause anyone, especially educators, to abandon your schools' guidance on the role of religion in public schools. My goal is to correct the widespread misunderstanding about the "wall of separation" language; namely, that it is not written in the U.S. Constitution and, as Justice Rehnquist stated, that the metaphor has "enslaved" our understanding of the Establishment Clause.

The philosophy of separation remains, but common sense must be applied. Justice Douglas, writing for the majority in an earlier Supreme Court decision, stated that "there cannot be the slightest doubt that the

The philosophy of separation remains, but common sense must be applied.

First Amendment reflects the philosophy that Church and State should be separated. And so far as interference with the 'free exercise' of religion and an 'establishment' of religion are concerned, the separation must be complete and unequivocal."[60] However, he wrote that common sense must be applied.

> Otherwise, the state and religion would be aliens to each other – hostile, suspicious, and even unfriendly. Churches could not be required to pay even property taxes. Municipalities would not be permitted to render police or fire protection to religious groups. Policemen who helped parishioners into their places of worship would violate the Constitution. Prayers in our legislative halls; the appeals to the Almighty in the messages of the Chief Executive; the proclamations making Thanksgiving Day a holiday; 'so help me God' in our courtroom oaths – these and all other references to the Almighty that run through our laws, our public rituals, our ceremonies would be flouting the First Amendment. A fastidious atheist or agnostic could even object to the supplication with which the Court opens each session: 'God save the United States and this Honorable Court.'[61]

There are compelling reasons why we should not allow the "wall of separation" metaphor to promote a strict separationist view of the Establishment Clause. It is historically unfounded and practically unworkable. Plus, it does not take into consideration the role of the Free Exercise Clause or how the two Religion Clauses work together. More importantly, the wall of separation metaphor has the potential to gut our laws, history, ceremonies, public rituals, and culture. As D. Elton Trueblood observed, such a move could render us a "cut-flower civilization," which after being removed from its roots, will look good for a time but eventually wither and die.[62]

Fortunately, today's majority of the U.S. Supreme Court is well aware of the historical and analytical shortcomings of the "wall of separation" metaphor. The abandonment of the *Lemon* Test, with its strict separationist approach, is strong evidence that the current majority has more of an accommodationist philosophy in Establishment Clause cases. As a result, there is less of a concern that the "wall of separation" metaphor will dominate the U.S. Supreme Court's interpretations of the Establishment Clause.

THE FREE SPEECH CLAUSE OF THE FIRST AMENDMENT

The First Amendment states:

> "Congress shall make no law respecting an establishment of religion, or prohibiting the free exercise thereof; *or abridging the freedom of speech* or of the press, or the right of the people peaceably to assemble, and to petition the Government for a redress of grievances."

U.S. CONST. amend. I (Emphasis added). The plain language of the Free Speech Clause restricts *federal* government regulation of speech. The Free Speech Clause has also been extended through caselaw to restrict *state* and *local* government regulation of speech.[63]

The Free Speech Clause protects against government regulation of an expansive array of speech and speech-related conduct. Since all speech is conveyed through conduct, the Free Speech Clause protects speaking, writing, typing, and distributing pamphlets. It also protects expressive conduct that constitutes speech, such as wearing a black armband to protest the Vietnam War,[64] or burning the American flag.[65] The Free Speech Clause provides overlapping protection with the Free Exercise Clause when religious activities are expressive.[66] The Free Speech Clause even protects the freedom not to speak and not be required to engage in conduct that conveys a message, such as the freedom not to salute the American flag and not say the Pledge of Allegiance in public schools.[67]

Moreover, government restrictions on the content of speech are presumed to be unconstitutional. To justify content-based restrictions on speech, the law or government action must pass strict scrutiny; the restriction must be narrowly tailored to achieve a compelling state interest.[68]

Nonetheless, the First Amendment does not protect all speech. The government can restrict and even punish some types of speech and speech-related conduct. Unprotected speech includes obscenity,[69] false or deceptive advertising,[70] fighting words,[71] and defamation (using state tort laws). These categories define the boundaries of the Free Speech Clause.

For example, in a case involving "fighting words," the U.S. Supreme Court described the breadth of the Free Speech Clause as follows:

> The vitality of civil and political institutions in our society depends on free discussion. As Chief Justice Hughes wrote in *De Jonge v. Oregon*, it is only through free debate and free exchange of ideas that government remains responsive to the will of the people and peaceful change is effected. **The right to speak freely and to promote diversity of ideas and programs is therefore one of the chief distinctions that sets us apart from totalitarian regimes.**
>
> Accordingly, a function of free speech under our system of government is to invite dispute. It may indeed best serve its high purpose when it induces a condition of unrest, creates dissatisfaction with conditions as they are, or even stirs people to anger. Speech is often provocative and challenging. It may strike at prejudices and preconceptions and have profound unsettling effects as it presses for acceptance of an idea. That is why freedom of speech, though not absolute, is nevertheless protected against censorship or punishment, unless shown likely to produce a clear and present danger of a serious substantive evil that rises far above public inconvenience, annoyance, or unrest. **There is no room under our Constitution for a more restrictive view. For the alternative would lead to standardization of ideas either by legislatures, courts, or dominant political or community groups.**[72]

After the 1949 case cited above, the U.S. Supreme Court continued to define the boundaries of fighting words. For example, in 2002, the U.S. Supreme Court held that "true threats" of imminent bodily harm are *not* protected speech.[73] Some of the Court's other decisions are in the footnote.[74] If you have additional questions about fighting words, please obtain legal counsel.

Defamation is another area of unprotected speech. Government can restrict free speech with defamation laws that allow individuals to bring civil cases against one another based on their speech. Defamation claims are not brought by the government. They are civil tort cases where the injured party sues the speaker and, if applicable, the publisher (newspaper, magazine, radio station, television, etc.) to recover money damages.

"Defamation" is the overarching category for libel (written speech that is defamatory) and slander (spoken speech that is defamatory). In a defamation case, the injured party must prove that the statement was defamatory. What is "defamatory" is a question of law for the courts of each state. However, some types of speech are identified in state law as being defamatory *per se* (on their face), such as accusing someone of a crime. The injured party may also be required to prove "damage" to their reputation. The speaker can then defend by proving that the statement was true. A higher standard of proof is required for cases involving "public officials" and "public figures," which is why they endure harsher criticism. In other words, defamatory speech is considered unprotected speech because it can be challenged under state defamation laws.

"Defamation" is the overarching category for libel (written speech that is defamatory) and slander (spoken speech that is defamatory).

Generally, media outlets such as newspapers, magazines, television, and radio who "publish" the statements are considered the "deep pocket" (the one with the most money) and, as a result, they must carefully write, review, and edit their publications, sometimes involving the advice of legal counsel. On the other hand, internet service providers and "discussion forums" (social media sites like Facebook, Instagram, and Twitter, for example), are not usually subject to state defamation laws.

Congress has allowed internet service providers and "discussion forums" to be exempt from defamation laws under Section 230 of the Communications Decency Act ("CDA") of 1996. 47 U.S.C. § 230. Section 230 states, **"No provider or user of an interactive computer service shall be treated as the publisher or speaker of any information provided by another information content provider"** and "[n]o cause of action may be brought and no liability may be imposed under any State or local law that is inconsistent with this section." While the actual person or entity (such as news media) that posts the statements is potentially liable, the "discussion forum" that is the "deep pocket" is not under Section 230. In other words, Congress' exemption for internet service providers in Section 230 of the CDA is at the root of why we see defamatory speech on discussion forums. Section 230 of the CDA preempts state defamation laws, which operate as the traditional check on what is acceptable speech in public discourse.

One concern for parents and educators is that children who spend a lot of time on the internet are learning the unbridled "rules of engagement" for internet discussion forums, which often *are not* subject to defamation laws. Then, when they function in public schools, through printed materials, and on radio or television, they have not been trained for the different "rules of engagement" for these forums, which *are* subject to state defamation laws. At this point, Congress seems unlikely to remove Section 230 of the CDA. Yet, for the time being, parents and educators can teach children about speech on discussion forums and limit their internet use with parental controls and in-school phone restrictions.

THE NEGATIVE FREE SPEECH RIGHT – THE FREEDOM NOT TO SPEAK[75]

The Free Speech Clause also protects the "concomitant" negative free speech right, the right not to speak, and the prohibition against compelled speech.[76] The freedom *not* to speak publicly "serves the same ultimate end as freedom of speech in its affirmative aspect."[77] In 2006, the U.S. Supreme Court stated "[s]ome of this Court's leading First Amendment precedents have established the principle that freedom of speech prohibits the government from telling people what they must say."[78] In 2021, the U.S. Supreme Court held that "[t]he government may not ... compel the endorsement of ideas that it approves."[79]

> The Free Speech Clause also protects the "concomitant" negative free speech right, the right not to speak, and the prohibition against compelled speech.

The freedom not to speak is best exemplified in the 1943 case of *W.Va. State Board of Education v. Barnett*, where the U.S. Supreme Court held that First Amendment's Free Speech Clause protects public school students from being forced to say the Pledge of Allegiance or salute the American flag. Justice Jackson, writing for the majority, stated:

> The right to freedom of thought and of religion as guaranteed by the Constitution against State action includes both the right to speak freely and the right to refrain from speaking at all....
>
> ***If there is any fixed star in our constitutional constellation, it is that no official, high or petty, can prescribe what shall be orthodox in politics, nationalism, religion, or other matters of opinion or force citizens to confess by word or act their faith therein.***[80]

In addition to the right *not* to say the Pledge of Allegiance, the U.S. Supreme Court protected the student's right *not* to salute the American flag. In other words, the freedom not to speak includes both words and conduct that constitutes speech.[81] The freedom not to speak has the potential to empower parents, students, and educators as they interact with public school systems, and more importantly, address some of the more recent curriculum changes that they believe violate their parental rights, right to free exercise, and right to free speech. Further, when combined with the right to free exercise of religion, the negative free speech right transforms a case to one of "hybrid rights," thus requiring strict scrutiny of any law or rule that abridges these freedoms.[82]

TIME PLACE AND MANNER RESTRICTIONS: THE PUBLIC FORUM DOCTRINE

The public forum doctrine is crucial to understanding the rights of parents at public school board meetings, educators in the workplace, and private speakers who are trying to gain access to students in public schools. Federal and state governments are permitted to restrict speech and speech-related conduct on government property, including public schools. The U.S. Supreme Court has created the public forum doctrine to determine what restrictions are permitted depending on the type of government property or "forum" involved.[83]

Traditional Public Forums
A traditional public forum is public property that has historically been open for speech-related conduct such as public parks, streets, and sidewalks. Speakers in public forums have the strongest protections of the First Amendment. In public forums, government cannot restrict the content of speech unless the restriction passes strict scrutiny. Also, the government cannot impose time, place, and manner restrictions, on speech unless they are: (1) content neutral (not based on the content of the speech); (2) viewpoint neutral (i.e., allow both candidates to speak in a political debate); (3) narrowly tailored to achieve an important or compelling government interest (traffic safety, noise and litter control, orderly crowd control); and (4) the leave open other alternative channels of communication. Additionally, the restrictions must not be overbroad, vague, or give government officials unfettered discretion.

Designated Public Forum
A designated public forum is public property that has not been historically open for speech-related conduct, but the government has temporarily allowed it through policy or practice (i.e., municipal buildings where school boards meet and allow public comment).[84] Once a designated public forum is opened, the government is not obligated to keep it open, but must follow the same rules as a public forum. In other words, state and local school boards cannot restrict speech based on viewpoint.

So, suppose you were prohibited from speaking at your state or local school board meeting. In that case, you can: (1) examine your state's open meetings law and your state and local rules to see if you and the board complied with the applicable laws and rules; (2) consider whether your speech was protected speech (i.e., not obscenity, not fighting words, not defamatory, etc.); and (3) if necessary, consult with an attorney regarding the constitutional implications of your situation.

Limited Public Forums

A limited public forum is a type of designated public forum that is opened for a specific speech-related activity (school gym opened in the evening to host a debate on a community concern). The government can reserve a limited public forum for its intended use and can discriminate against types of speech or classes of speakers if the restrictions are: (1) viewpoint neutral (i.e., allow both sides of an issue to be presented); and (2) reasonably related to a legitimate government interest. For example, a religious group cannot be excluded simply because they intend to express religious views.[85]

Nonpublic Forums

A nonpublic forum is government property that is not open for speech-related activities, such as public schools,[86] military bases,[87] and postal service properties,[88] to name a few. Nonpublic forums can be regulated to reserve them for their intended use (i.e., educating students). Government can restrict the *content* of speech in nonpublic forums if the laws and rules they enact are viewpoint neutral and rationally related to a legitimate governmental objective. A legitimate objective includes "educating students."[89]

Since the government can restrict content in public schools, the government may allow speech on some issues but not others. For example, public schools can control the content of school newspapers and students' speeches for legitimate educational reasons.[90] Public schools can prohibit speech (both in school and during school sponsored activities) that can be interpreted as celebrating or advocating illegal drug use.[91] Public schools can punish students who use profanity on the school campus.[92] Public schools can limit student speech if it bears the school's imprimatur (imprint or name of the name of the school such as a school sponsored newspaper or school uniform).[93] Public schools can also punish student speech that "materially and substantially disrupts" the school's educational mission or it invades the rights of another individual.[94] However, public schools cannot prohibit students from engaging in speech-related conduct (i.e., wearing black armbands

> *Since the government can restrict content in public schools, the government may allow speech on some issues but not others.*

to protest government) because this type of suppression is not related to a legitimate government interest.[95]

Regarding "private speakers" in public schools, their rights are limited. The public forum doctrine offers a compelling legal argument that may prevent advocacy groups, third-party vendors, and unapproved supplemental instructional materials providers from engaging in speech-related conduct in public schools. Legislators, school officials and educators may be able to use the nonpublic forum doctrine to enact laws and rules to prevent the plethora of private speech that is infiltrating the public schools and speaking to the impressionable and captive audience of students. For a more in-depth analysis of this issue, see Chapter 9 under the subsection titled, "The Public Forum Doctrine: Limiting Private Speech in Public Schools."

The U.S. Supreme Court continues to define the boundaries of the Free Speech Clause, the Religion Clauses, and Parental Rights. If you have questions about these and other federal and state constitutional rights, please obtain legal counsel.

HOW TO FIND WHAT YOU NEED:

Your Federal and State Constitutional Rights

- **NOTICE: Caselaw is continually changing based on new court decisions interpreting the laws. It is crucial to consult legal counsel before relying on caselaw.**
- If you read U.S. Supreme Court decisions on Justia.com, click the tab for the entire case, not just the syllabus or summary.
- Your state and local boards of education may have information on their websites about the role of parental rights, religious freedom, and freedom of speech in your school district.
- If you have specific legal questions, your state bar association may provide advice at a free or reduced cost. They can also direct you to a lawyer. I have listed the link to your state's bar association in Appendix C on the page for your state. If you need legal assistance,

please act immediately because time limitations called statutes of limitations may apply to your claims.
- **Also, some groups that work to protect religious freedom offer legal representation at a free or reduced cost.** Although I have not used or worked with any of these groups and cannot endorse them, the most well-known groups that represent clients in parental rights and religious freedom cases includes: (1) the Alliance Defending Freedom, (2) the American Center for Law and Justice, (3) the Becket Fund for Religious Liberty, (4) the Center for Law and Religious Freedom, (5) the Liberty Counsel, (6) the Liberty Institute, (7) the Pacific Justice Institute, (8) the Thomas More Law Center, and (9) the Thomas More Society. It is best to research and interview several firms and lawyers before choosing one.

HIRING LEGAL COUNSEL DOES NOT NECESSARILY MEAN YOU WILL GO TO COURT

Either you individually, or a group of like-minded parents, may choose to hire local legal counsel, but this does not necessarily mean that the matter will escalate to litigation. Most lawyers try to work things out without litigation. In fact, there are strong arguments that resolving school-related issues without litigation is the favored course. Your lawyer may begin with a letter to the local school board and local school superintendent: 1) requesting enforcement of state school laws and other rules that support your position; 2) requesting exemptions for your children from content and materials; 3) asserting your right to a public education guaranteed under your state constitution; and 4) asserting your constitutional rights guaranteed under the federal and state constitutions. You and your attorney may also speak before the local board of education. Hopefully, the local board and local school superintendent will respond to the requests and you can come to an amicable agreement with the school.

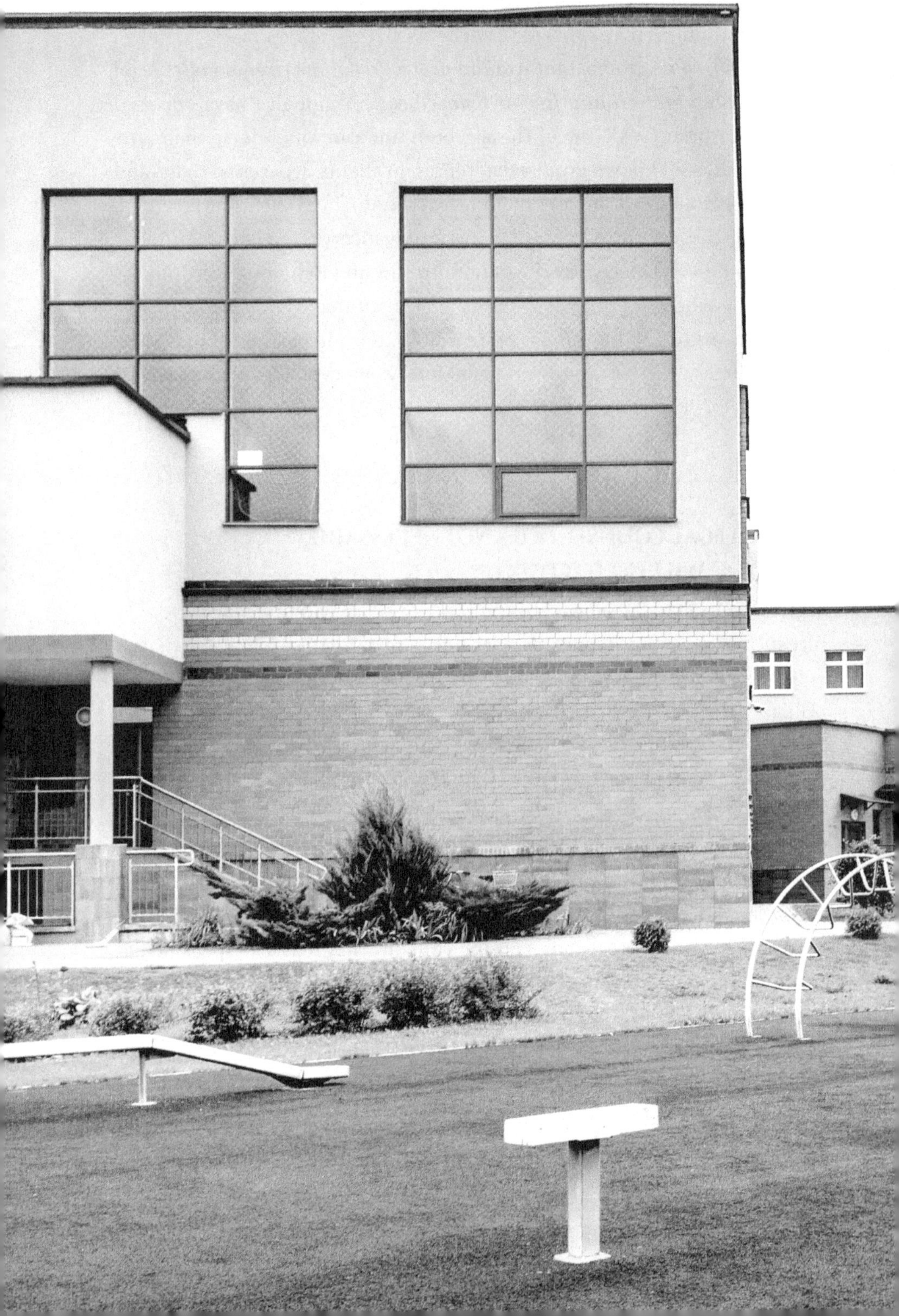

PART III

APPLYING
WHAT YOU HAVE LEARNED

CHAPTER 12

PROTECTING CHILDREN

Submit Opt-Out → Investigate & Research → Advocate with Facts → Connect with Others

"Start where you are, use what you have, do what you can."
— Arthur Ashe, World-Class Professional Tennis Player

If you are interested in applying this information individually or with others in your community, here are some ideas to get you started.

SUBMIT A PARENT OPT-OUT OF SPECIFIC INSTRUCTIONAL MATERIALS AND CONTENT

1. Parents can submit an opt-out based on parental rights, the right to free exercise of religion, and the right to freedom of speech, which are guaranteed under the federal and state constitutions. To see a blank sample opt-out, go to Appendix A.
2. If state school laws or state and local rules recognize parents' right to opt-out, that is just more reason for the opt-out to be recognized by the school.

Parents can submit an opt-out based on parental rights, the right to free exercise of religion, and the right to freedom of speech, which are guaranteed under the federal and state constitutions.

3. Hopefully, the school will honor the opt-out request. If the school denies the request, you can decide whether you want to challenge the school's denial. If so, the "denial" becomes the basis for the claim.
4. If you are concerned about what is being taught in sex education, the states that presume parental consent for sex education (opt-out states) include Alabama, Alaska, Arizona (HIV), California, Colorado, Connecticut, Florida, Georgia, Hawaii, Idaho, Illinois, Indiana, Iowa, Louisiana, Maine, Maryland, Massachusetts, Michigan, Missouri, Montana, New Hampshire, New Jersey, New Mexico, New York, Ohio, Oklahoma, Oregon, Pennsylvania, Rhode Island, South Carolina, Vermont, Virginia, Washington, West Virginia, and Wisconsin. For these states, parents must opt out of sex education in writing. The states that require parental consent for sex education (opt-in states) include Arizona, Mississippi, Nevada, Tennessee, Texas, and Utah. For these states, parents must opt-in to sex education in writing. If your state is not listed or you want more information on your state, see Guttmacher Institute *"Sex and HIV Education,"* as of February 1, 2023, at https://www.guttmacher.org/state-policy/explore/sex-and-hiv-education.
5. There is strength in numbers. If several families with children in the same school or the same class submit an opt-out, those children and their parents will have the support of one another as they assert their constitutional rights.

RESEARCH AND INVESTIGATE

Knowledge is power. You can begin by investigating what is being taught in your children's school and, simultaneously, research your state laws and rules. You may also want to form a group to divide the responsibilities. My suggestion is to begin with investigation and research:

1. Investigate what your children are being taught in the school. You can examine curriculum, textbooks, supplemental instructional material and content, online resources, third-party vendors, professional development for teachers and administrators, etc. This can be done informally or with an open records request.
2. Get involved on a textbook or curriculum approval committee.

3. Research *current* laws and rules. You can use a system that is organized by the various levels with several people researching a category (i.e., state school laws, state board of education rules, and local board of education rules). You can also use a system that is organized by topic.
4. Research *proposed* laws and rules following the same format above. This will involve attending local and state board of education meetings, and state legislative sessions.
5. Investigate "Released Time for Religious Instruction" programs in your state. These programs are permitted under a U.S. Supreme Court decision that allows students in public schools to be released during school hours for off-premises religious instruction — *if* the program meets certain criteria. *Zorach v. Clauson*, 343 U.S. 306 (1952).
6. Research whether your state and local boards of education have adopted the "National Sex Education Standards," which were published by the non-profit entity "SIECUS: Sex Ed for Social Change." To view SIECUS' standards, go to (https://siecus.org/). In addition to the standards, see the "Glossary of Sex Education Terms" on pages 53-68, which clarifies the content being taught to students.
7. Research what curriculum, courses, and activities require parental consent or whether parental consent is presumed and you must opt out. Remember that state parental consent requirements may be found in: (1) the state's parental rights amendment to the state constitution; (2) the state's parental rights laws; (3) the state's school laws; (4) the state and local board of education's rules; or (5) the state's case law. These provisions use the terms "parent," "legal guardian," "consent," "exempt," "excuse," "elect," "withdraw," "in writing" and "written." The state's laws do not tend to use the terms "opt-in" or "opt-out." In Georgia, the law that allows parents to give non-consent is stated: "Any parent or legal guardian of a child to whom the course of study set forth in this Code section is to be taught shall have the right to elect, in writing, that such child not receive such course of study." O.C.G.A. § 20-2-143(d). As you can see, this provision is not particularly clear to the average person.
8. Research the differences between a PTA and a PTO.
9. If you communicate your findings, include the citation and a link to the entire law. Reliance on summaries and soundbites can be misleading.

ADVOCATE WITH FACTS BEFORE YOUR STATE AND LOCAL BOARDS

Many local and state board members agree with the citizens who elected them but are either outnumbered on the board or are unsure of local support on tough issues. Therefore, before you begin advocating, consider the following:

1. If you want to advocate for a particular issue, email your local and state school board member and ask whether he or she agrees with you.
2. If the board member agrees with you, support him or her on the day of the vote. You may even want to speak in support of the issue.
3. If the board member disagrees with you, try to understand the reasons for the board member's position as well as the board dynamics. You can always persuade the board member to take a different position. Never threaten.
4. Speak at the local and state board meeting to garner support from other board members. Always be respectful.
5. Consider running for the local school board or supporting another candidate.
6. Regarding enforcement of state school laws and state and local board of education rules:
    a. If your school is not following them, you can respectfully request in writing that they do so.
    b. If they refuse, you can pursue the matter with the appropriate authority, which may be the local school board and local school superintendent or the state board of education and state school superintendent.
    c. If you are not successful at either of these levels, you can pursue the matter with the assistance of legal counsel.
7. Advocate with your time and money. Whether it is the professional associations we join, the stores where we shop, the tech providers we choose, the internet sites we visit, or the movies we watch, we are constantly supporting one thing or another. I am not suggesting a boycott. Instead, I am suggesting intentional choices with our time and money. Individually, our choices make little, if any difference. Yet, if we *all* do a little, it can make a big difference.

8. If you think you may need legal assistance to protect your children, immediately consult with legal counsel. Some types of cases require individuals to "exhaust their administrative remedies" before going to court. In other words, individuals may need to appeal through the chain of command within the public school system (i.e., begin at the school, appeal to the local board, and appeal to the state board of education), before going to the courts. Also, time limitations or statutes of limitations may apply at each of these levels! Therefore, it is important to have legal counsel involved at the ground level to guide you. When might such a situation arise? Although this list is not exhaustive, here are a few situations:
    - You think that your federal and/or state constitutional rights (i.e., right of privacy, parental rights, right to free exercise of religion, right to freedom of speech, and the accompanying right not to speak), have been violated and you are willing to challenge the school up the chain of command and in the legal system (if necessary).
    - Your child is exposed to instructional materials and content that is egregious and falls within your state's definition of "obscenity" or "material harmful to minors," and you are willing to challenge the state's exemption in the legal system by filing a police report (if necessary).
    - Your child is exposed to instructional materials and content that falls within your state's definition of "obscenity" or "material harmful to minors," there is a complaint process that you think violates your federal or state constitutional rights, and you are willing to challenge the policy up the chain of command and in the legal system (if necessary).
    - Your child experiences racial discrimination as defined in Title VI of the federal Civil Rights Act of 1964, or your state and local civil rights laws. Although legal counsel may not be required to file a complaint, it is highly recommended.
    - You are concerned about potential harm to students and want to know if you should give "legal notice" (supported by expert letters and reports) to your school and school district.

CONNECT WITH OTHERS

Numerous groups have information on protecting children in public schools. These groups take stances on *many* school-related issues. As a result, you may agree with 80% of what one group supports, 70% of what another supports, and 60% of another. Nonetheless, I encourage you to connect with others and learn about the issues that concern you. If you wait to find a group that you agree with 100% on school-related issues, you may have trouble finding one. Plus, your knowledge of how to protect children in public schools will be limited.

Also, learn the lesson of "The Hunter and the Quail," which is an ancient tale about the power of cooperation. In the story, a hunter regularly caught quail that lived along a riverbank. One day the wisest quail had an idea: "let's cooperate and fly upward together so that all of us can escape the net." The quail followed his advice and cooperated to resist the hunter's net. The hunter went home hungry. Days later, the flock stopped cooperating and began arguing among themselves. "You're squeezing my wing!" one shouted. "You're stepping on my feathers!" cried another. Then, when the hunter threw his net over the flock of quail, they were flying in different directions and unable to resist him. While in the net, they continued to argue about who was at fault – until they became dinner. The moral of the story is the power of cooperation.

A NOTE OF ENCOURAGEMENT

In January 2016, I was studying for the Georgia bar exam. Although I had been licensed to practice law in Pennsylvania and New Jersey since 1994, I had missed the cut-off for Georgia bar reciprocity when we moved south. It had been 22 years since I graduated from law school. Unfortunately, bar exam preparation courses are not designed nor timed for people in my situation. They kick off in December for the February exam.

So, I got serious. To minimize distractions, I began studying at the public library from the time it opened until it closed – every day. Believing that life is a marathon and not a sprint, I trudged through the material. With the support of my husband, I stuck with it and trusted my old study skills.

On February 23, 2016, I sat down to take the exam surrounded by people who were young enough to be my children. Then, just before the exam began, the firewall on my laptop prevented the bar exam software from downloading. The proctor handed me a stack of blank exam books and said, "You'll have to write." Hoping that the mishap might help me, I wrote until my hand hurt. Several months later I received the news – I passed.

So, why do I tell you this story? Because we all feel unsure of our abilities at times. Whether you are uncertain of your ability to apply the material in this book or advocate before a local board of education, you are not alone. Courage is moving forward *despite* being nervous – or afraid. The "butterflies" in your stomach mean that you care. Also, remember that you are setting an example for your children. As you prepare, do your best. You never know if that "extra" effort will give you the push you need to finish well. If you speak before the local board, remember that preparedness and good manners can do more than the best education.

> Wishing you all the best!
> *Kelly*

ACKNOWLEDGMENTS

Two people encouraged me to write this book – my parents – Paul and Susie Himes. As the holidays ended and 2022 began, the three of us talked about the ever-increasing number of parents fighting with public school officials. With each dispute, I retorted, "The parents just need to . . ." Then I explained the public school system and constitutional rights – again and again. Eventually, I said, "I think I might write a book." My father asked, "Do you have an outline?" "No," I said but I began to make one. Three weeks later, I started writing.

My family was my early editorial team. With enthusiasm, my parents edited and commented on several first drafts. My father, who also loves history, championed changes in the first chapter and recommended the section on measuring improvement in school discipline. My mother, who is affectionately known as the "grammar police," commented with southern charm. She and my sister were, and are, my go-to's for illustrations and color. My husband and children jumped into the mix with their suggestions and edits. A critical thinker and a master at consistency and details, my husband can spot an out-of-place bold period from afar. Our children's edits were substantive and thought-provoking – "how the turntables."[1] Some changes were tiny. Others affected the organization of the book.

I found my 2011 drawings of the building and columns explaining the structure of public schools. I thought it was critical to convey the information with illustrations. Fred Stark, an artist, brought them to life. Once the book and illustrations had taken shape, I garnered opinions and received encouragement from several trusted friends – Rhonda, Katie, Cliff, Ed, Lynn, Michelle, Terri, Kyle, and Jim. Judge Garmon, a family friend, and a retired Regional Chief Administrative Law Judge read two of the "finished" drafts. He provided tremendous support and encouragement. An unnamed constitutional lawyer provided input on new U.S. Supreme Court decisions. News outlets were a never-ending source of content.

ACKNOWLEDGMENTS

The people who helped me cross the finish line with this book are book designer Michelle M. White of MMW Books and publishing consultant Susie Schaeffer of Finish the Book Publishing. Michelle created a compelling cover design, created the logo, modernized the illustrations, and did a fabulous job laying out the text. During our first conversation, Michelle grasped my message and communicated it in the first draft of the cover design. Susie is well-versed in the technical aspects of book and e-book publishing. She walked me through the process and answered my questions. Michael Beylkin, Esquire of Fox Rothschild, LLP, my copyright and trademark attorney, kindly advised me in the unknown legal territory.

To my *Moms in Prayer International* group and others who pray for our schools — thank you. Some say our lives are like a tapestry. We see the underside with knots and messy dangling strings; yet God sees the topside that fits together perfectly. I am incredibly thankful that I have a tiny glimpse of the topside. The circumstances of my life taught me *exactly* what I needed to know to write this book. The timing seems right too. I am thankful.

With appreciation beyond words,
Kelly

APPENDIX A

BLANK SAMPLE PARENT OPT-OUT

Below is a blank sample parent opt-out to help parents apply the concepts in this book, preferably with the assistance of local legal counsel. Please see the disclaimer below and the note that this form is excluded from my copyright. To find an attorney, please see Appendix C and the link to the state bar on your state's information page.

PUBLIC SCHOOL OPT-OUT / NON-CONSENT FORM FOR THE PARENTS AND LEGAL GUARDIANS OF _____
FOR THE _____ SCHOOL YEAR

I/We, _____,
as parent(s) and/or legal guardian(s) of _____,
a minor child, who attends _____school, hereby respectfully request an opt-out/exemption based on my/our federal and state constitutional rights, which include: parental rights, free exercise of religion and conscience, freedom of speech, and negative freedom of speech or freedom not to speak. We are raising our children in accordance with my/our sincerely held religious beliefs and conscience. The specific content that we believe violates our rights is specified in Sections I-V below. Additionally, I/we are requesting that our child be exempt from the following class(es):_____.

Section I – CONTENT / SUBJECTMATTER
I/WE DO NOT CONSENT to my/our child being given instructional material or content, or being subjected to discussion or activities on any of the following topics:

APPENDIX A: SAMPLE PARENT OPT-OUT

Section II – COMMON SOURCES
I/WE DO NOT CONSENT to my/our child's participation in any instruction, discussion, or activity which is derived in whole or in part from, contains information from, or references to the following sources:

Section III – SURVEYS AND INQUIRIES
I/WE DO NOT CONSENT to my/our child being given any surveys.
I/WE DO NOT CONSENT to my/our child being questioned in any form or manner regarding the following:

Section IV – NON-EMERGENCY HEALTH/MEDICAL CARE
I/WE DO NOT CONSENT to my/our child being given any of the following health services:

Section V – DATA SHARING
I/WE DO NOT CONSENT to any data sharing regarding the following:

> Regarding Sections I, II, and III above, I/we request alternative academic instruction for my/our child during the same period that any instruction or activity listed above is provided, and without subjecting my/our child to any disciplinary action, academic penalty, ridicule, retaliation, retribution, or other sanction.

Section VI – LEGAL REFERENCES
I/WE make this request as permitted by the following:

The United States Constitution protects the people from federal and state government infringement of their rights to: free exercise of religion, freedom of speech, freedom to peacefully assemble, and freedom to petition the government for redress of grievances. U.S. Const., First Amendment; *Cantwell v. Connecticut*, 310 U.S. 296, 303 (1940); *McDonald v. Chicago*, 561 U.S. 742, 763-767 & nn. 12-13 (2010) (U.S. Supreme Court holding that "the Due Process Clause of the Fourteenth Amendment 'incorporates' the great majority of [1st-10th Amendments] and thus makes them equally applicable to the States").

The U.S. Supreme Court has held that the U.S. Constitution also "protects the fundamental right of parents to make decisions concerning the care, custody, and control of their children." *Troxel v. Granville,* 530 U.S. 57 (2000). **Parents also have the right "to direct the upbringing and education of children under their control."** *Pierce v. Society of Sisters,* 268 U.S. 510 (1925). See also, *Santosky v. Kramer,* 455 U.S. 745 (1982) (recognizing "fundamental liberty interest of natural parents in the care, custody, and management of their child"); *Wisconsin v. Yoder,* 406 U.S. 205 (1972) (recognizing "liberty of parents...to direct the upbringing and education of children"); *Meyer v. Nebraska,* 262 U.S. 390 (1923) (concluding that the state "legislature has attempted materially to interfere with . . . the power of parents to control the education of their own").

Our State Constitution includes: (1) a Bill of Rights or Declaration of Rights that reiterates the rights given to us in the U.S. Constitution, thus providing a second layer of state constitutional rights to the people; and (2) an "Education Article" that gives a state right to a free public education k-12.

State and local school superintendents and other state and local government officials have a duty to uphold the U.S. Constitution and the state constitution and to protect against violations of the people's federal and state constitutional rights.

I/We hereby request that this notification be provided to all people offering instruction to my/our child during the school year, including but not limited to teachers, substitute teachers, aides, counselors, and librarians.

Parent_____Date_____

Parent_____Date_____

Received at School by_____Date_____

IMPORTANT DISCLAIMER: *The information in this form is for educational purposes only. No information contained in this form should be construed as legal advice, nor is it intended to be a substitute for legal counsel on any subject matter. The purchase of this book and/or the use of this form does not create an attorney-client relationship. The information in this form may not reflect the current law in your jurisdiction, particularly where new laws were enacted in the most recent legislative session. Readers are encouraged to contact an education law attorney in their jurisdiction with any questions.* **The information in this form is excluded from the copyright for this book and is available for copying, additions, revisions, and use by you and your legal counsel.**

APPENDIX B

RELIGION CLAUSES IN THE STATE CONSTITUTIONS

Note: For simplicity, the introductory headings within the state constitutions have been removed. The term "[sic]" within a quote means that the spelling or grammar used in the quote was in the original document and is not an error by the person transcribing it.

Alabama Constitution, Article I, § 3
"That no religion shall be established by law; that no preference shall be given by law to any religious sect, society, denomination, or mode of worship; that no one shall be compelled by law to attend any place of worship; nor to pay any tithes, taxes, or other rate for building or repairing any place of worship, or for maintaining any minister or ministry; that no religious test shall be required as a qualification to any office or public trust under this state; and that the civil rights, privileges, and capacities of any citizen shall not be in any manner affected by his religious principles."

Alaska Constitution, Article I, § 4
"No law shall be made respecting an establishment of religion, or prohibiting the free exercise thereof."

Arizona Constitution, Article II, § 12
"The liberty of conscience secured by the provisions of this constitution shall not be so construed as to excuse acts of licentiousness, or justify practices inconsistent with the peace and safety of the state. No public money or property shall be appropriated for or applied to any religious worship, exercise, or instruction, or to the support of any religious establishment. No religious qualification shall be required for any public office or employment, nor shall any person be incompetent as a witness or juror in consequence of

his opinion on matters of religion, nor be questioned touching his religious belief in any court of justice to affect the weight of his testimony."

Arkansas Constitution, Article II, §§ 24-25

"All men have a natural and indefeasible right to worship Almighty God according to the dictates of their own consciences; no man can, of right, be compelled to attend, erect, or support any place of worship; or to maintain any ministry against his consent. No human authority can, in any case or manner whatsoever, control or interfere with the right of conscience; and no preference shall ever be given, by law, to any religious establishment, denomination or mode of worship, above any other."

"Religion, morality and knowledge being essential to good government, the General Assembly shall enact suitable laws to protect every religious denomination in the peaceable enjoyment of its own mode of public worship."

The Constitution of the State of California, Article I, § 4

"Free exercise and enjoyment of religion without discrimination or preference are guaranteed. This liberty of conscience does not excuse acts that are licentious or inconsistent with the peace or safety of the State. The Legislature shall make no law respecting an establishment of religion."

"A person is not incompetent to be a witness or juror because of his or her opinions on religious beliefs."

Colorado Constitution, Article II, § 4

"The free exercise and enjoyment of religious profession and worship, without discrimination, shall forever hereafter be guaranteed; and no person shall be denied any civil or political right, privilege or capacity, on account of his opinions concerning religion; but the liberty of conscience hereby secured shall not be construed to dispense with oaths or affirmations, excuse acts of licentiousness or justify practices inconsistent with the good order, peace or safety of the state. No person shall be required to attend or support any ministry or place of worship, religious sect or denomination against his consent. Nor shall any preference be given by law to any religious denomination or mode of worship."

Connecticut Constitution, Article First, § 3

"The exercise and enjoyment of religious profession and worship, without discrimination, shall forever be free to all persons in the state; provided, that the right hereby declared and established, shall not be so construed as to excuse acts of licentiousness, or to justify practices inconsistent with the peace and safety of the state."

Delaware Constitution, Article I, §§ 1-2

"Although it is the duty of all men frequently to assemble together for the public worship of Almighty God; and piety and morality, on which the prosperity of communities depends, are hereby promoted; yet no man shall or ought to be compelled to attend any religious worship, to contribute to the erection or support of any place of worship, or to the maintenance of any ministry, against his own free will and consent; and no power shall or ought to be vested in or assumed by any magistrate that shall in any case interfere with, or in any manner control the rights of conscience, in the free exercise of religious worship, nor a preference given by law to any religious societies, denominations, or modes of worship."

"No religious test shall be required as a qualification to any office, or public trust, under this State."

Florida Constitution, Article I, § 3

"There shall be no law respecting the establishment of religion or prohibiting or penalizing the free exercise thereof. Religious freedom shall not justify practices inconsistent with public morals, peace or safety. No revenue of the state or any political subdivision or agency thereof shall ever be taken from the public treasury directly or indirectly in aid of any church, sect, or religious denomination or in aid of any sectarian institution."

Georgia Constitution, Article I, § 3

"No inhabitant of this state shall be molested in person or property or be prohibited from holding any public office or trust on account of religious opinions; but the right of freedom of religion shall not be so construed as to excuse acts of licentiousness or justify practices inconsistent with the peace and safety of the state."

APPENDIX B: RELIGION CLAUSES IN THE STATE CONSTITUTIONS

The Constitution of the State of Hawaii, Article I, § 4
"No law shall be enacted respecting an establishment of religion, or prohibiting the free exercise thereof, or abridging the freedom of speech or of the press or the right of the people peaceably to assemble and to petition the government for a redress of grievances."

Idaho Constitution, Article I, § 4
"The exercise and enjoyment of religious faith and worship shall forever be guaranteed; and no person shall be denied any civil or political right, privilege, or capacity on account of his religious opinions; but the liberty of conscience hereby secured shall not be construed to dispense with oaths or affirmations, or excuse acts of licentiousness or justify polygamous or other pernicious practices, inconsistent with morality or the peace or safety of the state; nor to permit any person, organization, or association to directly or indirectly aid or abet, counsel or advise any person to commit the crime of bigamy or polygamy, or any other crime. No person shall be required to attend or support any ministry or place of worship, religious sect or denomination, or pay tithes against his consent; nor shall any preference be given by law to any religious denomination or mode of worship. Bigamy and polygamy are forever prohibited in the state, and the legislature shall provide by law for the punishment of such crimes."

Illinois Constitution, Article I, § 3
"The free exercise and enjoyment of religious profession and worship, without discrimination, shall forever be guaranteed, and no person shall be denied any civil or political right, privilege or capacity, on account of his religious opinions; but the liberty of conscience hereby secured shall not be construed to dispense with oaths or affirmations, excuse acts of licentiousness, or justify practices inconsistent with the peace or safety of the State. No person shall be required to attend or support any ministry or place of worship against his consent, nor shall any preference be given by law to any religious denomination or mode of worship."

Indiana Constitution, Article I, §§ 2-8
"All people shall be secured in the natural right to worship ALMIGHTY GOD, according to the dictates of their own consciences. No law shall, in any case

whatever, control the free exercise and enjoyment of religious opinions, or interfere with the rights of conscience. No preference shall be given, by law, to any creed, religious society, or mode of worship; and no person shall be compelled to attend, erect, or support, any place of worship, or to maintain any ministry, against his consent. No religious test shall be required, as a qualification for any office of trust or profit. No money shall be drawn from the treasury, for the benefit of any religious or theological institution. No person shall be rendered incompetent as a witness, in consequence of his opinions on matters of religion. The mode of administering an oath or affirmation, shall be such as may be most consistent with, and binding upon, the conscience of the person, to whom such oath or affirmation may be administered."

Iowa Constitution, Article I, §§ 3-4
"The general assembly shall make no law respecting an establishment of religion, or prohibiting the free exercise thereof; nor shall any person be compelled to attend any place of worship, pay tithes, taxes, or other rates for building or repairing places of worship, or the maintenance of any minister, or ministry."

"No religious test shall be required as a qualification for any office, or public trust, and no person shall be deprived of any of his rights, privileges, or capacities, or disqualified from the performance of any of his public or private duties, or rendered incompetent to give evidence in any court of law or equity, in consequence of his opinions on the subject of religion; and any party to any judicial proceeding shall have the right to use as a witness, or take the testimony of, any other person not disqualified on account of interest, who may be cognizant of any fact material to the case; and parties to suits may be witnesses, as provided by law."

Kansas Constitution, Article I, § 7
"The right to worship God according to the dictates of conscience shall never be infringed; nor shall any person be compelled to attend or support any form of worship; nor shall any control of or interference with the rights of conscience be permitted, nor any preference be given by law to any religious establishment or mode of worship. No religious test or property qualification

shall be required for any office of public trust, nor for any vote at any elections, nor shall any person be incompetent to testify on account of religious belief."

Kentucky Constitution, Article I, § 1
"All men are, by nature, free and equal, and have certain inherent and inalienable rights, among which may be reckoned: The right of worshiping Almighty God according to the dictates of their consciences."

Louisiana Constitution, Article I, § 8
"No law shall be enacted respecting an establishment of religion or prohibiting the free exercise thereof."

Maine Constitution, Article I, § 3
"Religious freedom; sects equal; religious tests prohibited; religious teachers. All individuals have a natural and unalienable right to worship Almighty God according to the dictates of their own consciences, and no person shall be hurt, molested or restrained in that person's liberty or estate for worshipping God in the manner and season most agreeable to the dictates of that person's own conscience, nor for that person's religious professions or sentiments, provided that that person does not disturb the public peace, nor obstruct others in their religious worship; – and all persons demeaning themselves peaceably, as good members of the State, shall be equally under the protection of the laws, and no subordination nor preference of any one sect or denomination to another shall ever be established by law, nor shall any religious test be required as a qualification for any office or trust, under this State; and all religious societies in this State, whether incorporate or unincorporate, shall at all times have the exclusive right of electing their public teachers, and contracting with them for their support and maintenance."

Maryland Constitution, Article 36
"That as it is the duty of every man to worship God in such manner as he thinks most acceptable to Him, all persons are equally entitled to protection in their religious liberty; wherefore, no person ought by any law to be molested in his person or estate, on account of his religious persuasion, or profession, or for his religious practice, unless, under the color of religion, he shall disturb the good order, peace or safety of the State, or shall infringe the

laws of morality, or injure others in their natural, civil or religious rights; nor ought any person to be compelled to frequent, or maintain, or contribute, unless on contract, to maintain, any place of worship, or any ministry; nor shall any person, otherwise competent, be deemed incompetent as a witness, or juror, on account of his religious belief; provided, he believes in the existence of God, and that under His dispensation such person will be held morally accountable for his acts, and be rewarded or punished therefor either in this world or in the world to come."

"Nothing shall prohibit or require the making reference to belief in, reliance upon, or invoking the aid of God or a Supreme Being in any governmental or public document, proceeding, activity, ceremony, school, institution, or place."

"Nothing in this article shall constitute an establishment of religion."

The Constitution of the Commonwealth of Massachusetts, Part of the First, Article III
"As the happiness of a people, and the good order and preservation of civil government, essentially depend upon piety, religion and morality; and as these cannot be generally diffused through a community, but by the institution of the public worship of God, and of public instructions in piety, religion and morality: Therefore, to promote their happiness and to secure the good order and preservation of their government, the people of this commonwealth have a right to invest their legislature with power to authorize and require, and the legislature shall, from time to time, authorize and require, the several towns, parishes, precincts, and other bodies politic, or religious societies, to make suitable provision, at their own expense, for the institution of the public worship of God, and for the support and maintenance of public Protestant teachers of piety, religion and morality, in all cases where such provision shall not be made voluntarily."

Michigan Constitution, Article I, §
"Every person shall be at liberty to worship God according to the dictates of his own conscience. No person shall be compelled to attend, or, against his consent, to contribute to the erection or support of any place of religious

worship, or to pay tithes, taxes or other rates for the support of any minister of the gospel or teacher of religion. No money shall be appropriated or drawn from the treasury for the benefit of any religious sect or society, theological or religious seminary; nor shall property belonging to the state be appropriated for any such purpose. The civil and political rights, privileges and capacities of no person shall be diminished or enlarged on account of his religious belief."

Minnesota Constitution, Article I, §§ 16-17
"The enumeration of rights in this constitution shall not deny or impair others retained by and inherent in the people. The right of every man to worship God according to the dictates of his own conscience shall never be infringed; nor shall any man be compelled to attend, erect or support any place of worship, or to maintain any religious or ecclesiastical ministry, against his consent; nor shall any control of or interference with the rights of conscience be permitted, or any preference be given by law to any religious establishment or mode of worship; but the liberty of conscience hereby secured shall not be so construed as to excuse acts of licentiousness or justify practices inconsistent with the peace or safety of the state, nor shall any money be drawn from the treasury for the benefit of any religious societies or religious or theological seminaries."

"No religious test or amount of property shall be required as a qualification for any office of public trust in the state. No religious test or amount of property shall be required as a qualification of any voter at any election in this state; nor shall any person be rendered incompetent to give evidence in any court of law or equity in consequence of his opinion upon the subject of religion."

Mississippi Constitution, Article III, § 18
"No religious test as a qualification for office shall be required; and no preference shall be given by law to any religious sect or mode of worship; but the free enjoyment of all religious sentiments and the different modes of worship shall be held sacred. The rights hereby secured shall not be construed to justify acts of licentiousness injurious to morals or dangerous to the peace and safety of the state, or to exclude the Holy Bible from use in any public school of this state."

Missouri Constitution, Article I, § 5
"That all men and women have a natural and indefeasible right to worship Almighty God according to the dictates of their own consciences; that no human authority can control or interfere with the rights of conscience; that no person shall, on account of his or her religious persuasion or belief, be rendered ineligible to any public office or trust or profit in this state, be disqualified from testifying or serving as a juror, or be molested in his or her person or estate; that to secure a citizen's right to acknowledge Almighty God according to the dictates of his or her own conscience, neither the state nor any of its political subdivisions shall establish any official religion, nor shall a citizen's right to pray or express his or her religious beliefs be infringed; that the state shall not coerce any person to participate in any prayer or other religious activity, but shall ensure that any person shall have the right to pray individually or corporately in a private or public setting so long as such prayer does not result in disturbance of the peace or disruption of a public meeting or assembly; that citizens as well as elected officials and employees of the state of Missouri and its political subdivisions shall have the right to pray on government premises and public property so long as such prayers abide within the same parameters placed upon any other free speech under similar circumstances; that the General Assembly and the governing bodies of political subdivisions may extend to ministers, clergypersons, and other individuals the privilege to offer invocations or other prayers at meetings or sessions of the General Assembly or governing bodies; that students may express their beliefs about religion in written and oral assignments free from discrimination based on the religious content of their work; that no student shall be compelled to perform or participate in academic assignments or educational presentations that violate his or her religious beliefs; that the state shall ensure public school students their right to free exercise of religious expression without interference, as long as such prayer or other expression is private and voluntary, whether individually or corporately, and in a manner that is not disruptive and as long as such prayers or expressions abide within the same parameters placed upon any other free speech under similar circumstances; and, to emphasize the right to free exercise of religious expression, that all free public schools receiving state appropriations shall display, in a conspicuous and legible manner, the text of the Bill of Rights of the Constitution of the United States; but this section shall not be construed

to expand the rights of prisoners in state or local custody beyond those afforded by the laws of the United States, excuse acts of licentiousness, nor to justify practices inconsistent with the good order, peace or safety of the state, or with the rights of others."

Montana Constitution, Article II, § 5
"The state shall make no law respecting an establishment of religion or prohibiting the free exercise thereof."

Nebraska Constitution, Article I, § 4
"All persons have a natural and indefeasible right to worship Almighty God according to the dictates of their own consciences. No person shall be compelled to attend, erect or support any place of worship against his consent, and no preference shall be given by law to any religious society, nor shall any interference with the rights of conscience be permitted. No religious test shall be required as a qualification for office, nor shall any person be incompetent to be a witness on account of his religious beliefs; but nothing herein shall be construed to dispense with oaths and affirmations. Religion, morality, and knowledge, however, being essential to good government, it shall be the duty of the Legislature to pass suitable laws to protect every religious denomination in the peaceable enjoyment of its own mode of public worship, and to encourage schools and the means of instruction."

Nevada Constitution, Article I, § 4
"Liberty of conscience. The free exercise and enjoyment of religious profession and worship without discrimination or preference shall forever be allowed in this State, and no person shall be rendered incompetent to be a witness on account of his opinions on matters of his religious belief, but the liberty of consciene [conscience] hereby secured, shall not be so construed, as to excuse acts of licentiousness or justify practices inconsistent with the peace, or safety of this State."

New Hampshire Constitution, Part First, § 5
"Every individual has a natural and unalienable right to worship God according to the dictates of his own conscience, and reason; and no subject shall be hurt, molested, or restrained, in his person, liberty, or estate, for

worshipping God in the manner and season most agreeable to the dictates of his own conscience; or for his religious profession, sentiments, or persuasion; provided he doth not disturb the public peace or disturb others in their religious worship."

New Jersey Constitution, Article I, §§ 4-5
"There shall be no establishment of one religious sect in preference to another; no religious or racial test shall be required as a qualification for any office or public trust."

"No person shall be denied the enjoyment of any civil or military right, nor be discriminated against in the exercise of any civil or military right, nor be segregated in the militia or in the public schools, because of religious principles, race, color, ancestry or national origin."

New Mexico Constitution, Article II, § 11
"Every man shall be free to worship God according to the dictates of his own conscience, and no person shall ever be molested or denied any civil or political right or privilege on account of his religious opinion or mode of religious worship. No person shall be required to attend any place of worship or support any religious sect or denomination; nor shall any preference be given by law to any religious denomination or mode of worship."

New York Constitution, Article I, § 3
"The free exercise and enjoyment of religious profession and worship, without discrimination or preference, shall forever be allowed in this state to all humankind; and no person shall be rendered incompetent to be a witness on account of his or her opinions on matters of religious belief; but the liberty of conscience hereby secured shall not be so construed as to excuse acts of licentiousness, or justify practices inconsistent with the peace or safety of this state."

North Carolina Constitution, Article I, § 13
"All persons have a natural and inalienable right to worship Almighty God according to the dictates of their own consciences, and no human authority shall, in any case whatever, control or interfere with the rights of conscience."

North Dakota Constitution, Article I, § 3
"The free exercise and enjoyment of religious profession and worship, without discrimination or preference shall be forever guaranteed in this state, and no person shall be rendered incompetent to be a witness or juror on account of his opinion on matters of religious belief; but the liberty of conscience hereby secured shall not be so construed as to excuse acts of licentiousness, or justify practices inconsistent with the peace or safety of this state."

The Constitution of the State of Ohio, Article I, § 7
"All men have a natural and indefeasible right to worship Almighty God according to the dictates of their own conscience. No person shall be compelled to attend, erect, or support any place of worship, or maintain any form of worship, against his consent; and no preference shall be given, by law, to any religious society; nor shall any interference with the rights of conscience be permitted. No religious test shall be required, as a qualification for office, nor shall any person be incompetent to be a witness on account of his religious belief; but nothing herein shall be construed to dispense with oaths and affirmations. Religion, morality, and knowledge, however, being essential to good government, it shall be the duty of the General Assembly to pass suitable laws, to protect every religious denomination in the peaceable enjoyment of its own mode of public worship, and to encourage schools and the means of instruction."

The Constitution of the State of Oklahoma, Article II, §2-5
"No public money or property shall ever be appropriated, applied, donated, or used, directly or indirectly, for the use, benefit, or support of any sect, church, denomination, or system of religion, or for the use, benefit, or support of any priest, preacher, minister, or other religious teacher or dignitary, or sectarian institution as such."

Oregon Constitution, Article II, §§ 2-7
"All men shall be secure in the Natural right, to worship Almighty God according to the dictates of their own consciences."

"No law shall in any case whatever control the free exercise, and enjoyment of religeous [sic] opinions, or interfere with the rights of conscience."

"No religious test shall be required as a qualification for any office of trust or profit."

"No money shall be drawn from the Treasury for the benefit of any religeous [sic], or theological institution, nor shall any money be appropriated for the payment of any religeous [sic] services in either house of the Legislative Assembly."

"No person shall be rendered incompetent as a witness, or juror in consequence of his opinions on matters of religeon [sic]; nor be questioned in any Court of Justice touching his religeous [sic] belief to affect the weight of his testimony."

"The mode of administering an oath, or affirmation shall be such as may be most consistent with, and binding upon the conscience of the person to whom such oath or affirmation may be administered."

The Constitution of the Commonwealth of Pennsylvania, Article I, §§ 3-4
"All men have a natural and indefeasible right to worship Almighty God according to the dictates of their own consciences; no man can of right be compelled to attend, erect or support any place of worship or to maintain any ministry against his consent; no human authority can, in any case whatever, control or interfere with the rights of conscience, and no preference shall ever be given by law to any religious establishments or modes of worship."

"No person who acknowledges the being of a God and a future state of rewards and punishments shall, on account of his religious sentiments, be disqualified to hold any office or place of trust or profit under this Commonwealth."

The Constitution of the State of Rhode Island, Article I, § 3
"Freedom of religion. -- Whereas Almighty God hath created the mind free; and all attempts to influence it by temporal punishments or burdens, or by civil incapacitations, tend to beget habits of hypocrisy and meanness; and whereas a principal object of our venerable ancestors, in their migration to this country and their settlement of this state, was, as they expressed it, to hold forth a lively experiment that a flourishing civil state may stand and be

best maintained with full liberty in religious concernments; we, therefore, declare that no person shall be compelled to frequent or to support any religious worship, place, or ministry whatever, except in fulfillment of such person's voluntary contract; nor enforced, restrained, molested, or burdened in body or goods; nor disqualified from holding any office; nor otherwise suffer on account of such person's religious belief; and that every person shall be free to worship God according to the dictates of such person's conscience, and to profess and by argument to maintain such person's opinion in matters of religion; and that the same shall in no wise diminish, enlarge, or affect the civil capacity of any person."

The Constitution of the State of South Carolina, Article I, § 2

"The General Assembly shall make no law respecting an establishment of religion or prohibiting the free exercise thereof, or abridging the freedom of speech or of the press; or the right of the people peaceably to assemble and to petition the government or any department thereof for a redress of grievances."

The Constitution of the State of South Dakota, Article VI, § 3

"Freedom of religion--Support of religion prohibited. The right to worship God according to the dictates of conscience shall never be infringed. No person shall be denied any civil or political right, privilege or position on account of his religious opinions; but the liberty of conscience hereby secured shall not be so construed as to excuse licentiousness, the invasion of the rights of others, or justify practices inconsistent with the peace or safety of the state."

"No person shall be compelled to attend or support any ministry or place of worship against his consent nor shall any preference be given by law to any religious establishment or mode of worship. No money or property of the state shall be given or appropriated for the benefit of any sectarian or religious society or institution."

The Constitution of the State of Tennessee, Article I, §§ 3-4

"That all men have a natural and indefeasible right to worship Almighty God according to the dictates of their own conscience; that no man can of right be compelled to attend, erect, or support any place of worship, or to maintain any minister against his consent; that no human authority can, in any case whatever, control or interfere with the rights of conscience; and that no preference shall ever be given, by law, to any religious establishment or mode of worship."

"That no political or religious test, other than an oath to support the Constitution of the United States and of this state, shall ever be required as a qualification to any office or public trust under this state."

The Constitution of the State of Texas, Article I, §§ 4-7
"No religious test shall ever be required as a qualification to any office, or public trust, in this State; nor shall any one be excluded from holding office on account of his religious sentiments, provided he acknowledge the existence of a Supreme Being."

"No person shall be disqualified to give evidence in any of the Courts of this State on account of his religious opinions, or for the want of any religious belief, but all oaths or affirmations shall be administered in the mode most binding upon the conscience, and shall be taken subject to the pains and penalties of perjury."

"All men have a natural and indefeasible right to worship Almighty God according to the dictates of their own consciences. No man shall be compelled to attend, erect or support any place of worship, or to maintain any ministry against his consent. No human authority ought, in any case whatever, to control or interfere with the rights of conscience in matters of religion, and no preference shall ever be given by law to any religious society or mode of worship. But it shall be the duty of the Legislature to pass such laws as may be necessary to protect equally every religious denomination in the peaceable enjoyment of its own mode of public worship."

"No money shall be appropriated, or drawn from the Treasury for the benefit of any sect, or religious society, theological or religious seminary; nor shall property belonging to the State be appropriated for any such purposes."

The Constitution of the State of Utah, Article I, § 4
"The rights of conscience shall never be infringed. The State shall make no law respecting an establishment of religion or prohibiting the free exercise thereof; no religious test shall be required as a qualification for any office of public trust or for any vote at any election; nor shall any person be incompetent as a witness or juror on account of religious belief or the absence thereof. There shall be no union of Church and State, nor shall any church dominate the State or interfere with its functions. No public money or property shall be appropriated for or applied to any religious worship, exercise or instruction, or for the support of any ecclesiastical establishment."

The Constitution of the State of Vermont, Article I, § 3
"That all persons have a natural and unalienable right, to worship Almighty God, according to the dictates of their own consciences and understandings, as in their opinion shall be regulated by the word of God; and that no person ought to, or of right can be compelled to attend any religious worship, or erect or support any place of worship, or maintain any minister, contrary to the dictates of conscience, nor can any person be justly deprived or abridged of any civil right as a citizen, on account of religious sentiments, or peculia[r] mode of religious worship; and that no authority can, or ought to be vested in, or assumed by, any power whatever, that shall in any case interfere with, or in any manner control the rights of conscience, in the free exercise of religious worship. Nevertheless, every sect or denomination of christians ought to observe the sabbath or Lord's day, and keep up some sort of religious worship, which to them shall seem most agreeable to the revealed will of God."

The Constitution of the State of Virginia, Article I, § 16
"That religion or the duty which we owe to our Creator, and the manner of discharging it, can be directed only by reason and conviction, not by force or violence; and, therefore, all men are equally entitled to the free exercise of religion, according to the dictates of conscience; and that it is the mutual duty of all to practice Christian forbearance, love, and charity towards each other. No man shall be compelled to frequent or support any religious worship, place, or ministry whatsoever, nor shall be enforced, restrained, molested, or burthened in his body or goods, nor shall otherwise suffer on account of his religious opinions or belief; but all men shall be free to profess and by argument

to maintain their opinions in matters of religion, and the same shall in nowise diminish, enlarge, or affect their civil capacities. And the General Assembly shall not prescribe any religious test whatever, or confer any peculiar privileges or advantages on any sect or denomination, or pass any law requiring or authorizing any religious society, or the people of any district within this Commonwealth, to levy on themselves or others, any tax for the erection or repair of any house of public worship, or for the support of any church or ministry; but it shall be left free to every person to select his religious instructor, and to make for his support such private contract as he shall please."

The Constitution of the State of Washington, Article I, § 11
"Absolute freedom of conscience in all matters of religious sentiment, belief and worship, shall be guaranteed to every individual, and no one shall be molested or disturbed in person or property on account of religion; but the liberty of conscience hereby secured shall not be so construed as to excuse acts of licentiousness or justify practices inconsistent with the peace and safety of the state. No public money or property shall be appropriated for or applied to any religious worship, exercise or instruction, or the support of any religious establishment: PROVIDED, HOWEVER, That this article shall not be so construed as to forbid the employment by the state of a chaplain for such of the state custodial, correctional, and mental institutions, or by a county's or public hospital district's hospital, health care facility, or hospice, as in the discretion of the legislature may seem justified. No religious qualification shall be required for any public office or employment, nor shall any person be incompetent as a witness or juror, in consequence of his opinion on matters of religion, nor be questioned in any court of justice touching his religious belief to affect the weight of his testimony."

The Constitution of the State of West Virginia, Article III, § 15-15a
"No man shall be compelled to frequent or support any religious worship, place or ministry whatsoever; nor shall any man be enforced, restrained, molested or burthened, in his body or goods, or otherwise suffer, on account of his religious opinions or belief, but all men shall be free to profess and by argument, to maintain their opinions in matters of religion; and the same shall, in nowise, affect, diminish or enlarge their civil capacities; and the Legislature shall not prescribe any religious test whatever, or confer any peculiar

privileges or advantages on any sect or denomination, or pass any law requiring or authorizing any religious society, or the people of any district within this state, to levy on themselves, or others, any tax for the erection or repair of any house for public worship, or for the support of any church or ministry, but it shall be left free for every person to select his religious instructor, and to make for his support, such private contracts as he shall please."

"Public schools shall provide a designated brief time at the beginning of each school day for any student desiring to exercise their right to personal and private contemplation, meditation or prayer. No student of a public school may be denied the right to personal and private contemplation, meditation or prayer nor shall any student be required or encouraged to engage in any given contemplation, meditation or prayer as a part of the school curriculum."

The Constitution of the State of Wisconsin, Article I, § 18
"The right of every person to worship Almighty God according to the dictates of conscience shall never be infringed; nor shall any person be compelled to attend, erect or support any place of worship, or to maintain any ministry, without consent; nor shall any control of, or interference with, the rights of conscience be permitted, or any preference be given by law to any religious establishments or modes of worship; nor shall any money be drawn from the treasury for the benefit of religious societies, or religious or theological seminaries."

The Constitution of the State of Wyoming, Article I, § 18-19
"The free exercise and enjoyment of religious profession and worship without discrimination or preference shall be forever guaranteed in this state, and no person shall be rendered incompetent to hold any office of trust or profit, or to serve as a witness or juror, because of his opinion on any matter of religious belief whatever; but the liberty of conscience hereby secured shall not be so construed as to excuse acts of licentiousness or justify practices inconsistent with the peace or safety of the state."

"No money of the state shall ever be given or appropriated to any sectarian or religious society or institution."

APPENDIX C

STATE AND LOCAL RESOURCES

NOTICE: State laws and state and local board of education rules are continually changing. It is crucial to check and recheck several sources to confirm that you have the most current version of the law or rule.

ALABAMA

The Constitution of the State of Alabama
Article I – Declaration of Rights (Sections 1-36)
Article XIV – Education (Sections 256-270)
https://law.justia.com/constitution/alabama/

Alabama State Legislature – https://alison.legislature.state.al.us/
Alabama State Laws – https://law.justia.com/alabama/
Alabama School Laws (Title 16 – Education) –
  https://law.justia.com/codes/alabama/2022/title-16/

Sample of Alabama Education-Related Laws
To locate the laws below, go to the Alabama School Laws link above and search for the citation that interests you by clicking on the appropriate chapters and subchapters as you wind your way to the law. You can also enter the terms "Justia," "Alabama," and the "numeric portion of the citation" in your search bar. Be sure to look at the most recent version of the law.

Alabama Education Council – Ala. Code § 16-44-2
Alabama Religious Freedom Amendment – Ala. Const. amend. 622
AL Sample FOIA Request – National Freedom of Information Coalition
Core Curriculum – Ala. Code § 16-6B-2
Crimes, Obscenity – Ala. Code §§ 13A-12-200.1 to 13A-12-200.12; Material Harmful to Minors – 13A-12-200.5; Affirmative Defenses – 13A-12-200.4
County Superintendent Duties and Bond – AL Code § 16-8-7
Open Meetings Act – Ala. Code §§ 36-25A-1 to 36-25A-11
Open Records Act – Ala. Code §§ 36-12-40 to 36-12-41
Released Time for Religious Instruction – Ala. Code § 16-1-20.6
Responsible Sexual Behavior ... Illegal Drugs – Ala. Code § 16-40A-1 to 16-40A-4
State Courses of Study Committee – Ala. Code § 16-35-1 to 16-35-5

Student Religious Liberties Act of 2015 – Ala. Code § 16-1- 20.5
U.S. and State Flag – Ala. Code § 16-43-1

Alabama Administrative Code (Title 290 – State Board of Education)
https://regulations.justia.com/states/alabama/title-290/
Alabama State Board & Department of Education –
   https://www.alabamaachieves.org/
Alabama State Bar – https://www.alabar.org/

ALASKA

The Constitution of the State of Alaska
Article I – Declaration of Rights (Sections 1-25)
Article VII – Health, Education & Welfare; Section 1. Public Education (Section 1)
https://law.justia.com/constitution/alaska/

Alaska State Legislature – https://akleg.gov/
Alaska State Laws – https://law.justia.com/codes/alaska/
Alaska School Laws (Title 14. Education, Libraries, & Museums) –
   https://law.justia.com/codes/alaska/2021/title-14/

Sample of Alaska Education-Related Laws
To locate the laws below, go to the Alaska School Laws link above and search for the citation that interests you by clicking on the appropriate chapters and subchapters as you wind your way to the law. You can also enter the terms "Justia," "Alaska," and the "numeric portion of the citation" in your search bar. Be sure to look at the most recent version of the law.

AK Sample FOIA Request – National Freedom of Information Coalition
Charter Schools – AK Stat. §§ 14.03.250 to 14.03.290
Flags and Pledge of Allegiance – AK Stat. § 14.03.130
Harassment, Intimidation, and Bullying – AK Stat. § 14.33.200
Open Records Act – AK Stat. §§ 40.25.100 to 40.25.295
Open Meetings Act – AK Stat. §§ 44.62.310 to 44.62.320
Parent's Rights– AK Stat. § 14.03.016
Partisan and Sectarian Doctrines Prohibited – AK Stat. § 14.03.090
Psychiatric and Behavioral Evaluations – AK Stat. §§ 14.30.171 to 14.30.179
Questionnaires and Surveys– AK Stat. § 14.03.110
State Board Duties – AK Stat. § 14.07.165

Alaska Administrative Code (Title 4 – Education and Early Development) –
   https://regulations.justia.com/states/alaska/title-4/
Alaska Department of Education & Early Development –
   https://education.alaska.gov/

Alaska State Board of Education – https://education.alaska.gov/State_Board
Alaska Bar Association – https://alaskabar.org/

ARIZONA

The Constitution of the State of Arizona
Article II – Declaration of Rights
Article XI – Education
https://law.justia.com/constitution/arizona/

Arizona State Legislature – https://www.azleg.gov/arstitle/
Arizona State Laws – https://law.justia.com/codes/arizona/
Arizona School Laws (Title 15. Education) –
   https://law.justia.com/codes/arizona/2022/title-15/

Sample of Arizona Education-Related Laws
To locate the laws below, go to the Arizona School Laws link above and search for the citation that interests you by clicking on the appropriate chapters and subchapters as you wind your way to the law. You can also enter the terms "Justia," "Arizona," and the "numeric portion of the citation" in your search bar. Be sure to look at the most recent version of the law.

American History– AZ Rev Stat § 15-717
Arizona Free Exercise of Religion Act – AZ Rev Stat § 41-1493.01 to 41-1493.02
AZ Sample FOIA Request – National Freedom of Information Coalition
Character Education– AZ Rev Stat § 15-719
Course of Study and Textbooks – AZ Rev Stat § 15-721
Mental Health Screening and Exemptions – AZ Rev Stat § 15-104
Open Meetings Act – AZ Rev Stat § 38-431.01
Prohibited Courses and Classes – AZ Rev Stat § 15-112
Public Records Law – AZ Rev Stat §§ 39-121 to 39-121-128
Rights of Parents – AZ Rev Stat § 15-113
Sex Education – AZ Rev Stat § 15-711
Surveys, Pupil Information, and Parent Permission – AZ Rev Stat § 15-117
U.S. and State Constitutions– AZ Rev Stat § 15-710

Arizona Administrative Code (Title 7 – Education) –
   https://regulations.justia.com/states/arizona/title-7/
Arizona Department of Education – https://www.azed.gov/
Arizona State Board of Education – https://azsbe.az.gov/
State Bar of Arizona – https://www.azbar.org/

ARKANSAS

The Constitution of the State of Arkansas
Article II – Declaration of Rights
Article XIV – Education
https://law.justia.com/constitution/arkansas/

Arkansas State Legislature – https://www.arkleg.state.ar.us/
Arkansas State Laws – https://law.justia.com/codes/arkansas/
Arkansas School Laws (Title 6 – Education) –
  https://law.justia.com/codes/arkansas/2020/title-6/

Sample of Arkansas Education-Related Laws
To locate the laws below, go to the Arkansas School Laws link above and search for the citation that interests you by clicking on the appropriate chapters and subchapters as you wind your way to the law. You can also enter the terms "Justia," "Arkansas," and the "numeric portion of the citation" in your search bar. Be sure to look at the most recent version of the law.

AR Sample FOIA Request –National Freedom of Information Coalition
Arkansas Religious Freedom Restoration Act – AR Code §§ 16-123-401 to 16-123-407
Crimes, Obscenity – AR Code §§ 5-68-301 to 5-68-308; Defenses– AR Code § 5-68-308
Curriculum, American Heritage – AR Code § 6-16-122
Emergency Plans and Panic Button – AR Code § 6-15-1302
Open Meetings Law – AR Code § 25-19-106
Open Records Law– AR Code §§ 25-19-101 to 25-19-111
Parental Involvement – AR Code § 6-15-1702
Public School Libraries – AR Code § 6-25-105
School Leadership Coordinating Council – AR Code § 6-1-403
U.S. Citizenship Civics Test – AR Code § 6-16-149; U.S. Flag – AR Code § 6-16-105
Use of Personal Electronic Devices – AR Code § 6-18-515

Arkansas Administrative Code (Agency 005 – Department of Education) –
  https://regulations.justia.com/states/arkansas/agency-005/
Arkansas State Board & Div. of Elem. & Sec. Education –
  https://dese.ade.arkansas.gov/
Arkansas Bar Association – https://www.arkbar.com/home

CALIFORNIA

The Constitution of the State of California
Article I – Declaration of Rights
Article IX – Education
https://law.justia.com/constitution/california/

California State Legislature – https://leginfo.legislature.ca.gov/

California State Laws – https://law.justia.com/codes/california/
California School Laws (Titles 1-2 – Elementary & Secondary Education) –
https://law.justia.com/codes/california/2021/code-edc/

Sample of California Education-Related Laws

To locate the laws below, go to the California School Laws link above and search for the citation that interests you by clicking on the appropriate chapters and sub-chapters as you wind your way to the law. You can also enter the terms "Justia," "California," and the "numeric portion of the citation" in your search bar. Be sure to look at the most recent version of the law.

CA Sample FOIA Request – National Freedom of Information Coalition
Charter Schools – CA Educ Code §§ 47600 to 47604.5
Crimes, Obscenity, Harmful Matter – CA Penal Code §§ 313 to 313.5; Defense – CA Penal Code § 313.3
Notification to Parent or Guardian – CA Educ Code §§ 48980 to 48985
Open Meetings Act – CA Govt Code §§ 54950 to 54960.5
Open Records Act – CA Govt Code §§ 6250 to 6268
Parent Review – CA Educ Code §§ 49091.10 to 49091.19
Parental Involvement – CA Educ Code §§ 51100 to 51102
Prohibited Instruction and Materials – CA Educ Code §§ 51500 to 51540
Required Courses – CA Educ Code §§ 51200 to 51206.4
Speech and Communication – CA Educ Code § 48950
Student Organizations – CA Educ Code § 48930

California Code of Regulations (Title 5 – Education) –
https://regulations.justia.com/states/california/title-5/
California Department of Education – https://www.cde.ca.gov/
California State Board of Education – https://www.cde.ca.gov/be/
State Bar of California – https://www.calbar.ca.gov/

COLORADO

The Constitution of the State of Colorado
Article II – Bill of Rights
Article IX – Education
https://law.justia.com/constitution/colorado/

Colorado General Assembly – https://leg.colorado.gov/
Colorado State Laws – https://law.justia.com/codes/colorado/
Colorado School Laws (Title 22 – Education) –
https://law.justia.com/codes/colorado/2021/title-22/

Sample of Colorado Education-Related Laws

To locate the laws below, go to the Colorado School Laws link above and search for the citation that interests you by clicking on the appropriate chapters and subchapters as you wind your way to the law. You can also enter the terms "Justia," "Colorado," and the "numeric portion of the citation" in your search bar. Be sure to look at the most recent version of the law.

Children's Internet Protection – CO Rev Stat §§ 22-87-101 to 22-87-107
CO Sample FOIA Request – National Freedom of Information Coalition
Comprehensive Sex Education – CO Rev Stat § 22-1-128
Crimes, Harmful Materials – CO Rev Stat §§ 18-7-501 to 18-7-5.4; Exemption – 18-7-503
History and Government – CO Rev Stat §§ 22-1-104; U.S. Constitution –CO Rev Stat § 22-1-108
K-5 Social and Emotional Health– CO Rev Stat §§ 22-102-101 to 22-102-108
Open Meetings Law – CO Stat §§ 24-6-401 to 24-6-402
Open Records Law – CO Rev Stat §§ 24-72-200.1 to 24-72-206
Rights of Free Expression for Students – CO Rev Stat § 22-1-120
Student Data and Security – CO Rev Stat §§ 22-16-101 to 22-16-112
Use of Flag – CO Rev Stat § 22-1-106

Code of Colorado Regulations (300 – Department of Education) –
https://regulations.justia.com/states/colorado/300/
Colorado Department of Education & State Board of Education –
https://www.cde.state.co.us/
Colorado Bar Association – https://www.cobar.org/

CONNECTICUT

The Constitution of the State of Connecticut
Article I – Declaration of Rights
Article VIII – Education
https://law.justia.com/constitution/connecticut/

Connecticut General Assembly – https://www.cga.ct.gov/
Connecticut State Laws – https://law.justia.com/codes/connectocut/
Connecticut School Laws (Title 10 – Education and Culture) –
https://law.justia.com/codes/connecticut/2020/title-10/

Sample of Connecticut Education-Related Laws
To locate the laws below, go to the Connecticut School Laws link above and search for the citation that interests you by clicking on the appropriate chapters and subchapters as you wind your way to the law. You can also enter the terms "Justia," "Connecticut," and the "numeric portion of the citation" in your search bar. Be sure to look at the most recent version of the law.

Board of Education Hearings – CT Gen Stat § 10-238
Connecticut Religious Freedom Restoration Act – CT Gen Stat § 52-571b
CT Sample FOIA Request – National Freedom of Information Coalition
Disciplinary Policies – CT Gen Stat § 10-233e

Duties of Boards – CT Gen Stat § 10-220
Open Meetings Law – CT Gen Stat § 1-225
Open Records Law – CT Gen Stat § 1-210
Parental and Community Involvement – CT Gen Stat §10-4g
Penal Code, Obscenity Offenses (1991) – CT Gen Stat §§ 53a-193 to 53a-196; Defense – 53a-195 (The offense and defense are not listed in the recent code)
School Governance Councils – CT Gen Stat § 10-223j
Social and Emotional Learning – CT Gen Stat § 10-222q
Student Data Privacy – CT Gen Stat §§ 10-234bb to 10-234gg

Connecticut Administrative Code (Title 10 – Education and Culture) –
https://regulations.justia.com/states/connecticut/title-10/
Connecticut State Board and Department of Education – https://portal.ct.gov/SDE/
Connecticut Bar Association – https://www.ctbar.org/

DELAWARE

The Constitution of the State of Delaware
Article I – Bill of Rights
Article X – Education
https://law.justia.com/constitution/delaware/

Delaware General Assembly – https://legis.delaware.gov/
Delaware State Laws – https://law.justia.com/codes/delaware/
Delaware School Laws (Title 14 – Education) –
https://law.justia.com/codes/delaware/2022/title-14/

Sample of Delaware Education-Related Laws
To locate the laws below, go to the Delaware School Laws link above and search for the citation that interests you by clicking on the appropriate chapters and sub-chapters as you wind your way to the law. You can also enter the terms "Justia," "Delaware," and the "numeric portion of the citation" in your search bar. Be sure to look at the most recent version of the law.

Charter Schools – 14 DE Code §§ 501 to 518
Crimes, Obscenity – 11 DE Code §§ 1361 to 1365; Defenses – 11 DE Code § 1362
DE Sample FOIA Request – National Freedom of Information Coalition
Department of Education Powers & Duties – 14 DE Code § 122
District Libraries – 14 DE Code §§ 7101 to 7108
Interscholastic Athletic Association – 14 DE Code §§ 301 to 312
Open Meetings Law – 29 DE Code § 10004
Open Records Law – 29 DE Code § 10003
Parental Involvement – 14 DE Code § 157
Parents' Right to Know – 14 DE Code §§ 3001B to 3003B
Part-Time School/Class – 14 DE Code §§ 3501 to 515
School Shared Decision-Making – 14 DE Code §§ 801 to 808

Delaware Administrative Code (Title 14 - Education)
https://regulations.justia.com/states/delaware/title-14/
Delaware State Board & Department of Education –
   https://education.delaware.gov/
Delaware State Bar Association – https://www.dsba.org/

FLORIDA

The Constitution of the State of Florida
Article I – Declaration of Rights
Article IX – Education
https://law.justia.com/constitution/florida/

Florida State Legislature – http://www.leg.state.fl.us/
Florida State Laws – https://law.justia.com/codes/florida/
Florida School Laws (Title XLVIII – Early Learning – 20 Education Code) –
   https://law.justia.com/codes/florida/2022/title-xlviii/

Sample of Florida Education-Related Laws
To locate the laws below, go to the Florida School Laws link above and search for the citation that interests you by clicking on the appropriate chapters and subchapters as you wind your way to the law. You can also enter the terms "Justia," "Florida," and the "numeric portion of the citation" in your search bar. Be sure to look at the most recent version of the law.

Crimes, Obscenity – FL Stat § 847.001 to 847.202; Exemption for "approved instructional materials" – FL Stat § 847.012
District School Board Operation and Control – FL Stat § 1003.02
FL Sample FOIA Request – National Freedom of Information Coalition
Florida Religious Freedom Restoration Act – FL Stat §§ 761.01 to 761.05
Maximum Class Size – FL Stat § 1003.03
Open Meetings and Records Laws – FL Stat §§ 286.011 & 286.0114
Parents' Bill of Rights – FL Stat §§ 1014.01 to 1014.06
Patriotic Programs – FL Stat § 1003.44
Public K-12 Instruction – FL Stat §§ 1003.41 to 1003.49965
State Board Oversight and Enforcement – FL Stat § 1008.32
Student and Parental Rights and Choices – FL Stat §§ 1002.01 to 1002.995
Student Conduct and Parental Involvement – FL Stat § 1003.04
Student and Personnel Religious Liberties Act – FL Stat § 1002.206

Florida Administrative Code (6 – Department of Education)
   https://regulations.justia.com/states/florida/6/
Florida State Board of Education & Florida Department of Education –
   https://www.fldoe.org/
Florida State Bar – https://www.floridabar.org/

GEORGIA

The Constitution of the State of Georgia
Article I – Bill of Rights
Article VIII – Education
https://law.justia.com/constitution/georgia/

Georgia General Assembly – https://www.legis.ga.gov/
Georgia State Laws – https://law.justia.com/codes/georgia/
Georgia School Laws (Title 20 – Education)
  https://law.justia.com/codes/georgia/2021/

Sample of Georgia Education-Related Laws
To locate the laws below, go to the Georgia School Laws link above and search for the citation that interests you by clicking on the appropriate chapters and subchapters as you wind your way to the law. You can also enter the terms "Justia," "Georgia," and the "numeric portion of the citation" in your search bar. Be sure to look at the most recent version of the law.

Crimes, Harmful Material – O.C.G.A. § 16-12-103; Exceptions – O.C.G.A. § 16-12-104
Exclusion of Partisan or Sectarian Material – O.C.G.A. § 20-2-1011
GA Sample FOIA Request – National Freedom of Information Coalition
Georgia's New Mental Health Law – O.C.G.A. § 37-1-20(28); 37-3-4(a); 49-5-24(b)
High School Athletic Association – O.C.G.A. § 20-1-2103
Open Meetings Act – O.C.G.A. §§ 50-14-1 to 50-14-6
Open Records Act – O.C.G.A. §§ 50-18-70 to 50-18-77
Prohibition Against Divisive Concepts – O.C.G.A. § 20-1-11(a)
Sex Education, Exemption – O.C.G.A. § 20-2-143
Student Discipline – O.C.G.A. §§ 20-2-735 to 20-2-742
U.S. and GA History – O.C.G.A. §§ 20-2-142; 20-2-142.1; 20-2-1020; 20-2-1021; 20-2-1022

Georgia Administrative Rules & Regulations (160 – Department of Education) –
  https://regulations.justia.com/states/georgia/department-160/
Georgia State Board of Education & Department Education –
  https://www.gadoe.org/
State Bar of Georgia – https://www.gabar.org/

HAWAII

The Constitution of the State of Hawaii
Article I – Bill of Rights
Article X – Education
https://law.justia.com/constitution/hawaii/

Hawaii State Legislature – https://www.capitol.hawaii.gov/
Hawaii State Laws – https://law.justia.com/codes/hawaii/

Hawaii School Laws (Title 18 – Education) –
https://law.justia.com/codes/hawaii/2022/title-18/

Sample of Hawaii Education-Related Laws
To locate the laws below, go to the Hawaii School Laws link above and search for the citation that interests you by clicking on the appropriate chapters and subchapters as you wind your way to the law. You can also enter the terms "Justia," "Hawaii," and the "numeric portion of the citation" in your search bar. Be sure to look at the most recent version of the law.

Administration of Medication – HI Rev Stat § 302A-853
Compact for Education – HI Rev Stat §§ 311-1 to 311-6
Curriculum – HI Rev Stat §§ 302A-251 to 302A-323
Early Learning Board – HI Rev Stat § 302L-1.6
HI Sample FOIA Request – National Freedom of Information Coalition
Libraries – HI Rev Stat §§ 312-1 to 312-8
Open Meetings and Records Law – HI Rev Stat §§ 92-1 to 92-13
Penal Code, Promoting Pornography, Exemptions – HI Rev Stat § 712-1215
Public Charter Schools – HI Rev Stat §§ 302D-1 to 302D-40
Statewide Performance Standards – HI Rev Stat § 302A-201

Hawaii Administrative Rules (Title 8 – Department of Education) –
https://regulations.justia.com/states/hawaii/title-8/
Hawaii State Department of Education – https://www.hawaiipublicschools.org/
State of Hawaii Board of Education – https://boe.hawaii.gov/
Hawaii State Bar – https://hsba.org/

IDAHO

The Constitution of the State of Idaho
Article I – Declaration of Rights
Article IX – Education and School Lands
https://law.justia.com/constitution/idaho/

Idaho Legislature – https://legislature.idaho.gov/
Idaho State Laws – https://law.justia.com/codes/idaho/
Idaho School Laws (Title 33 – Education) – https://law.justia.com/codes/idaho/2022/

Sample of Idaho Education-Related Laws
To locate the laws below, go to the Idaho School Laws link above and search for the citation that interests you by clicking on the appropriate chapters and subchapters as you wind your way to the law. You can also enter the terms "Justia," "Idaho," and the "numeric portion of the citation" in your search bar. Be sure to look at the most recent version of the law.

Courses of Instruction – ID Code §§ 33-1601 to 33-1636

Crimes, Material Harmful to Minors – ID Code §§ 18-1513 to 18-1517; Defenses – ID Code § 18-1517
Fairness in Women's Sports – ID Code § 33-6201 to 33-6206
Family Life Policy – ID Code § 33-1608
ID Sample FOIA Request – National Freedom of Information Coalition
Open Meetings Law – ID Code §§ 74-201 to 74-208
Open Records Act – ID Code §§ 74-101 to 74-126
Parental Rights – ID Code § 33-6001
Religious Freedom Restoration Act – ID Code §§ 73-401 to 73-404
School Elections – ID Code §§ 33-401 to 33-405
Sex Education, Exemptions – ID Code § 33-1611
Teachers – ID Code §§ 33-1201 to 1280
U.S. Constitution and Flag, and National Anthem – ID Code § 33-1602

Idaho Administrative Code (Title IDAPA 08 – Education, Board and Department) – https://regulations.justia.com/states/idaho/08/
Idaho State Department of Education – https://www.sde.idaho.gov/
Idaho State Board of Education – https://boardofed.idaho.gov/
Idaho State Bar – https://isb.idaho.gov/

ILLINOIS

The Constitution of the State of Illinois
Article I – Bill of Rights
Article X – Bill Education
https://law.justia.com/constitution/illinois/

Illinois General Assembly – https://www.ilga.gov/
Illinois State Laws – https://law.justia.com/codes/illinois/
Illinois School Laws (Chapter 105 – Schools) – https://law.justia.com/codes/illinois/2021/chapter-105/

Sample of Illinois Education-Related Laws
To locate the laws below, go to the Illinois School Laws link above and search for the citation that interests you by clicking on the appropriate chapters and subchapters as you wind your way to the law. You can also enter the terms "Justia," "Illinois," and the "numeric portion of the citation" in your search bar. Be sure to look at the most recent version of the law.

Care of Students with Diabetes Act – 105 ILCS 145/5
Charter Schools – 105 ILCS 5/27A
Comprehensive Health Education Act – 105 ILCS 110/1
Courses of Study and Special Instruction – 105 ILCS 5/27
Crimes, Obscenity, and Affirmative Defenses – 720 ILCS 5/11-20(f)
IL Sample FOIA Request – National Freedom of Information Coalition

APPENDIX C: STATE AND LOCAL RESOURCES

Interscholastic Athletics – 105 ILCS 25/1
Open Meetings Act – 5 ILCS 120/1
Open Records Act – 5 ILCS 140/1
Religious Freedom Restoration Act – 775 ILCS § 35/1 to 35/99
School Health Center – 105 ILCS 129/5
Speech Rights of Student Journalists – 105 ILCS 80/5
Student Records – 105/ ILCS 10/1

Illinois Administrative Code (Title 23 – Education & Cultural Resources) –
https://regulations.justia.com/states/illinois/title-23/
Illinois State Board & Department of Education – https://www.isbe.net/
Illinois State Bar Association – https://www.isba.org/

INDIANA

The Constitution of the State of Indiana
Article I – Bill of Rights
Article VIII – Education
https://law.justia.com/constitution/indiana/

Indiana General Assembly – https://iga.in.gov/
Indiana State Laws – https://law.justia.com/codes/indiana/
Indiana School Laws (Title 20 – Education) –
https://law.justia.com/codes/indiana/2021/title-20/

Sample of Indiana Education-Related Laws
To locate the laws below, go to the Indiana School Laws link above and search for the citation that interests you by clicking on the appropriate chapters and sub-chapters as you wind your way to the law. You can also enter the terms "Justia," "Indiana," and the "numeric portion of the citation" in your search bar. Be sure to look at the most recent version of the law.

Charter Schools – IN Code §§ 20-24-1 to 20-24-13
Crimes, Obscenity – IN Code § 35-49-3-3; Defenses – IN Code § 35-49-3-4
Curriculum Materials– IN Code §§ 20-20-5.5-2 to 20-20-5.5-3
IN Sample FOIA Request – National Freedom of Information Coalition
Mandatory Curriculum – IN Code §§ 20-30-5-0.5 to 20-30-5-23
Optional Curriculum – IN Code §§ 20-30-6.1-1 to 20-30-6.1-3
Open Meetings Law – IN Code § 5-14-1.5-1 to 5-14-1.5-8
Open Records Law – IN Code §§ 5-14-3-1 to 5-14-3-10
Religious Freedom Restoration Act – IN Code § 1.IC34-13-9
Social, Emotional and Behavioral Health Plan – IN Code §§ 20-19-5-1 and 2
Student Discipline – IN Code §§ 20-33-8-0.2 to 20-33-8-34
Student Religious Civil Liberties – IN Code §§ 20-33-12-1 to 20-33-12-8
Student Standards, and Assessments – IN Code §§ 20-32-1-1 to 20-32-9-4

Indiana Administrative Code (Titles 510 and 512) –
  https://regulations.justia.com/states/indiana/title-510/
  https://regulations.justia.com/states/indiana/title-512/
Indiana Department of Education – https://www.in.gov/doe/
Indiana State Board of Education – https://www.in.gov/sboe/
Indiana State Bar Association – https://www.inbar.org/

IOWA

The Constitution of the State of Iowa
Article I – Bill of Rights
Article IX – Education and School Lands
https://law.justia.com/constitution/iowa/

Iowa Legislature – https://www.legis.iowa.gov/
Iowa State Laws – https://law.justia.com/codes/iowa/
Iowa School Laws (Title VII – Education & Cultural Affairs) –
  https://law.justia.com/codes/iowa/2022/title-vii/

Sample of Iowa Education-Related Laws
To locate the laws below, go to the Iowa School Laws link above and search for the citation that interests you by clicking on the appropriate chapters and subchapters as you wind your way to the law. You can also enter the terms "Justia," "Iowa," and the "numeric portion of the citation" in your search bar. Be sure to look at the most recent version of the law.

Behavioral Health Services– IA Code §§ 280A.1 to 280A.4
Charter Schools – IA Code §§ 256F.1 to 256F.11
Crimes, Obscenity – IA Code §§ 728.1 to 728.15; Defenses – 728.7
Educational Standards – IA Code § 256.11
IA Sample FOIA Request – National Freedom of Information Coalition
Open Meetings Law – IA Code §§ 21.1 to 21.11
Open Records Law– IA Code §§ 22.1 to 22.16
Online Learning Requirements – IA Code § 256.1
Religious Books – IA Code § 280.6
Student Exercise of Free Expression – IA Code § 280.22
Textbooks – IA Code §§ 301.1 to 301.30
Uniform School Requirements – IA Code §§ 280.1 to 280.30

Iowa Administrative Code (Agency 281 – Education Department) –
  https://regulations.justia.com/states/iowa/agency-281/
Iowa State Board/Department of Education – https://educateiowa.gov/
Iowa State Bar Association – https://www.iowabar.org/

KANSAS

The Constitution of the State of Kansas
Kansas Bill of Rights
Article VI - Education
https://law.justia.com/constitution/kansas/

Kansas State Legislature - http://www.kslegislature.org/
Kansas State Laws - https://law.justia.com/codes/kansas/
Kansas School Laws (Chapter 72 - Schools) -
    https://law.justia.com/codes/kansas/2021/chapter-72/

Sample of Kansas Education-Related Laws
To locate the laws below, go to the Kansas School Laws link above and search for the citation that interests you by clicking on the appropriate chapters and subchapters as you wind your way to the law. You can also enter the terms "Justia," "Kansas," and the "numeric portion of the citation" in your search bar. Be sure to look at the most recent version of the law.

Crimes, Obscenity to Minors, and Defense - KS Stat § 21-6401
Curriculum - KS Stat §§ 72-3214 to 72-3254; Required - 72-3214; 72-3217
Employment of Lobbyists - KS Stat § 72-9935
High School Activities - KS Stat §§ 72-7114 to 72-7120; Records and Meetings - 72-7114
KS Sample FOIA Request - National Freedom of Information Coalition
Mental Health Intervention Pilot Program - KS Stat §72-9943
Open Meetings Law - KS Stat § 75-4317 et seq.; 75-4317
Open Records Law - KS Stat §§ 45-215 to 254; Requests - 45-218
Patriotism, Flags, and Holidays - KS Stat § 72-9928
Religious Freedom Restoration Act - KS Stat §§ 60-5301 to 60-5305
Student Health - KS Stat §§ 72-7114 to 72-7120; Assessments - 72-6267
Test, Questionnaires, Surveys ... Questions Prohibited - KS Stat § 72-6316

Kansas Administrative Regulations (Agency 91 - Department of Education) -
    https://regulations.justia.com/states/kansas/agency-91/
Kansas State Board & Department of Education - https://www.ksde.org/
Kansas Bar Association - https://ksbar.org/

KENTUCKY

The Constitution of the Commonwealth of Kentucky
Bill of Rights - Sections 1-26
Education - Sections 183-189
https://law.justia.com/constitution/kentucky/

Kentucky General Assembly - https://legislature.ky.gov/
Kentucky Laws - https://law.justia.com/codes/kentucky/

Kentucky School Laws (Title XIII – Education) –
https://law.justia.com/codes/kentucky/2021/ (scroll to Title XIII – Education)

Sample of Kentucky Education-Related Laws
To locate the laws below, go to the Kentucky School Laws link above and search for the citation that interests you by clicking on the appropriate chapters and subchapters as you wind your way to the law. You can also enter the terms "Justia," "Kentucky," and the "numeric portion of the citation" in your search bar. Be sure to look at the most recent version of the law.

Confidentiality of Student Records – KY Rev Stat § 160.705
Evaluation of Textbooks and Programs – KY Rev Stat § 156.410
Family Rights and Privacy – KY Rev Stat §§ 160.700 to 160.730
KY Sample FOIA Request – National Freedom of Information Coalition
Local Superintendent Advisory Councils – KY Rev Stat § 156.007
Open Meetings Act – KY Rev Stat §§ 61.800 to 61.850; 61.800
Open Records Act – KY Rev Stat §§ 61.870 to 61.884; 61.872
Pornography – KY Rev Stat § 531; Exemptions – KY Rev Stat § 531.070
Public Charter Schools – KY Rev Stat §§ 160.1590 to 160.1599
Religious Freedom Restoration Act – KY Rev Stat § 446.350
School Districts Powers and Duties – KY Rev Stat § 160.290
State Board of Education – KY Rev Stat § 156.029
Student Health Services – KY Rev Stat § 156.501

Kentucky Administrative Regulations (Titles 701 through 725 Education) –
https://regulations.justia.com/states/kentucky/
Kentucky Department of Education & Board of Education –
https://education.ky.gov/
Kentucky Bar Association – https://www.kybar.org/

LOUISIANA

The Constitution of the State of Louisiana
Article I – Declaration of Rights
Article VIII – Education
https://law.justia.com/constitution/louisiana/

Louisiana State Legislature – https://legis.la.gov/
Louisiana State Laws – https://law.justia.com/codes/louisiana/
Louisiana School Laws (Title 17 – Education) –
https://law.justia.com/codes/louisiana/2021/revised-statutes/title-17/

Sample of Louisiana Education-Related Laws
To locate the laws below, go to the Louisiana School Laws link above and search for the citation that interests you by clicking on the appropriate chapters and subchapters as you wind your way to the law. You can also enter the terms "Justia,"

"Louisiana," and the "numeric portion of the citation" in your search bar. Be sure to look at the most recent version of the law.

Crimes, Obscenity, and Exemptions – LA Rev Stat § 14:106(D)(1)
Duties of State Board – LA Rev Stat § 17:7; Powers – LA Rev Stat § 17:6
Election of Parish Board Members – LA Rev Stat § 17:52
LA Sample FOIA Request – National Freedom of Information Coalition
Open Meetings Law – LA Rev Stat §§ 42:11 to 28; 42:14
Open Records Law – LA Rev Stat §§ 44:1 et seq.; 44:31
Parents' Bill of Rights – LA Rev Stat § 17:406.9
Permitted Courses – LA Rev Stat §§ 17:281 to 17:286
Powers of Local School Boards – LA Rev Stat § 17:81
Preservation of Religious Freedom Act – LA Rev Stat § 13:5231 to 13:5242
Required Courses – LA Rev Stat §§ 17:261 to 280; History – 17:261, 262, 265, 268, 277
Sex Education, Exemptions – § 17:281(D)
State Superintendent Functions – LA Rev Stat § 17:21; Duties – 17:22
Textbooks and Instructional Materials – LA Rev Stat §17:351.1

Louisiana Administrative Code (Title 28 – Education) –
https://regulations.justia.com/states/louisiana/title-28/
Louisiana Department of Education – https://www.louisianabelieves.com/
Louisiana State Board of Elem. & Sec. Education – https://bese.louisiana.gov/
Louisiana State Bar Association – https://www.lsba.org/

MAINE

The Constitution of the State of Maine
Article I – Declaration of Rights
Article VIII – Education
https://law.justia.com/constitution/maine/

Maine State Legislature – https://legislature.maine.gov/
Maine State Laws – https://law.justia.com/codes/maine/
Maine School Laws (Title 20-A – Education) –
https://law.justia.com/codes/maine/2021/title-20-a/

Sample of Maine Education-Related Laws
To locate the laws below, go to the Maine School Laws link above and search for the citation that interests you by clicking on the appropriate chapters and subchapters as you wind your way to the law. You can also enter the terms "Justia," "Maine," and the "numeric portion of the citation" in your search bar. Be sure to look at the most recent version of the law.

Charter Schools – 20-A ME Rev Stat §§ 2401 to 2415
Crimes, Obscenity to Minors, and Exemption – 17 ME Rev Stat § 2911(2)
Elementary Course of Study – 20-A ME Rev Stat § 4711

Health and P.E. – 20-A ME Rev Stat § 4723
History Instruction – 20-A ME Rev Stat § 4706; beginning 7/1/2023 see § 4706
Instruction Requirements – 20-A ME Rev Stat §§ 4701 to 4710-B
Junior / Middle School Course of Study – 20-A ME Rev Stat § 4712
ME Sample FOIA Request – National Freedom of Information Coalition
Open Meetings – 1 ME Rev Stat §§ 400 to 521
Open Records Act – 1 ME Rev Stat § 408-A
Policy on Education – 20-A ME Rev Stat § 2
Secondary Schools, Requirements – 20-A ME Rev Stat § 4721

Code of Maine Rules (05 – Department of Education) –
https://regulations.justia.com/states/maine/05/
Maine Department of Education & State Board of Education –
https://www.maine.gov/doe/
Maine State Bar Association – https://www.mainebar.org/

MARYLAND

The Constitution of the State of Maryland
Declaration of Rights
Article VIII – Education
https://law.justia.com/constitution/maryland/

Maryland General Assembly – https://mgaleg.maryland.gov/
Maryland State Laws – https://law.justia.com/codes/maryland/
Maryland School Laws (Education Code) –
https://law.justia.com/codes/maryland/2021/education/

Sample of Maryland Education-Related Laws
To locate the laws below, go to the Maryland School Laws link above and search for the citation that interests you by clicking on the appropriate chapters and subchapters as you wind your way to the law. You can also enter the terms "Justia," "Maryland," and the "numeric portion of the citation" in your search bar. Be sure to look at the most recent version of the law.

Behavioral Health Service – MD Educ Code Ann § 7-438
Course Descriptions and Alternatives – MD Educ Code Ann § 7-112
Criminal Law; Obscenity – MD Criminal Law Code Ann § 11-201 to 211; Exemption – MD Criminal Law Code Ann § 11-210
Employee Right to Engage in Political Activity – MD Educ Code Ann § 4-129; Political Activities of Employees – MD Local Govt Code Ann §§ 1-301 to 306; Restrictions on Political Activities – MD Local Govt Code Ann § 1-304
Governor's P-20 Leadership Council – MD Educ Code Ann § 24-801
MD Sample FOIA Request – National Freedom of Information Coalition
Open Meetings Act – MD Gen Provisions Code Ann §§ 3-101 to 3-501; § 3-303
Open Records Act – MD Gen Provisions Code Ann §§ 4-101 to 4-601; § 4-201

APPENDIX C: STATE AND LOCAL RESOURCES

Public Charter Schools – MD Educ Code Ann §§ 9-101 to 112
Student Data Privacy – MD Educ Code Ann § 4-131
Textbooks and Materials – MD Educ Code Ann § 7-106
World-Class Education – MD Educ Code Ann § 1-303

Code of Maryland Regulations (Title 13A – State Board of Education) –
https://regulations.justia.com/states/maryland/title-13a/
Maryland State Board and Department of Education –
https://www.marylandpublicschools.org/
Maryland State Bar Association – https://www.msba.org/

MASSACHUSETTS

The Constitution of the Commonwealth of Massachusetts
Part of the First – Declaration of Rights
Article VIII – Education
https://law.justia.com/constitution/massachusetts/

Massachusetts Legislature – https://malegislature.gov/
Massachusetts Laws of the Commonwealth –
https://law.justia.com/codes/maryland/
Massachusetts School Laws (Part I, Title XII – Education) –
https://law.justia.com/codes/massachusetts/2021/part-i/title-xii/

Sample of Massachusetts Education-Related Laws
To locate the laws below, go to the Massachusetts School Laws link above and search for the citation that interests you by clicking on the appropriate chapters and subchapters as you wind your way to the law. You can also enter the terms "Justia," "Massachusetts," and the "numeric portion of the citation" in your search bar. Be sure to look at the most recent version of the law.

Charter Schools – MA Gen L ch 71 § 89
Commissioner Duties – MA Gen L ch 69 § 1a; 6A § 16s
Crimes, Obscenity, Defense – MA Gen L ch 272 § 29; 272 § 31
Curriculum Framework – MA Gen L ch 69 § 1e
History and Social Science – MA Gen L ch 71 § 2; Genocide – 71 § 98
MA Sample FOIA Request – National Freedom of Information Coalition
Open Meetings Law – MA Gen L ch 30a §§ 18 to 25; 30a § 20
Open Records Law – MA Gen L ch 66 §§ 1 to 21; 66 § 10
Requested Courses, Approval – MA Gen L ch 71 § 13
Restrictions on Teachers' Political Rights – MA Gen L ch 71 § 44
Sex Education and Notice to Parents – MA Gen L ch 71 § 32a; Advisory Committees – 71 § 38o (38 followed by lower case letter "o")

Code of Massachusetts Regulations (603 – Department of Elementary and
Secondary Education) –
https://regulations.justia.com/states/massachusetts/603-cmr/
Massachusetts State Board and Department of Education –
https://www.doe.mass.edu/
Massachusetts Bar Association – https://www.masslawhelp.com/

MICHIGAN

The Constitution of the State of Michigan
Article I – Declaration of Rights
Article VIII – Education
https://law.justia.com/constitution/michigan/

Michigan Legislature – https://legislature.mi.gov/
Michigan State Laws – https://law.justia.com/codes/michigan/
Michigan School Laws (Chapters 380 and 388 – Revised School Code and
School Aid) – https://law.justia.com/codes/michigan/2021/chapter-380/

Sample of Michigan Education-Related Laws
To locate the laws below, go to the Michigan School Laws link above and search for the citation that interests you by clicking on the appropriate chapters and sub-chapters as you wind your way to the law. You can also enter the terms "Justia," "Michigan," and the "numeric portion of the citation" in your search bar. Be sure to look at the most recent version of the law.

Compact for Education – MI Comp L §§ 388.1301 to 388.1304; 388.1301
Crimes, Obscenity – MI Comp L §§ 751.361 to 370; 752.365; Exemption – 752.367
Critical Health Problems Education Act – MI Comp L §§ 388.381 to 388.385; 388.383
MI Sample FOIA Request – National Freedom of Information Coalition
Oath of All Teachers – MI Comp L §§ 388; 388.401; 388.402
Open Meetings Act – MI Comp L §§ 15.261 to 15.275; 15.263
Open Records Act – MI Comp L §§ 15.231 to 15.236; Public Records – 15.233
Private, Denominational, and Parochial Schools – MI Comp L § 388.551 to 388.558
Save Our Students Act – MI Comp L §§ 380.1891 to 380.1895; 380.1893
State Board of Education – MI Comp L §§ 388.1001 to 388.1017; Rules – 388.1015
Student Online Personal Protection – MI Comp L § 388.1291 to 1295; 388.1295
Transfer of Powers and Duties to P-20 Leadership Council – MI Comp L § 388.1581

Michigan Administrative Code (Department of Education)
https://regulations.justia.com/states/michigan/education/
Michigan Department of Education & State Board of Education –
https://www.michigan.gov/mde/
State Bar of Michigan – https://www.michbar.org/

MINNESOTA

The Constitution of the State of Minnesota
Article I – Bill of Rights
Article XIII – Miscellaneous Subjects, Section I. Uniform System of Public Schools
https://law.justia.com/constitution/minnesota/

Minnesota State Legislature – https://www.leg.mn.gov/
Minnesota State Laws – https://law.justia.com/codes/minnesota/
Minnesota School Laws (Chapter 120-129C – Education Code: Prekindergarten – Grade 12) – https://law.justia.com/codes/minnesota/2022/chapters-120-129c/

Sample of Minnesota Education-Related Laws
To locate the laws below, go to the Minnesota School Laws link above and search for the citation that interests you by clicking on the appropriate chapters and sub-chapters as you wind your way to the law. You can also enter the terms "Justia," "Minnesota," and the "numeric portion of the citation" in your search bar. Be sure to look at the most recent version of the law.

American Heritage, No censorship – MN Stat § 120B.235
Charter Schools – MN Stat §§ 124E.01 to 124E.26
Computers Contracts – MN Stat § 125B.022; Advertising Opt-Out – MN Stat § 25B.022(a)(5)
Crimes, Obscenity – MN Stat § 617.293; 617.294; Definitions – 617.292; Exemptions – 617.295
Limits on Testing – MN Stat § 120B.301
Mental Health Education – MN Stat § 120B.21
MN Sample FOIA Request – National Freedom of Information Coalition
Open Records Law – MN Stat § 15.17; Data Access – MN Stat § 13.03; Records – 138.17
Open Meeting Law – MI Stat §§ 13D.001 to 13D.08; 13D.01
Parental Curriculum Review – MN Stat § 120B.20
Required Academic Standards – MN Stat § 120B.021

Minnesota Administrative Rules (Agency 129 & 130 – Education Department & State Board) – https://regulations.justia.com/states/minnesota/
Minnesota State Board & Department of Education – https://education.mn.gov/MDE/
Minnesota State Bar Association – https://www.mnbar.org/

MISSISSIPPI

The Constitution of the State of Mississippi
Article III – Bill of Rights
Article VIII – Education
https://law.justia.com/constitution/mississippi/

Mississippi Legislature – http://www.legislature.ms.gov/
Mississippi State Laws – https://law.justia.com/codes/mississippi/
Mississippi School Laws (Title 37 – Education) –
   https://law.justia.com/codes/mississippi/2020/title-37/

Sample of Mississippi Education-Related Laws
To locate the laws below, go to the Mississippi School Laws link above and search for the citation that interests you by clicking on the appropriate chapters and sub-chapters as you wind your way to the law. You can also enter the terms "Justia," "Mississippi," and the "numeric portion of the citation" in your search bar. Be sure to look at the most recent version of the law.

Charter Schools – MS Code §§ 37-28-1 to 37-28-63
Crimes, Morals and Decency – MS Code §§ 97-29-101 to 97-29-109;
   Exemption – 97-101-107
Duties of State Superintendent – MS Code § 37-3-11
Duties District Superintendent – MS Code § 37-9-14
Health – 37-13-131 to 37-13-137
MS Sample FOIA Request – National Freedom of Information Coalition
Open Meetings Law – MS Code §§ 25-41-1 to 25-41-17; 25-41-5
Open Records Law – MS Code §§ 25-61-1 to 25-61-19; 25-61-5
Religious Freedom Restoration Act – MS Code § 11-61-1
Sex Education – MS Code §§ 37-13-171 to 37-13-175; Parent Notice– 37-12-173
State Board of Education Appeals – MS Code § 37-1-5
Student Religious Liberties Act – MS Code §§ 37-12-1 to 37-12-15
Textbooks – MS Code §§ 37-43-1 to 37-43-59; Rating Committee – 37-43-21; Retention of Copies – 37-43-25; Selection by Local School District – 37-43-31

Mississippi Administrative Code (Titles 7 & 9 – Education) –
   https://regulations.justia.com/states/mississippi/title-7/
Mississippi State Board & Department of Education – https://www.mdek12.org/
Mississippi Bar Association – https://www.msbar.org/

MISSOURI

The Constitution of the State of Missouri
Article I – Bill of Rights
Article IX – Education
https://law.justia.com/constitution/missouri/

Missouri General Assembly – https://www.mo.gov/government/legislative-branch/
Missouri State Laws – https://law.justia.com/codes/missouri/
Missouri School Laws (Title XI – Education and Libraries) –
   https://law.justia.com/codes/missouri/2021/title-xi/

Sample of Missouri Education-Related Laws
To locate the laws below, go to the Missouri School Laws link above and search for the citation that interests you by clicking on the appropriate chapters and subchapters as you wind your way to the law. You can also enter the terms "Justia," "Missouri," and the "numeric portion of the citation" in your search bar. Be sure to look at the most recent version of the law.

American History and Constitutions – MO Rev Stat § 170.011
Antibullying Policy Required – MO Rev Stat § 160.775
Duties of Commissioner – MO Rev Stat § 161.122
Human Sexuality and Parental Rights – MO Rev Stat § 170.015
Instruction Materials and Subjects – MO Rev Stat §§ 170.005 to 170.350
MO Sample FOIA Request – National Freedom of Information Coalition
Oath of Office – MO Rev Stat § 161.042
Open Records Law – MO Rev Stat §§ 610.010 to 610.035; MO Rev Stat § 610.023
Open Meetings Law – MO Rev Stat § 610.020
Religious Freedom Restoration Act – MO Rev Stat § 1.302
School Laws, Neglect/Refusal to Comply, Misdemeanor – MO Rev Stat § 162.091
Social and Emotional Education, Voluntary Pilot Project – MO Rev Stat § 170.020
State Board Powers and Duties– MO Rev Stat § 161.092
Student Religious Liberties Act – MO Rev Stat § 160.2500
U.S. Flag, Pledge of Allegiance, and Exemption – MO Rev Stat § 171.021

Missouri Code of State Regulations (Title 5 – Department of Elementary & Secondary Education) – https://regulations.justia.com/states/missouri/title-5/
Missouri State Board & Department of Education – https://dese.mo.gov/
Missouri Bar – https://mobar.org/

MONTANA

The Constitution of the State of Montana
Article II – Declaration of Rights
Article X – Education & Public Lands
https://law.justia.com/constitution/montana/

Montana State Legislature – https://leg.mt.gov/
Montana State Laws – https://law.justia.com/codes/montana/
Montana School Laws (Title 20 – Education) –
https://law.justia.com/codes/montana/2022/title-20/

Sample of Montana Education-Related Laws
To locate the laws below, go to the Montana School Laws link above and search for the citation that interests you by clicking on the appropriate chapters and subchapters as you wind your way to the law. You can also enter the terms "Justia," "Montana," and the "numeric portion of the citation" in your search bar. Be sure to look at the most recent version of the law.

Board of Education Powers and Duties – MT Code § 20-2-121
Crimes, Obscenity, Minors – MT Code § 45-8-201; 45-8-206; Exemption – 45-8-206(2)(b)
Immunizations Required – MT Code § 20-5-403; Exemption – 20-5-405
MT Sample FOIA Request – National Freedom of Information Coalition
Open Meetings Law – MT Code §§ 2-3-201 to 2-3-221; 2-3-203; Public – 2-3-103
Open Records Law – MT Code §§ 2-6-1001 to 1033; 2-6-1003
Religious Freedom Restoration Act – MT Code § 27-33-101 to 105
School Elections and Elector Challenges – MT Code §§ 20-20-303; 13-13-301(2)
School Library Book Selection – MT Code § 20-7-204
Superintendent Powers & Duties – MT Code § 20-3-106
U.S. Civics Test – MT Code § 20-7-119
Violation of School Laws – MT Code §§ 20-1-207; Enforcement – 20-1-209

Administrative Rules of Montana (Department 10 – Education) –
https://regulations.justia.com/states/montana/department-10/
Montana Office of Public Instruction – https://opi.mt.gov/
Montana Board of Public Education – https://bpe.mt.gov/
State Bar of Montana – https://www.montanabar.org/

NEBRASKA

The Constitution of the State of Nebraska
Article I – Personal Rights
Article VII – Education
https://law.justia.com/constitution/nebraska/

Nebraska Legislature – https://nebraskalegislature.gov/
Nebraska State Laws – https://law.justia.com/codes/nebraska/
Nebraska School Laws (Chapter 79 – Schools) –
https://law.justia.com/codes/nebraska/2022/chapter-79/

Sample of Nebraska Education-Related Laws
To locate the laws below, go to the Nebraska School Laws link above and search for the citation that interests you by clicking on the appropriate chapters and subchapters as you wind your way to the law. You can also enter the terms "Justia," "Nebraska," and the "numeric portion of the citation" in your search bar. Be sure to look at the most recent version of the law.

Academic Content Standards – NE Code §§ 79-760.01; 79-760.02
Commissioner Powers and Duties – NE Code § 79-305
Committee on American Civics – NE Code § 79-724
Crimes, Obscenity to Minors – NE Code §§ 28-807 et seq.; 28-808; Defense – 28-815(1)
NE Sample FOIA Request – National Freedom of Information Coalition
Open Meetings Law – NE Code §§ 84-1407 to 84-1415; 84-1408
Open Records Law – NE Code §§ 84-712 to 84-712.09; 84-712
Parent Involvement – NE Code §§ 79-530; 79-531; 79-532; 79-533

Rule, Regulation, or Policy, Waiver Authorized – NE Code § 79-750
School Textbooks – NE Code § 79-734; Textbook Contracts – 79-734.01
State Board Powers and Duties – NE Code § 79-318

Nebraska Administrative Code (Department of Education) –
https://regulations.justia.com/states/nebraska/education-department-of/
Nebraska Department of Education & State Board of Education –
https://www.education.ne.gov/
Nebraska State Bar Association – https://www.nebar.com/

NEVADA

The Constitution of the State of Nevada
Article I – Declaration of Rights
Article XI – Education
https://law.justia.com/constitution/nevada/

Nevada Legislature – https://www.leg.state.nv.us/
Nevada State Laws – https://law.justia.com/codes/nevada/
Nevada School Laws (Title 34 – Education) –
https://law.justia.com/codes/nevada/2021/ (scroll to Title 34 – Education)

Sample of Nevada Education-Related Laws
To locate the laws below, go to the Nevada School Laws link above and search for the citation that interests you by clicking on the appropriate chapters and subchapters as you wind your way to the law. You can also enter the terms "Justia," "Nevada," and the "numeric portion of the citation" in your search bar. Be sure to look at the most recent version of the law.

Academics and Textbooks – NV Rev Stat §§ 389.003 to 389.880
Charter Schools – NV Rev Stat §§ 388A.010 to 388A.740
Crimes, Obscenity – NV Rev Stat §§ 201.015 et seq.; Exemptions – 201.237
Development of Academic Plan – NV Rev Stat §§ 388.165 to 388.227; 388.165
Educational Leader (Enforcement) – NV Rev Stat § 385.175
NV Sample FOIA Request – National Freedom of Information Coalition
Open Meetings Law – NV Stat §§ 241.015 to 241.040; 241-020
Open Records Law – NV Rev Stat §§ 239.001 to 239.340; 239.010
P-20W Advisory – NV Rev Stat §§ 400.010 to 400.045; 400.027
Required Instruction and Exceptions – NV Rev Stat §§ 389.054 to 389.077; 389.054
Written Notice of Courses – NV Rev Stat § 392.018

Nevada Administrative Code (Chapter 385 – Education State Administration) –
https://regulations.justia.com/states/nevada/chapter-385/
Nevada Department of Education & State Board of Education –
https://doe.nv.gov/
State Bar of Nevada – https://doe.nv.gov/

NEW HAMPSHIRE

The Constitution of the State of New Hampshire
Part First – Bill of Rights
Part Second – Form of Government, Encouragement of Literature, Trade, etc. Art. 83
https://law.justia.com/constitution/new-hampshire/

General Court of New Hampshire – https://www.gencourt.state.nh.us/
New Hampshire State Laws – https://law.justia.com/codes/new-hampshire/
New Hampshire School Laws (Title XV – Education) –
https://law.justia.com/codes/new-hampshire/2021/title-xv/

Sample of New Hampshire Education-Related Laws
To locate the laws below, go to the New Hampshire School Laws link above and search for the citation that interests you by clicking on the appropriate chapters and sub-chapters as you wind your way to the law. You can also enter the terms "Justia," "New Hampshire," and the "numeric portion of the citation" in your search bar. Be sure to look at the most recent version of the law.

Access to Public School Programs, Home Educated – NH Rev Stat § 193:1-c
Chartered Public Schools – NH Rev Stat §§ 194-B:1 to 194-B:22
Crimes, Obscenity – NH Rev Stat §§ 650:1 to 650:6; Exemption – 650:3
Educational Content – NH Rev Stat § 193-E:2-a
NH Sample FOIA Request – National Freedom of Information Coalition
Open Meetings Law – NH Rev Stat § 91-A:4
Open Records Law – NH Rev Stat § 91-A:2
Performance and Accountability – NH Rev Stat §§ 193-H:1 to 193-H:5
Prohibition on Teaching Discrimination – NH Rev Stat §§ 193:38 to 193:40
Rulemaking Authority and Standards – NH Rev Stat § 186:8
School Patriot Act – NH Rev Stat § 194:15-c
State Board Duties – NH Rev Stat § 186:11

New Hampshire Code of Administrative Rules (Board of Education) –
https://regulations.justia.com/states/new-hampshire/ed/
New Hampshire State Board & Department of Education –
https://www.education.nh.gov/
New Hampshire Bar Association – https://www.nhbar.org/

NEW JERSEY

The New Jersey State Constitution
Article I – Rights & Privileges
Article 8, § IV, ¶ 1.
https://law.justia.com/constitution/new-jersey/

New Jersey Legislature – https://www.njleg.state.nj.us/

New Jersey State Laws – https://law.justia.com/codes/new-jersey/
New Jersey School Laws (Title 18A – Education) –
https://law.justia.com/codes/new-jersey/2021/title-18a/

Sample of New Jersey Education-Related Laws
To locate the laws below, go to the New Jersey School Laws link above and search for the citation that interests you by clicking on the appropriate chapters and subchapters as you wind your way to the law. You can also enter the terms "Justia," "New Jersey," and the "numeric portion of the citation" in your search bar. Be sure to look at the most recent version of the law.

AIDS Prevention– NJ Rev Stat §§ 18A:35-4.19 to 18A:35-4.22
Charter Schools – NJ Rev Stat §§ 18A:36A-1 to 18A:36A-18; 18A:36A-2
Courses of Study – NJ Rev Stat §§ 18A:35-1 to 18A:35-42; Noncompliance – 18A:35-38
Medical Treatment, Parent Objections – NJ Rev Stat § 18A:35-4.8
NJ Sample FOIA Request – National Freedom of Information Coalition
Open Public Meetings Act – NJ Rev Stat §§ 10:4-6 to 10:4-21; 10:4-7
Open Public Records Act – NJ Rev Stat §§ 47:1A-1 to 47:1A-18; 47:1A-1
Parent's Conflict with Conscience – NJ Rev Stat § 18A:35-4.7
School Ethics – NJ Rev Stat §§ 18A:12-21 to 18A:12-34; 18A:12-24.1
Student's Right to Freedom of Speech and Press – NJ Rev Stat § 18A:36-44
School Surveys, Parent Consent – NJ Rev Stat §§ 18A:36-34; Voluntary 18A:36-34.1
Textbook Selection – NJ Rev Stat § 18A:34-1

New Jersey Administrative Code (Title 6A – Education) –
https://regulations.justia.com/states/new-jersey/title-6a/
New Jersey State Board & State Department of Education –
https://www.nj.gov/education/
New Jersey State Bar Association – https://tcms.njsba.com/

NEW MEXICO

The Constitution of the State of New Mexico
Article II – Bill of Rights
Article XII – Education
https://law.justia.com/constitution/new-mexico/

New Mexico Legislature – https://www.nmlegis.gov/
New Mexico State Laws – https://law.justia.com/codes/new-mexico/
New Mexico School Laws (Chapter 22 – Public Schools) –
https://law.justia.com/codes/new-mexico/2021/chapter-22/

Sample of New Mexico Education-Related Laws
To locate the laws below, go to the New Mexico School Laws link above and search for the citation that interests you by clicking on the appropriate chapters and subchapters as you wind your way to the law. You can also enter the terms "Justia,"

"New Mexico," and the "numeric portion of the citation" in your search bar. Be sure to look at the most recent version of the law.

Charter School Districts – NM Stat §§ 22-8E-1 to 22-8E-8
Charter Schools – NM Stat §§ 22-8B-1 to 22-8B-17.1
Core Curriculum – NM Stat § 22-13-1.5
Course of Instruction– NM Stat §§ 22-13-1 to 22-13-34
Instructional Material, Review – NM Stat § 22-15-8
Local School Board Powers and Duties – NM Stat § 22-5-4
Meditation in Public School – NM Stat § 22-27-2
NM Sample FOIA Request – National Freedom of Information Coalition
Open Meetings Act – NM Stat §§ 10-15-1 to 10-15-4; 10-15-1
Open Records Act – NM Stat §§ 14-2-1 to 14-2-12; 14-2-8
Religious Freedom Restoration Act – NM Stat §§ 28-22-1 to 28-22-5
School Athletics Equity – NM Stat §§ 22-31-1 to 22-31-6
Subject Areas Required – NM Stat § 22-13-1

New Mexico Administrative Code (Title 5 – Primary and Secondary Education) –
https://regulations.justia.com/states/new-mexico/title-6/
New Mexico State Board & Public Education Department –
https://webnew.ped.state.nm.us/
State Bar of New Mexico – https://www.sbnm.org/

NEW YORK

The Constitution of the State of New York
Article I – Bill of Rights
Article XI – Education
https://law.justia.com/constitution/new-york/

New York State Assembly – https://nyassembly.gov/
New York State Laws – https://law.justia.com/codes/new-york/
New York School Laws (EDN- Education) –
https://law.justia.com/codes/new-york/2021/edn/

Sample of New York Education-Related Laws
To locate the laws below, go to the New York School Laws link above and search for the citation that interests you by clicking on the appropriate chapters and subchapters as you wind your way to the law. You can also enter the terms "Justia," "New York," and the "numeric portion of the citation" in your search bar. Be sure to look at the most recent version of the law.

Charter Schools – NY Educ L §§ 2850 to 2857
Discrimination Prohibited – NY Educ L §§ 3201; 3201A
Instruction Required – NY Educ L § 3204
Medical and Health Service – NY Educ L §§ 901 to 923; 901

NY Sample FOIA Request – National Freedom of Information Coalition
Open Meetings Law – NY Pub Off L §§ 100 to 111; 103
Open Records Law – NY Pub Off L §§ 84 to 90; Purpose – 84
Parental Duties – NY Educ L § 3212
Penal Law, Obscenity to Minors – NY Educ L § 235; Defense – NY Educ L § 235.15(1)
Standardized Testing – NY Educ L §§ 340 to 348
Textbook Access – NY Educ L §§ 720 to 724

New York Codes, Rules, and Regulations (Title 8 – Education Department) –
https://regulations.justia.com/states/new-york/title-8/
New York State Board of Education & State Education Department –
http://www.nysed.gov/
New York State Bar Association – https://nysba.org/

NORTH CAROLINA

The Constitution of the State of North Carolina
Article I – Declaration of Rights
Article IX – Education
https://law.justia.com/constitution/north-carolina/

North Carolina General Assembly – https://www.ncleg.gov/
North Carolina State Laws – https://law.justia.com/codes/north-carolina/
North Carolina School Laws (Chapter 115C – Elementary & Secondary Education) –

https://law.justia.com/codes/north-carolina/2021/chapter-115c/

Sample of North Carolina Education-Related Laws
To locate the laws below, go to the North Carolina School Laws link above and search
for the citation that interests you by clicking on the appropriate chapters and subchapters as you wind your way to the law. You can also enter the terms "Justia,"
"North Carolina," and the "numeric portion of the citation" in your search bar. Be
sure to look at the most recent version of the law.

B-3 Interagency Council – NC Gen Stat §§ 115C-64.25 to 115C-64.28; 115C-64.25
Charter Schools – NC Gen Stat §§ 115C-218 to 115C-218.115
Crimes, Harmful Material to Minors – NC Gen Stat §§ 14-190.13 to 14-190.20; Defenses –
14-190.15(c)(2)
NC Sample FOIA Request – NC FOIA National Freedom of Information Coalition
Open Meetings Law – NC Gen Stat §§ 143-318.9 to 143-318.18; 143-318.10
Open Records Law – NC Gen Stat §§ 132-1 to 132-11; 132-1
Parent Advisory Council – NC Gen Stat § 115C-238.69
Reproductive Health and Safety – NC Gen Stat § 115C-81.30
State Board Powers and Duties – NC Gen Stat § 115C-12
Student Prayer and Religious Activity – NC Gen Stat §§ 115C-407.30 to 115C-407.33

Textbooks – NC Gen Stat §§ 115C-85 to 115C-102; 115C-98

North Carolina Administrative Code (Title 16 – State Board of Education) –
https://regulations.justia.com/states/north-carolina/title-16/
North Carolina Department of Public Instruction – https://www.dpi.nc.gov/
North Carolina State Board of Education –
https://www.dpi.nc.gov/about-dpi/state-board-education
North Carolina Bar Association – https://www.ncbar.org/

NORTH DAKOTA

The Constitution of the State of North Dakota
Article I – Declaration of Rights
Article VIII – Education
https://law.justia.com/constitution/north-dakota/

North Dakota Legislative Branch – https://www.ndlegis.gov/
North Dakota State Laws – https://law.justia.com/codes/north-dakota/
North Dakota School Laws (Title 15.1 – Elementary & Secondary Education) –
https://law.justia.com/codes/north-dakota/2021/title-15/

Sample of North Dakota Education-Related Laws
To locate the laws below, go to the North Dakota School Laws link above and search for the citation that interests you by clicking on the appropriate chapters and subchapters as you wind your way to the law. You can also enter the terms "Justia," "North Dakota," and the "numeric portion of the citation" in your search bar. Be sure to look at the most recent version of the law.

Criminal Code, Obscenity – N.D.C.C. §§ 12.1-27.1; Exceptions – 12.1-27.1-11
Curriculum and Testing – N.D.C.C. §§ 15.1-21-01 to 15.1-21-27
Home Education – N.D.C.C. §§ 15.1-23-01 to 15.1-23-19
ND Sample FOIA Request – National Freedom of Information Coalition
Open Meetings / Records Law – N.D. Const. art XI, § 5; N.D.C.C. §§ 44-04-01 to 44-04-33
Patriotic Society – N.D.C.C. § 15.1-06-14.1
Protection of Student Data – N.D.C.C. § 15.1-07-25.3
School Boards – N.D.C.C. §§ 15.1-09-01 to 15.1-09-60
State Board of Education – N.D.C.C. §§ 15.1-01-01 to 15.1-01-04
Students and Safety – N.D.C.C. §§ 15.1-19-01 to 15.1-19-28
Superintendent – N.D.C.C. §§ 15.1-02-01 to 15.1-02-22

North Dakota Administrative Code (Title 68 – Public School Education)
https://regulations.justia.com/states/north-dakota/title-68/
North Dakota Department of Public Instruction – https://www.nd.gov/dpi/
North Dakota State Board of Education – https://www.nd.gov/dpi/familiescommunity/community/boards-and-committees/state-board-public-school-education

State Bar Association of North Dakota - https://www.sband.org/

OHIO

The Constitution of the State of Ohio
Article I - Bill of Rights
Article VI - Education
https://law.justia.com/constitution/ohio/

Ohio Legislature - https://www.legislature.ohio.gov/
Ohio State Laws - https://law.justia.com/codes/ohio/
Ohio School Laws (Title 33 - Education-Libraries) -
 https://law.justia.com/codes/ohio/2021/title-33/

Sample of Ohio Education-Related Laws
To locate the laws below, go to the Ohio School Laws link above and search for the citation that interests you by clicking on the appropriate chapters and subchapters as you wind your way to the law. You can also enter the terms "Justia," "Ohio," and the "numeric portion of the citation" in your search bar. Be sure to look at the most recent version of the law.

Academic Standards, Curriculum - Ohio Rev Code § 3301.079
Charter or Community Schools - Ohio Rev Code §§ 3304.01 to 33014.99
Crimes, Sex Offenses, Pandering Obscenity, Defenses - Ohio Rev Code § 2907.32(B)
No Agreements to Cede Control of Content Standards; No Purchase of PARCC
 Assessments - Ohio Rev Code § 3301.078
OH Sample FOIA Request - National Freedom of Information Coalition
Parental Review of Instructional Materials - Ohio Rev Code § 3313.212
Open Meetings Law - Ohio Rev Code §§ 121.22; Education - 3301.05
Open Records Law (including some Nonprofits) - Ohio Rev Code § 149.431
Selection of Textbooks by Board - Ohio Rev Code § 3329.08
State Board Powers and Duties - Ohio Rev Code § 3301.07
Student Religious Liberties Act - Ohio Rev Code §§ 3320.01 to 3320.03; 3320.03

Ohio Administrative Code (Title 3301 - Department of Education) -
 https://regulations.justia.com/states/ohio/title-3301
Ohio Department of Education - https://education.ohio.gov/
Ohio State Board of Education - https://education.ohio.gov/State-Board
Ohio State Bar Association - https://www.ohiobar.org/

OKLAHOMA

The Constitution of the State of Oklahoma
Article II - Bill of Rights
Article VIII - Education
https://law.justia.com/constitution/oklahoma/

Oklahoma State Legislature – http://www.oklegislature.gov/
Oklahoma State Laws – https://law.justia.com/codes/oklahoma/
Oklahoma School Laws (Title 70 – Schools) –
   https://law.justia.com/codes/oklahoma/2022/title-70/

Sample of Oklahoma Education-Related Laws
To locate the laws below, go to the Oklahoma School Laws link above and search for the citation that interests you by clicking on the appropriate chapters and subchapters as you wind your way to the law. You can also enter the terms "Justia," "Oklahoma," and the "numeric portion of the citation" in your search bar. Be sure to look at the most recent version of the law.

Charter Schools – 70 OK Stat §§ 70-3-130 to 70-3-145.8; 70-3-131
Courses for Instruction – 70 OK Stat § 70-11-103
Local Textbook Committee – 70 OK Stat §§ 70-16-111; 70-16-111.1
OK Sample FOIA Request – National Freedom of Information Coalition
Open Meetings Act – 25 OK Stat §§ 25-301 to 25-314; 25-302
Open Records Act – 51 OK Stat §§ 24A.1 to 24A.33; 51-24A.2
Plan of Education Development – 70 OK Stat § 70-3-104.5
Psychiatric / Psychological Exams, Parent Consent – 70 OK Stat § 70-11-107
Religious Freedom Act – 51 OK Stat §§ 251 to 258
School Districts – 70 OK Stat §§ 70-5-106; Powers and Duties – 70-5-117
Sex Education – 70 OK Stat § 70-11-105.1
State Department of Education – 70 OK Stat § 70-1-105
State Superintendent Powers and Duties – 70 OK Stat § 70-1-107.1

Oklahoma Administrative Code (Title 210 – State Department of Education) –
   https://regulations.justia.com/states/oklahoma/title-210/
Oklahoma State Board & Department of Education – https://sde.ok.gov/
Oklahoma Bar Association – https://www.okbar.org/

OREGON

The Constitution of the State of Oregon
Article I – Bill of Rights
Article VIII – Education & School Lands
https://law.justia.com/constitution/oregon/

Oregon State Legislature – https://www.oregonlegislature.gov/
Oregon State Laws – https://law.justia.com/codes/oregon/
Oregon School Laws (Volume 9 – Education & Culture) –
   https://law.justia.com/codes/oregon/2021/volume-09/

Sample of Oregon Education-Related Laws
To locate the laws below, go to the Oregon School Laws link above and search for the citation that interests you by clicking on the appropriate chapters and subchapters as you wind your way to the law. You can also enter the terms "Justia," "Oregon,"

and the "numeric portion of the citation" in your search bar. Be sure to look at the most recent version of the law.

Books and Instructional Materials – OR Rev Stat § 337
Constitution and U.S. History – OR Rev Stat § 336.057
Crimes, Harmful Materials– OR Rev Stat §§ 167.051 to .105; Defenses – 167.085(2)
Mental Health Screenings and Opt-Out – OR Rev Stat § 336.216
Nondiscriminatory Curriculum – OR Rev Stat § 336.082
Open Meetings Law – OR Rev Stat § 192.630
Open Records Law – OR Rev Stat §§ 192.311 to 192.513; 192.314
OR Sample FOIA Request – National Freedom of Information Coalition
Public Charter Schools – OR Rev Stat § 338
Released Time for Religious Instruction – OR Rev Stat § 339.420
Required Courses and Excusal – OR Rev Stat § 336.035(2)

Oregon Administrative Rules (Chapters 414, 423, 581, 586, and 705) –
    https://regulations.justia.com/states/oregon/
Oregon Department of Education – https://www.oregon.gov/ode/
Oregon State Board of Education –
    https://www.oregon.gov/ode/about-us/stateboard/
Oregon State Bar – https://www.osbar.org/

PENNSYLVANIA

The Constitution of the Commonwealth of Pennsylvania
Article I – Declaration of Rights
Article III – Legislation; B. Education; Section 14 – Public School System
https://law.justia.com/constitution/pennsylvania/

Pennsylvania General Assembly – https://www.legis.state.pa.us/
Pennsylvania Commonwealth Laws – https://law.justia.com/codes/pennsylvania/
Pennsylvania School Laws (Title 24 – Education) –
    https://law.justia.com/codes/pennsylvania/2021/title-24/

Sample of Pennsylvania Education-Related Laws
To locate the laws below, go to the Pennsylvania School Laws link above and search for the citation that interests you by clicking on the appropriate chapters and subchapters as you wind your way to the law. You can also enter the terms "Justia," "Pennsylvania," and the "numeric portion of the citation" in your search bar. Be sure to look at the most recent version of the law.

Crimes, Obscenity – 18 PA Cons Stat § 5903; Exemptions – 5903(j)
Open Meetings Law – 65 PA Con Stat §§ 701 to 716; 65 PA Con Stat § 704
Open Records Law – 65 PA Con Stat §§ 67.101 et seq.
PA Sample FOIA Request – National Freedom of Information Coalition
Religious Freedom Protection Act – 71 PA Con Stat §§ 2401 to 2407

Unlike most states, Pennsylvania school laws are few. Most guidance on Pennsylvania public schools is provided in the **Pennsylvania Code (Title 22 – Education)**. https://regulations.justia.com/states/pennsylvania/title-22/. Go to the Pennsylvania Code link above and search for the citation that interests you by clicking on the appropriate chapters and subchapters as you wind your way to the rule. You can also enter the terms "Justia," "Pennsylvania," and the "numeric portion of the citation" in your search bar. Be sure to look at the most recent version of the rule.

Academic Standards, Curriculum, and Instruction – 22 PA Code §§ 4.20 to 4.29
Charter Schools and Cyber Charter Schools – 22 PA Code §§ 711.1 to 711.10
Educators' Code of Practice and Conduct – 22 PA Code §§ 235.1 to 235.5c
Freedom of Expression – 22 PA Code § 12.9
Purpose of Public Education – 22 PA Code § 4.11
Safe Schools – 22 PA Code §§ 10.1 to 10.25
Student Rights and Responsibilities – 22 PA. Code § 12.1

Pennsylvania Code (Title 22 – Education) –
https://regulations.justia.com/states/pennsylvania/title-22/
Pennsylvania Department of Education – https://www.education.pa.gov/
Pennsylvania State Board of Education – https://www.stateboard.education.pa.gov/
Pennsylvania Bar Association – https://www.pabar.org/

RHODE ISLAND

The Constitution of the State of Rhode Island
https://law.justia.com/constitution/rhode-island/
Article I – Declaration of Certain Constitutional Rights & Principles
Article XII – Of Education

Rhode Island Gen. Assembly – https://www.rilegislature.gov/
Rhode Island State Laws – https://law.justia.com/codes/rhode-island/
Rhode Island School Laws (Title 16 – Education) –
https://law.justia.com/codes/rhode-island/2022/title-16/

Sample of Rhode Island Education-Related Laws
To locate the laws below, go to the Rhode Island School Laws link above and search for the citation that interests you by clicking on the appropriate chapters and subchapters as you wind your way to the law. You can also enter the terms "Justia," "Rhode Island," and the "numeric portion of the citation" in your search bar. Be sure to look at the most recent version of the law.

AIDS Education Program and Exemption – RI Gen L § 16-22-17
Board of Education – RI Gen L §§ 6-97-1 to 16-97-10
Charter Public Schools – RI Gen L §§ 16-77-1 to16-77-6.1
Curriculum – RI Gen L §§ 16-22-1 to 16-22-33

Duties of Commission – RI Gen L § 16-1-5
Duties of Commissioner – RI Gen L § 16-2-11
Internet Filtering in Schools – RI Gen L § 16-21-6.1
Open Meetings Law – RI Gen L §§ 42-46-1 to 42-46-14; 42-46-3
Open Records Law – RI Gen L § 38-2-3
Religious Freedom Restoration Act – RI Gen L § 42-80.1-1 to 42-80.1-4
RI Sample FOIA Request – National Freedom of Information Coalition
Rights and Duties of Teachers – RI Gen L §§ 16-12-1 to 16-12-11

Rhode Island Code of Regulations (Title 200 – Board of Education) –
https://regulations.justia.com/states/rhode-island/title-200/
Rhode Island Department of Education – https://www.ride.ri.gov/
Rhode Island State Board of Education – https://www.ride.ri.gov/boardofeducation/
Rhode Island Bar Association – https://ribar.com/

SOUTH CAROLINA

The Constitution of the State of South Carolina
Article I – Declaration of Rights
Article XI – Public Education
https://law.justia.com/constitution/south-carolina/

South Carolina Legislature – https://www.scstatehouse.gov/
South Carolina State Laws – https://law.justia.com/codes/south-carolina/
South Carolina School Laws (Title 59 – Education) –
https://law.justia.com/codes/south-carolina/2021/title-59/

Sample of South Carolina Education-Related Laws
To locate the laws below, go to the South Carolina School Laws link above and search for the citation that interests you by clicking on the appropriate chapters and subchapters as you wind your way to the law. You can also enter the terms "Justia," "South Carolina," and the "numeric portion of the citation" in your search bar. Be sure to look at the most recent version of the law.

Charter Schools – SC Code §§ 59-40-10 to 59-40-240
Crimes, Harmful Material to Minors, Exemption – SC Code § 16-15-385(c)(2)
Health Education – SC Code §§ 59-25-5 to 59-25-90; Exemptions 59-25-50
Open Records Law– SC Code §§ 30-4-10 to 30-4-165; Meetings – 30-4-60; 30-4-70
Parental Involvement Program – SC Code § 59-1-454
Religious Freedom Restoration Act – SC Code §§ 1-32-10 to 1-32-60
Religious Viewpoints Anti-Discrimination Act – SC Code § 59-1-435
SC Sample FOIA Request – National Freedom of Information Coalition
State Superintendent Duties – SC Code § 59-3-30
Subjects of Instruction – SC Code §§ 59-29-10 to 59-29-570

Textbooks – SC Code §§ 59-31-10 to 610; Public Review and Hearings – 59-31-610
U.S. and State Flags – SC Code § 59-1-320

South Carolina Code of Regulations (Chapter 43 – State Board of Education) –
https://regulations.justia.com/states/south-carolina/chapter-43/
South Carolina Department of Education – https://ed.sc.gov/
South Carolina State Board of Education – https://ed.sc.gov/state-board/
South Carolina Bar Association – https://www.scbar.org/

SOUTH DAKOTA

The Constitution of the State of South Dakota
Article VI – Bill of Rights
Article VIII – Education & School Lands
https://law.justia.com/constitution/south-dakota/

South Dakota Legislature – https://sdlegislature.gov/
South Dakota State Laws – https://law.justia.com/codes/south-dakota/
South Dakota School Laws (Title 13 – Education) –
https://law.justia.com/codes/south-dakota/2021/title-13/

Sample of South Dakota Education-Related Laws
To locate the laws below, go to the South Dakota School Laws link above and search for the citation that interests you by clicking on the appropriate chapters and subchapters as you wind your way to the law. You can also enter the terms "Justia," "South Dakota," and the "numeric portion of the citation" in your search bar. Be sure to look at the most recent version of the law.

Character Development Instruction – SD Codified L §13-33-6.1
Crimes, Obscenity – SD Codified L §§ 22-24-27 to 22-24-30; Defenses – 22-24-31(4)
Curriculum and Courses – SD Codified L §§ 13-33-1 to 13-33-30
High School Activities – SD Codified L §§ 13-36-1 to 13-36-14
Open Meetings Law – SD Codified L § 1-25-1
Open Records Law – SD Codified L §§ 1-27-1 to 1-27-48; 1-27-37
Released Time for Religious Instruction – SD Codified L § 13-33-10
Religious Freedom Restoration Act – SD Codified L §§ 1-1A-1 to 1-1A-4
Secretary of Education Duties – SD Codified L §§ 13-3-1 to 13-3-97
SD Sample FOIA Request – National Freedom of Information Coalition
Supervision of Students and Conduct – SD Codified L §§ 13-32-1 to 13-32-20
U.S. & State Constitutions – SD Codified L § 13-33-4

South Dakota Administrative Rules (Title 24 – Education) –
https://regulations.justia.com/states/south-dakota/title-24/
South Dakota Department of Education – https://doe.sd.gov/
South Dakota State Board of Education – https://boardsandcommissions.sd.gov/
State Bar of South Dakota – https://www.statebarofsouthdakota.com/

TENNESSEE

The Constitution of the State of Tennessee
Article I - Declaration of Rights
Article XI - Miscellaneous Provisions; Section 12 (Education Article)
https://law.justia.com/constitution/tennessee/

Tennessee General Assembly - https://www.capitol.tn.gov/
Tennessee State Laws - https://law.justia.com/codes/tennessee/
Tennessee School Laws (Title 49 - Education) -
https://law.justia.com/codes/tennessee/2021/title-49/

Sample of Tennessee Education-Related Laws
To locate the laws below, go to the Tennessee School Laws link above and search for the citation that interests you by clicking on the appropriate chapters and subchapters as you wind your way to the law. You can also enter the terms "Justia," "Tennessee," and the "numeric portion of the citation" in your search bar. Be sure to look at the most recent version of the law.

Approved Textbooks and Materials - TN Code § 49-6-2202
Charter Schools - TN §§ 49-13-101 to 49-13-116
Crimes, Obscene Material to Minors, and Exception - TN Code § 39-17-902(e)
Curriculum - TN Code §§ 49-6-1001 to 49-6-1035
Extracurricular Activities - TN Code § 49-6-1031
Local Board Powers and Duties - TN Code § 49-2-203
Open Meetings Law - TN §§ 8-44-101 to 8-44-111
Open Records Law - TN §§ 10-7-501 to 10-7-517
Religious Freedom Restoration Act - TN Code § 4-1-407
State Board Powers and Duties - TN Code § 49-1-302
Student Religious Liberty Act - TN §§ 49-6-2901 to 46-6-2907
TN Sample FOIA Request - National Freedom of Information Coalition
Use of Unapproved Books Materials - TN Code § 49-6-2006

Rules & Regulations of the State of Tennessee (Title 520 - Education) -
https://regulations.justia.com/states/tennessee/title-0520/
Tennessee Department of Education - https://www.tn.gov/education/
Tennessee State Board of Education - https://www.tn.gov/sbe/
Tennessee Bar Association - https://www.tba.org/

TEXAS

The Constitution of the State of Texas
Article I - Bill of Rights
Article VII - Education
https://law.justia.com/constitution/texas/

Texas Legislature – https://capitol.texas.gov/
Texas State Laws – https://law.justia.com/codes/texas/
Texas School Laws (Education Code) –
   https://law.justia.com/codes/texas/2022/education-code/

Sample of Texas Education-Related Laws
To locate the laws below, go to the Utah School Laws link above and search for the citation that interests you by clicking on the appropriate chapters and subchapters as you wind your way to the law. You can also enter the terms "Justia," "Texas," and the "numeric portion of the citation" in your search bar. Be sure to look at the most recent version of the law.

Charter Schools – TX Educ Code §§ 12.001 to 12.265
Extracurricular Activities – TX Educ Code §§ 33.081 to 33.097
Instructional Material – TX Educ Code § 31.023
Instructional Requirements and Prohibitions – TX Educ Code § 28.0022
Obscenity, Harmful Material, Defenses – TX Penal Code § 43.24(c)
Open Government – TX Govt Code § 557.022
Open Meetings Law – TX Govt Code §§ 551.001 to 551.007
Open Records Law – TX Govt Code §§ 552.221 to 552.235
Parental Rights and Responsibilities – TX Educ Code §§ 26.001 to 26.015
Religious Freedom Restoration Act – TX Civ Prac & R Code §§ 110.001 to 110.012
Required Curriculum – TX Educ Code § 28.002
TX Sample FOIA Request – National Freedom of Information Coalition

Texas Administrative Code (Title 19 – Education) –
   https://regulations.justia.com/states/texas/title-19/
Texas Education Agency – https://tea.texas.gov/
Texas State Board of Education –
   https://tea.texas.gov/about-tea/leadership/state-board-of-education
State Bar of Texas – https://www.texasbar.com/

UTAH

The Constitution of the State of Utah
Article I – Declaration of Rights
Article X – Education
https://law.justia.com/constitution/untah/

Utah State Legislature – https://le.utah.gov/
Utah State Laws – https://law.justia.com/codes/utah/
Utah School Laws (Titles 53E and 53G – State and Local Public Education) –
   https://law.justia.com/codes/utah/2021/title-53e/
   https://law.justia.com/codes/utah/2021/title-53g/

APPENDIX C: STATE AND LOCAL RESOURCES

Sample of Utah Education-Related Laws
To locate the laws below, go to the Utah School Laws link above and search for the citation that interests you by clicking on the appropriate chapters and subchapters as you wind your way to the law. You can also enter the terms "Justia," "Utah," and the "numeric portion of the citation" in your search bar. Be sure to look at the most recent version of the law.

Activities Prohibited, Written Parent Consent – UT Code § 53E-9-203
Charter Schools – UT Code §§ 53G-5-101 to 53G-5-609
Crimes, Harmful Materials to Minors – UT Code §§ 76-10-1206; Defenses – 76-10-1208
Discipline and Safety – UT Code §§ 53G-8-101 to 53G-8-802
Local School Board Powers and Duties – UT Code §§ 53G-4-401 to 53G-4-411
Maintaining Constitutional Freedom – UT Code § 53G-10-202
Open Meetings Act – UT Code §§ 52-4-201 to 52-4-210
Open Records Act – UT Code § 63G-2-201
Parental Participation – UT Code § 53E-2-303
Powers of the State Board, Enforcement – UT Code § 53E-3-401
State Instructional Materials Commission – UT Code §§ 53E-4-401 to 53E-4-408
Student Clubs, Parental Consent – UT Code § 53G-7-709
UT Sample FOIA Request – National Freedom of Information Coalition

Utah Administrative Code (Education) –
https://regulations.justia.com/states/utah/education/
Utah Education Department – https://www.utah.gov/education/
Utah State Board of Education – https://www.schools.utah.gov/
Utah State Bar – https://www.utahbar.org/

VERMONT

The Constitution of the State of Vermont
Chapter I – Declaration of Rights
Chapter II – Plan or Frame of Government, Section 68 Laws to Encourage Virtue and Prevent Vice; Schools; Religious Activities
https://law.justia.com/constitution/vermont/

Vermont General Assembly – https://legislature.vermont.gov/
Vermont State Laws – https://law.justia.com/codes/vermont/
Vermont School Laws (Title 16 – Education) –
https://law.justia.com/codes/vermont/2021/title-16/

Sample of Vermont Education-Related Laws
To locate the laws below, go to the Vermont School Laws link above and search for the citation that interests you by clicking on the appropriate chapters and subchapters as you wind your way to the law. You can also enter the terms "Justia," "Vermont," and the "numeric portion of the citation" in your search bar. Be sure to look at the most recent version of the law.

Application of Laws to School Districts – 16 V.S.A. § 551
Attendance and Discipline – 16 V.S.A. §§ 1071 to 1167
Comprehensive Health – 16 V.S.A. §§ 131 – 136; Religious Exemption – § 134
Courses of Study – 16 V.S.A. §§ 906 to 947
Crimes, Obscenity – 13 V.S.A. §§ 2801 – 2813; Defense – § 2805
Open Meetings Law – 1 V.S.A. §§ 310 to 314; § 312
Open Records Law – 1 V.S.A. §§ 315 to 320; § 316
School Board Meetings – 16 V.S.A. § 554
State Board Powers and Duties – 16 V.S.A. § 164
State Board, Staff, Meetings – 16 V.S.A. § 163
Student Rights, Freedom of Expression – 16 V.S.A. § 1623
VT Sample FOIA Request – National Freedom of Information Coalition

Code of Vermont Rules (Agency 22 – Department of Education) –
https://regulations.justia.com/states/vermont/agency-22/
State of Vermont Agency of Education – https://education.vermont.gov/
Vermont State Board of Education –
https://education.vermont.gov/state-board-councils/state-board
Vermont Bar Association – https://www.vtbar.org/

VIRGINIA

The Constitution of the Commonwealth of Virginia
Article I – Bill of Rights
Article VIII – Education
https://law.justia.com/constitution/virginia/
Virginia General Assembly – https://virginiageneralassembly.gov/
Virginia Commonwealth Laws – https://law.justia.com/codes/virginia/
Virginia School Laws (Title 22.1 – Education) –
https://law.justia.com/codes/virginia/2021/title-22-1/

Sample of Virginia Education-Related Laws
To locate the laws below, go to the Virginia School Laws link above and search for the citation that interests you by clicking on the appropriate chapters and subchapters as you wind your way to the law. You can also enter the terms "Justia," "Virginia," and the "numeric portion of the citation" in your search bar. Be sure to look at the most recent version of the law.

Charter Schools – VA Code §§ 22.1-212.5 to 22.1-212.16
Courses and Textbooks – VA Code §§ 22.1-199 to 22.1-212.3
Crimes, Obscenity – VA Code §§ 18.2-372 to 18.2-389; Exceptions – 18.2-383
Culturally Relevant and Inclusive Practices Advisory – VA Code § 22.1-208.02
Family Life, Review and Opt-Out – VA Code §§ 22.1-207.1 to 22.1-207.2; 22.1-207.2
Judicial Review, School Board Decisions – VA Code § 22.1-87
Open Meetings Law – VA Code §§ 2.2-3707

Open Records Law – VA Code §§ 2.2-3704; VA Code §§ 2.2-3700 to 2.2-3714
Religious Freedom Restoration Act – VA Code §§ 57-1 to 57-2.1
Religious Viewpoint Expression – VA Code § 22.1-203.3
School Boards Powers and Duties – VA Code §§ 22.1-71 to 22.1-87
VA Sample FOIA Request – National Freedom of Information Coalition
Virginia and U.S. History, Flag – VA Code §§ 22.1-201 to 22.1-202

Virginia Administrative Code (Title 8 – Education) –
   https://regulations.justia.com/states/virginia/title-8/
Virginia Department of Education – https://www.doe.virginia.gov/
Virginia State Board of Education – https://www.doe.virginia.gov/
Virginia Bar Association – https://www.vba.org/

WASHINGTON

The Constitution of the State of Washington
Article I – Declaration of Rights
Article IX – Education
https://law.justia.com/constitution/washington/

Washington State Legislature – https://leg.wa.gov/
Washington State Laws – https://law.justia.com/codes/washington/
Washington School Laws (Title 28A – Common School Provisions) –
   https://law.justia.com/codes/washington/2021/title-28a/

Sample of Washington Education-Related Laws
To locate the laws below, go to the Washington School Laws link above and search for the citation that interests you by clicking on the appropriate chapters and sub-chapters as you wind your way to the law. You can also enter the terms "Justia," "Washington," and the "numeric portion of the citation" in your search bar. Be sure to look at the most recent version of the law.

Appeals From Board – WA Rev Code §§ 28A.645.010 to 28A.645.040
Charter Schools – WA Rev Code §§ 28A.710.010 to 28A.710.901
Compulsory Coursework – WA Rev Code §§ 28A.230.010 to 28A.230.320
Crimes, Obscenity – WA Rev Code §§ 9.68.015 to 9.68.900; Exemptions –§ 9.68.015
Health and Screening – WA Rev Code §§ 28A.210.010 to 28A.210.420
Observance of Veterans' Day – WA Rev Code § 28A.230.160
Open Meetings Act – WA Rev Code §§ 42.30.010 to 42.30.910
Open Records Act – WA Rev Code §§ 42.56.001 to 42.56.904; Atty Gen – § 42.56
Parent Access – WA Rev Code §§ 28A.605.010 to 28A.605.040
Students' Rights of Religious Expression – WA Rev Code § 28A.600.025
WA Sample FOIA Request –National Freedom of Information Coalition

Washington Administrative Code: Title 180 – State Board of Education –
https://regulations.justia.com/states/washington/title-180/
Washington State Board of Education – https://www.sbe.wa.gov/
Washington State Bar Association – https://www.wsba.org/

WEST VIRGINIA

The Constitution of the State of West Virginia
Article III – Bill of Rights
Article VII – Education
https://law.justia.com/constitution/west-virginia/

West Virginia Legislature – https://www.wvlegislature.gov/
West Virginia State Laws – https://law.justia.com/codes/west-virginia/
West Virginia School Laws (Chapter 18 and 18A – Education) –
https://law.justia.com/codes/west-virginia/2021/chapter-18/
https://law.justia.com/codes/west-virginia/2021/chapter-18a/

Sample of West Virginia Education-Related Laws
To locate the laws below, go to the West Virginia School Laws link above and search for the citation that interests you by clicking on the appropriate chapters and subchapters as you wind your way to the law. You can also enter the terms "Justia," "West Virginia," and the "numeric portion of the citation" in your search bar. Be sure to look at the most recent version of the law.

Adoption of Textbooks – WV Code §§ 18-2A-1 to 18-2A-10
Charter Schools – WV Code §§ 18-5G-1 to 18-5G-15
County Board of Education – WV Code §§ 18-5-1 to 18-5-49; Authority – 18-5-13
Crimes, Obscenity, Minors – WV Code §§ 61-8A-1 to 61-8A-7; Exemptions– 61-8A-3
Duties of County Superintendent – WV Code § 18-4-10
Local School Involvement – WV Code §§ 18-5A-1 to 18-5A-6
Open Governmental Proceedings Act – WV Code §§ 6-9A-1 to 6-9A-12
Open Records Act – WV Code §§ 29B-1-1 to 29B-1-7
Pledge of Allegiance, Flag – WV Code § 18-5-15b
State Board Duties – WV Code § 18-2E-1a
Student Religious Liberties – WV Code §§ 18-33-1 to 18-33-8
WV Sample FOIA Request –National Freedom of Information Coalition

West Virginia Code of State Rules (Agency 126 – Education) –
https://regulations.justia.com/states/west-virginia/agency-126/
West Virginia Department of Education – https://wvde.us/
West Virginia State Board of Education – https://wvde.us/state-board-of-education/
West Virginia State Bar – https://wvbar.org/

WISCONSIN

The Constitution of the State of Wisconsin
Article I – Declaration of Rights
Article X – Education
https://law.justia.com/constitution/wisconsin/

Wisconsin State Legislature – https://legis.wisconsin.gov/
Wisconsin State Laws – https://law.justia.com/codes/wisconsin/
Wisconsin School Laws (Chapters 115-121 – Public Instruction) –
https://law.justia.com/codes/wisconsin/2022/ (scroll to Chapter 115)

Sample of Wisconsin Education-Related Laws
To locate the laws below, go to the Wisconsin School Laws link above and search for the citation that interests you by clicking on the appropriate chapters and subchapters as you wind your way to the law. You can also enter the terms "Justia," "Wisconsin," and the "numeric portion of the citation" in your search bar. Be sure to look at the most recent version of the law.

Athletics – WI Stat. § 118.133
Charter Schools – WI Stat. § 118.40
Crimes, Obscenity, Exemption – WI Stat. § 994.21(8)(b)
Flag, Pledge of Allegiance, National Anthem – WI Stat. § 118.06
Human Growth and Development – WI Stat. § 118.019
Open Meetings Law – WI Stat. §§ 19.81 to 19.98
Open Records Law – WI Stat. §§ 19.31 to 19.39
Reading Instruction – WI Stat. § 118.015
Released Time for Religious Instruction – WI Stat. § 118.155
School Board Duties and Powers – WI Stat. § 120.12; WI Stat. § 120.13
School Board Meetings and Reports – WI Stat. § 120.11
WI Sample FOIA Request – National Freedom of Information Coalition

Wisconsin Administrative Code (Educational Approval Board) –
https://regulations.justia.com/states/wisconsin/educational-approval-board/
Wisconsin Department of Public Instruction – https://dpi.wi.gov/
State Bar of Wisconsin – https://www.wisbar.org/

WYOMING

The Constitution of the State of Wyoming
Article I – Declaration of Rights
Article VII – Education; State Institutions; Promotion of Health
https://law.justia.com/constitution/wyoming/

State of Wyoming Legislature – https://www.wyoleg.gov/
Wyoming State Laws – https://law.justia.com/codes/wyoming/

Wyoming School Laws (Title 21 – Education) –
https://law.justia.com/codes/wyoming/2022/title-21/

Sample of Wyoming Education-Related Laws
To locate the laws below, go to the Wyoming School Laws link above and search for the citation that interests you by clicking on the appropriate chapters and sub-chapters as you wind your way to the law. You can also enter the terms "Justia," "Wyoming," and the "numeric portion of the citation" in your search bar. Be sure to look at the most recent version of the law.

Charter Schools – WY Stat §§ 21-3-301 to 314
Core Knowledge and Skills – WY Stat § 21-9-101
Crimes, Obscenity, Exemption – WY Stat. § 6-4-302
Open Meetings Act – WY Stat §§ 16-4-401 to 16-4-408
Open Records Act – WY Stat §§ 16-4-201 to 16-4-205
State Board Duties – WY Stat § 21-2-304
State and U.S. Constitutions – WY Stat § 21-9-102; Penalty – WY Stat § 21-9-103
Reading Assessment and Intervention – WY Stat § 21-3-411
Right to Attend School – WY Stat §§ 21-4-301 to 316
WY Sample FOIA Request –National Freedom of Information Coalition

Wyoming Administrative Code (Agency 206 – Education Department) –
https://regulations.justia.com/states/wyoming/agency-206/
Wyoming Department of Education – https://edu.wyoming.gov/
Wyoming State Board of Education – https://edu.wyoming.gov/board/
Wyoming State Bar – https://www.wyomingbar.org/

Core Knowledge and Skills – WY Stat § 21-9-101
Crimes, Obscenity, Exemption – WY Stat. § 6-4-302
Open Meetings Act – WY Stat §§ 16-4-401 to 16-4-408
Open Records Act – WY Stat §§ 16-4-201 to 16-4-205
State and U.S. Constitutions – WY Stat § 21-9-102; Penalty – WY Stat § 21-9-103
State Board Duties – WY Stat § 21-2-304
Reading Assessment and Intervention – WY Stat § 21-3-411
Right to Attend School – WY Stat §§ 21-4-301 to 316
WY Sample FOIA Request –National Freedom of Information Coalition

NOTES

INTRODUCTION

1. At that time, there were two Montessori accrediting bodies: The American Montessori International (AMI) and the American Montessori Society (AMS). We chose the AMI school near our home. To apply Montessori principles at home with preschoolers, see Hainstock, Elizabeth G., *Teaching Montessori in the Home*, Plume Books, New York City, NY, 1997.
2. Engelman, Siegfried, Haddox, Phyllis, and Bruner, Elaine, *Teach your Child to Read in 100 Easy Lessons*, Simon & Schuster, New York City, NY, 1983.
3. Technically, "curricula" is plural, and "curriculum" is singular. Yet, because school systems and state laws use the term "curriculum" interchangeably, I have done the same.
4. Bauer, Susan Wise, *The Story of the World, History for the Classical Child*, Volumes 1-4, Well-Trained Mind Press, Charles City, VA, 2001-2005.
5. Bradford, William, *Of Plymouth Plantation, Bradford's History of the Plymouth Settlement 1608-1650*, Vision Forum, San Antonio, TX, 1998, which is the original manuscript rendered into modern English by Harold Paget in 1909. I read excerpts to our children. Interestingly, the Plymouth settlement attempted communal living but it failed. pp. 115-116. For a Thanksgiving story see, Bulla, Clyde Robert, *Squanto, Friend of the Pilgrims*, New York City, NY, Scholastic Paperbacks, 1990. For additional history materials, Hillsdale College offers a free downloadable *Hillsdale 1776 Curriculum*.
6. Wise, Jesse, and Bauer, Susan Wise, *The Well-Trained Mind: A Guide to Classical Education at Home*, W.W. Norton & Co., Inc., New York, NY, 1999. Wise, Jesse, *First Language Lessons for the Well-Trained Mind*, Well-Trained Mind Press, Charles City, VA, 2003.
7. *Adventures in Odyssey*, by Focus on the Family.
8. *Troxel v. Granville*, 530 U.S. 57 (2000); *Pierce v. Soc'y of Sisters*, 268 U.S. 510 (1925); *Meyer v. Nebraska*, 262 U.S. 390 (1923).
9. *Wisconsin v. Yoder*, 406 U.S. 205 (1972).
10. I describe a situation when I objected to a book one of our children was required to read. I also discuss my concerns with state laws that exempt public schools and libraries from state criminal obscenity laws.
11. According to the National Education Association, "Only 25 percent of U.S. students reach the 'proficient' standard on the NAEP Civics Assessment." *See* Litvinov, Amanda, NEA News, "*Forgotten Purpose: Civics Education in Public Schools*," (2017).
12. Postman, Neil, *Amusing Ourselves to Death, Public Discourse in the Age of Showbusiness*, Penguin Books, London, England, 1985.
13. The links to constitutions, laws, and caselaw, are through Justia.com, which is a free online resource. The links may not be the most recent version, in part because legislatures are continually passing new laws. To remedy this problem, compare the citations with Findlaw.com, which is a similar resource, and your state legislature's website.

CHAPTER 1: THE UNITED STATES CONSTITUTION AND THE TENTH AMENDMENT

1. *San Antonio v. Rodriguez*, 411 U.S. 1 (1973).
2. *Brown v. Bd. of Educ.*, 347 U.S. 483, 493 (1954). *See also, Wisconsin v. Yoder*, 406 U.S. 205, 213 (1972) (stating that "[p]roviding public schools ranks at the very apex of the function of a state").
3. The Declaration of Independence, dated July 4, 1776, states, "We hold these truths to be self-evident, that all men are created equal, that they are endowed by their Creator with certain unalienable Rights, that among these are Life, Liberty and the pursuit of Happiness. –That to secure these rights, Governments are instituted among Men, *deriving their just powers from the consent of the governed*...." Declaration of Independence (July 4, 1776) (emphasis added). "The people" give

government power under the natural rights theory. "The people's" rights are "unalienable" (impossible to take away).
4 An individual may have "standing" to allege that a federal law or action violates the Tenth Amendment because it interferes with powers reserved to the states. *See Bond v. U.S.*, 564 U.S. 211 (2011) (stating that "in a proper case, an individual may 'assert injury from governmental action taken in excess of the authority that federalism defines'").
5 *U.S. v. Am. Library Ass'n*, 539 U.S. 194, 203 (2003) (internal citation omitted).
6 *South Dakota v. Dole*, 483 U.S. 203, 206 (1987)
7 *Nat'l Fed'n of Indep. Bus. v. Sebelius*, 567 U.S. 519 (2012).
8 National Center for Education Statistics, Institute of Education Sciences, Finance Tables, "*Revenues and Expenditures for Public Elementary and Secondary Education: FY 19*," June 2021. (https://nces.ed.gov/pubs2021/2021302.pdf).
9 The Common Core State Standards Initiative ("Common Core"), is not a federal program. It is a 2010 initiative sponsored by the National Governors Ass'n and the Council of Chief State School Officers that details what students (K-12) should know after each grade in certain subjects. Many states have become members of Common Core in one or more subjects. Recently, some states have abandoned Common Core, and others have passed legislation prohibiting Common Core in their state.
10 *Meyer v. Nebraska*, 262 U.S. 390, 401 (1923).
11 *Pierce v. Soc'y of Sisters*, 268 U.S. 510, 534 (1925).
12 *Wisconsin v. Yoder*, 406 U.S. 205, 233 (1972).
13 *Santosky v. Kramer*, 455 U.S. 745, 753 (1982).
14 *Troxel v. Granville*, 530 U.S. 57, 60 (2000).
15 *Meyer v. Nebraska*, 262 U.S. 390 (1923); *Pierce v. Soc'y of Sisters*, 268 U.S. 510 (1925); *Wisconsin v. Yoder*, 406 U.S. 205 (1972); *Santosky v. Kramer*, 455 U.S. 745 (1982); *Troxel v. Granville*, 530 U.S. 57 (2000).

CHAPTER 2: THE STATE CONSTITUTION

1 The Supremacy Clause states: "This Constitution, and the Laws of the United States which shall be made in Pursuance thereof; and all Treaties made, or which shall be made, under the Authority of the United States, shall be the supreme Law of the Land; and the Judges in every State shall be bound thereby, any Thing in the Constitution or Laws of any State to the Contrary notwithstanding." U.S. CONST. art. VI, § 2.

CHAPTER 3: STATE SCHOOL LAWS

1 i.e., Truth in Education, https://truthineducation.org/opt-out-forms/.
2 *Troxel v. Granville*, 530 U.S. 57, 60 (2000) (holding that the U.S. Constitution "protects the fundamental right of parents to make decisions concerning the care, custody, and control of their children"); *Santosky v. Kramer*, 455 U.S. 745, 753 (1982) (recognizing the "fundamental liberty interest of natural parents in the care, custody, and management of their child"); *Wisconsin v. Yoder*, 406 U.S. 205, 233 (1972) (recognizing the "liberty of parents ... to direct the upbringing and education of children"); *Pierce v. Soc'y of Sisters*, 268 U.S. 510, 534 (1925) (stating that parents have the right "to direct the upbringing and education of children under their control"); *Meyer v. Nebraska*, 262 U.S. 390, 401 (1923) (concluding that the state "legislature has attempted materially to interfere with ... the power of parents to control the education of their own"). *See also, Zorach v. Clauson*, 343 U.S. 306 (1952) (upholding the constitutionality of released time programs for religious instruction for public school students during the school day).
3 Alaska has a similar law. AK Stat § 14.03.090.
4 "Partisan" means "an adherent to a particular party or cause as opposed to the public interest at large." "Partisan," *Black's Law Dictionary, Sixth Edition*, West Publishing Co. 1990, p. 1119.
5 "Sectarian" means "denominational" or "religious," which is its most common use today. *Black's Law Dictionary, Sixth Edition*, West Publishing Co. 1990, p. 1353.
6 O.C.G.A. § 20-2-143(d); Georgia's Parents' Bill of Rights, O.C.G.A. § 20-2-786(f)(3); Georgia State Bd. of Educ. Rule 160-4-2-.12; and local school district rules.
7 According to public records, SIECUS was founded in 1964 by Mary Calderone, medical director at Planned Parenthood.
8 *Pierce v. Soc'y of Sisters*, 268 U.S. 510, 534 (1925).
9 Wise, Jesse, and Bauer, Susan Wise, *The Well-Trained Mind: A Guide to Classical Education at Home*, W.W. Norton & Co., Inc., New York, NY, book cover inside flap.
10 O.C.G.A. §§ 20-1-11(b) and (e).

11 *Pierce v. Soc'y of Sisters*, 268 U.S. 510, 534 (1925).
12 *See also, Plainfield Consol. Sch. Dist. v. Cook*, 173 Ga. 447, 160 S.E. 617 (1931) (regarding mandamus order as a remedy to citizens); *Citizens Bank v. Am. Surety Co.*, 174 Ga. 852, 164 S.E. 817 (1932).
13 The U.S. Supreme Court expressly abandoned the Lemon Test for alleged violations of the Establishment Clause in Kennedy v. Bremerton Sch. Dist., 597 U.S. ___, 142 S. Ct. 2407, 2428 (2022). See also, Am. Legion v. Am. Humanist Ass'n., 588 U.S. ___, 139 S. Ct. 2067, 2087 (2019) (plurality opinion) (slip op., at 12–13); Town of Greece v. Galloway, 572 U.S. 565, 575–577 (2014); and Zelman v. Simmons-Harris, 536 U.S. 639, 652 (2002) (holding that a benefits program that allows private citizens to "direct government aid to religious schools wholly as a result of their own genuine and independent private choice" does not violate the Establishment Clause).
14 Georgia's new mental health law was formerly known as GA H.B. (House Bill) 1013 (Regular Session, 2021-2022).

CHAPTER 4: OTHER STATE LAWS THAT AFFECT PUBLIC SCHOOLS K-12

1 Senate Bill 588 (2022) amended this law. The new law requires local boards to establish meeting rules of conduct and permit members of the public to be removed for an "actual disruption" of the meeting. O.C.G.A. §§ 20-2-58(c)(3) and (4). There may be constitutional challenges to this new law based on the designated public forum doctrine, which does not allow for a "heckler's veto" of constitutionally protected speech. *Gregory v. Chicago*, 394 U.S. 111 (1969). *See* Chapter 11, Free Speech Clause.
2 Reisman, Judith A., and McAlister, Mary E., *"Materials Deemed Harmful to Minors Are Welcomed into Classrooms and Libraries via Educational "Obscenity Exemptions,"* Liberty University Law Review, Vol 12: Iss. 3, Article 3, 2018. See footnote n. 43 on page 527 for the 44 states that enacted exemptions as of 2018: ALA. CODE § 13A-12-200.4; ARK. CODE ANN. § 5-68-308; CAL. PENAL CODE § 313.3; COLO. REV. STAT. § 18-7-503; CONN. GEN. STAT. § 53a-195; DEL. CODE ANN. tit. 11, § 1362; D.C. CODE § 22-2201(c); FLA. STAT. § 847.011 (2008); GA. CODE ANN. § 16-12-104; HAW. REV. STAT. § 712-1215(2); IDAHO CODE § 18-1517; 720 ILL. COMP. STAT. 5/11-20(f) (2011); IND. CODE § 35-49-3-4; IOWA CODE § 728.7; KAN. STAT. ANN. § 21-6401(g); KY. REV. STAT. ANN. § 531.070; LA. REV. STAT. § 14:106 (2014); ME. STAT. tit. 17 § 2911 (2012); MD. CODE ANN., CRIM. LAW, § 11-210; MASS. GEN. LAWS ch. 272, § 29; MICH. COMP. LAWS § 752.367; MINN. STAT. § 617.295; MISS. CODE ANN. § 97-29-107; MONT. CODE ANN. § 45-8-201; NEB. REV. STAT. § 28-815; NEV. REV. STAT. § 201.237; N.H. REV. STAT. ANN. § 650:4; N.M. STAT ANN. § 30-37-5; N.Y. PENAL LAW § 235.15; N.C. GEN. STAT. § 14-190.15; N.D. CENT. CODE § 12.1-27.1-11; OHIO REV. CODE ANN. § 2907.32(B); OR. REV. STAT. § 167.085; 18 PA. CONS. STAT. § 5903(j) (2012); S.C. CODE ANN. § 16-15-385(C); S.D. CODIFIED LAWS § 22-24-31; TENN. CODE ANN. § 39-17-902(e) (2014); TEX. PENAL CODE § 43.24(c) (West 2011); UTAH CODE ANN. § 76-10-1208; VT. STAT. ANN. tit. 13, § 2805; VA. CODE ANN. § 18.2-383 (2017); WASH. REV. CODE § 9.68.015; W. VA. CODE § 61-8A-3; WIS. STAT. § 944.21(8)(b) (2017); WYO. STAT.ANN. § 6-4-302(c).
3 An "exemption" prevents school and library representatives from being prosecuted for violating the state's obscenity law. Some states give school and library representatives an "affirmative defense" instead. An "affirmative defense" does not prevent prosecution. Instead, after the prosecution puts forth its evidence, the burden of proof shifts to the school or library personnel to establish their "affirmative defense," i.e., that the person was teaching the curriculum, etc.
4 Wis. Stat. § 948.11 (4)(b).
5 The Florida law states, "This [obscenity law] does not apply to the distribution or posting of *school-approved instructional materials that by design serve as a major tool for assisting in the instruction of a subject or course* by school officers, instructional personnel, administrative personnel, school volunteers, educational support employees, or managers as those terms are defined in § 1012.01." FL Stat § 847.012. (emphasis added). The Florida exemption is more narrowly tailored than other states.
6 When the U.S. Supreme Court holds that a state law is unconstitutional because it infringes on a "fundamental right" (such as the right to marry or parental rights), the Court's decision has the potential to overturn *all* state laws that infringe on that fundamental right — nationwide.
7 Search for GA H.B. 1013, (Regular Session, 2021-2022) at p. 2 of the link.
8 GA H.B. 1013, lines 1-5.
9 GA H.B. 1013, lines 1146-1466, amending O.C.G.A. § 37-2-4(a).
10 GA H.B. 1013, lines 1528-1532; and 1663-1679, amending O.C.G.A. § 37-1-20(28) (emphasis added).
11 O.C.G.A. § 49-5-24(b).
12 Another important aspect of mental health laws is *involuntary commitment. See* GA H.B. 1013, lines 849-1214, which amends O.C.G.A. §§ 37-1-120 through 37-7-101. Evaluators (physicians) are addressed at GA H.B. 1013, lines 1075-1086, which amends O.C.G.A. § 37-3-42. *See* links to evaluators at O.C.G.A. § 37-3-41. That link states, "(d) Any psychologist, clinical social worker, or clinical nurse specialist in

psychiatric/mental health may perform any act specified by this Code section to be performed by a physician. Any reference in any part of this chapter to a physician acting under this Code section shall be deemed to refer equally to a psychologist, a clinical social worker, or a clinical nurse specialist in psychiatric/mental health acting under this Code section." O.C.G.A. § 37-3-41(d).
13 Regarding public school mental health counseling and psychiatric services, see if your state has a law prohibiting licensed counselors (including those in public and private schools), from discussing specific topics with minors, regardless of the child's and family's religious beliefs. Approximately 20 states have enacted laws affecting counselors' speech rights. Several others are considering them. I am not aware of any challenges to the constitutionality of these laws (i.e., by counselors based on the Contract Clause, the Free Exercise Clause, the Free Speech Clause, or the negative Free Speech Clause; or the parents based on parental rights, the Free Exercise Clause, the Free Speech Clause, and the negative Free Speech Clause, etc.). Tennessee appears to be the only state with a Counseling Protection Act.

CHAPTER 5: THE STATE BOARD OF EDUCATION AND THE STATE SCHOOL SUPERINTENDENT

1 A "bond" is an amount of money the superintendent must post to guarantee that he or she will faithfully discharge his or her duties. Lawyers sometimes "attach" or make a claim on the bonds during a dispute.
2 *See Plainfield Consol. Sch. Dist. v. Cook*, 173 Ga. 447, 160 S.E. 617 (1931) (regarding mandamus order as a remedy to citizens).

CHAPTER 7: CHARTER ENTITIES

1 When courts examine contracts and laws to determine what they mean, they apply certain "rules of construction." One rule is *expressio unius est exclusio alterius*, which Latin for "when one or more things of a class are expressly mentioned, others of the same class are excluded" (Merriam-Webster .com/legal/). In simple terms, if the charter document lists the laws that are not waived, one can argue that those are the *only* laws that are not waived. In the end, the courts make the final decision.
2 The lack of notice may deprive a person's right to procedural due process under the Fourteenth Amendment. *Goss v. Lopez*, 419 U.S. 565 (1975) (recognizing a property interest in public education that requires procedural due process under some circumstances).
3 O.C.G.A. § 20-2-212.6
4 O.C.G.A. § 20-2-182
5 O.C.G.A. § 20-2-989.2
6 O.C.G.A. § 20-2-218
7 Hillsdale College's Barney Charter School Initiative is an outreach program that launches and supports classical K-12 charter schools throughout the U.S., (https://k12.hillsdale.edu/About/BCSI/).
8 To review the referenced Charter School Renewal Application, go to https://www.gadoe.org/External-Affairs-and-Policy/Charter-Schools/Pages/Charter-Petition-Application.aspx.

CHAPTER 8: MAGNET SCHOOLS

1 In 1954, the U.S. Supreme Court held that racial segregation in public schools was unconstitutional. *Brown v. Bd. of Educ. of Topeka*, 347 U.S. 483 (1954). This decision *overturned* the previous "separate but equal" racial segregation doctrine permitted by *Plessy v. Ferguson*, 163 U.S. 537 (1896). After *Brown v. Bd. of Educ.*, public schools were required to desegregate. A year later, the U.S. Supreme Court decided *Brown v. Bd. of Educ. II (Brown II)*, which required public schools to desegregate "with all deliberate speed." *Brown v. Bd. of Educ. of Topeka II*, 349 U.S. 294 (1955).

CHAPTER 9: CONTROVERSIAL MATERIAL AND CONTENT

1 Private universities and colleges that do not receive state funding do not have these constraints.
2 *Hazelwood Sch. Dist. v. Kuhlmeier*, 484 U.S. 260, 273 (1988).
3 *Cantwell v. Connecticut*, 310 U.S. 296, 303 (1940) (discussing incorporation of these rights through the Due Process Clause of the Fourteenth Amendment).
4 *Bethel Sch. Dist. v. Fraser*, 478 U.S. 675 (1986); *Morse v. Frederick*, 551 U.S. 393 (2007).
5 *U.S. v. Am. Library Ass'n*, 539 U.S. 194 (2003).
6 *Bethel Sch. Dist. v. Fraser*, 478 U.S. 675 (1986); *Morse v. Frederick*, 551 U.S. 393 (2007).

7   "Torts" include: intentional torts (i.e., intentional infliction of emotional distress); unintentional torts (i.e., negligence); and others (i.e., defamation), to name a few.
8   Federal Tort Claims Act, Title 28 U.S.C. §§ 1346, 2671-2680, and states that follow the federal standards.

PART II: FEDERAL AND STATE CONSTITUTIONAL RIGHTS

1   *Considering the Role of Judges Under the Constitution of the United States: Hearing before the S. Comm. On the Judiciary, 112th Cong. 6-8 (2011) (statement of Hon.* Antonin Scalia, Associate Justice, Supreme Court of the United States). *See also,* Mortenson, Chris, *"Scalia: Portrait of a Man & Jurist,"* Mad Universe Prod. Co., 2017.
2   *Morrison v. Olson,* 487 U.S. 654 (1988) (stating that "the system of separated powers and checks and balances established in the Constitution was regarded by the Framers as 'a self-executing safeguard against the encroachment or aggrandizement of one branch at the expense of the other'" citing *Buckley v. Valeo,* 424 U.S. 1 (1976)).
3   *Wisconsin v. Yoder,* 406 U.S. 205 (1972).
4   Litvinov, Amanda, NEA News, *"Forgotten Purpose: Civics Education in Public Schools,"* (2017).
5   *Masterpiece Cake Shop Ltd., v. Colorado Civil Rts. Comm',* 585 U.S. ___, 138 S. Ct. 1719 (2018); Colo. Rev. Stat. §24-34-601 (2017). This case involved Colorado's Anti-Discrimination Act, which prohibits discrimination in places of "public accommodation," including cake shops. When the cake shop owner declined to make a wedding cake for a same-sex couple because of his religious convictions, the couple filed a complaint with the Colorado Civil Rights Division ("Commission"). The Commission decided against the cake shop. The cake shop owner then challenged the Commission's decision, alleging a violation of his constitutional rights of free speech and free exercise of religion. After a series of rulings in state court affirming the Commission's decision, the U.S. Supreme Court reversed and agreed with the cake shop owner. The U.S. Supreme Court held that the Commission's actions violated the cake shop owner's constitutional rights under the Free Exercise Clause. *In other words, the Commission was the government actor. The Commission's decision against the cake shop owner was the basis for his constitutional claim. See also,* Phillips, Jack, *The Cost of My Faith: How a Decision in My Cake Shop Took Me to the Supreme Court,* Salem Books, 2021.
6   Constitutional challenges can be brought under 42 U.S. Code § 1983, which is a federal civil rights statute. This statute allows individuals to sue state and local officials who violate their rights "under color of state law." The phrase "under color of state law" means the state or local official was enforcing a law that is allegedly unconstitutional. *See also, Ex parte Young,* 209 U.S. 123 (1908).

CHAPTER 10: STATE CONSTITUTIONAL RIGHTS

1   *San Antonio v. Rodriguez,* 411 U.S. 1 (1973). Although there is no federal constitutional right to a public education, "equal access to education" is protected under the Equal Protection Clause of the Fourteenth Amendment. *Brown v. Bd. of Educ.,* 347 U.S. 483 (1954).
2   *Crim v. McWhorter,* 242 Ga. 863 (1979).
3   Matters of "conscience" are protected under the following state constitutions: Arizona (Article II, § 12), Arkansas (Article II, § 24), California (Article I, §24), Colorado (Article II, § 4), Delaware (Article I, § 1), Georgia (Article I, § 1), Idaho (Article I, § 4), Illinois (Article I, § 3), Indiana (Article I, § 2), Kansas (Article I, § 7), Kentucky (Article I, § 1), Maine (Article I, § 3), Michigan (Article I, § 4), Minnesota (Article I, § 16), Missouri (Article I, § 5), Nebraska (Article I, § 4), Nevada (Article I, § 4), New Hampshire (Part First, § 5), New Mexico (Article II, § 11), New York (Article I, § 3), North Carolina (Article I, § 13), North Dakota (Article I, § 3), Ohio (Article I, § 7), Oregon(Article II, § 6), Pennsylvania (Article I, § 3), Rhode Island (Article I, § 8), South Dakota (Article I, § 3), Tennessee (Article I, § 3), Texas (Article I, § 6), Utah (Article I, § 4), Virginia (Article I, § 16), Washington (Article I, § 11), Wisconsin (Article I, § 18), and Wyoming (Article I, § 18).
4   The breadth of "religion" and "conscience" are also *limited* in the state constitutions of Arizona, California, Colorado, Connecticut, Idaho, Illinois, Mississippi, Missouri, Nevada, New York, North Dakota, South Dakota, Washington, and Wyoming. These state constitutions provide that "liberty of conscience does not excuse acts of licentiousness, or justify (or excuse) practices inconsistent with the peace (good order) (morality), and safety of the state (or invading the rights of others")." *See also,* Idaho (Article I § 4) (stating that liberty of conscience cannot be construed to justify "polygamous or other pernicious practices"); Mississippi (Article I, § 18) (stating that the rights secured cannot be construed to "exclude the Holy Bible from use in any public school of this state").

CHAPTER 11: FEDERAL CONSTITUTIONAL RIGHTS

1. U.S. CONST. amend. XIV. The Fourteenth Amendment includes a "fair process" and a "substantive component that provides heightened protection against government interference with certain fundamental rights and liberty interests." *Troxel v. Granville*, 530 U.S. 57, 65 (2000).
2. *W.Va. State Bd. of Educ. v. Barnett*, 319 U.S. 624, 633-34 (1943); *Wooley v. Maynard*, 430 U.S. 705, 714 (1977).
3. *McDonald v. Chicago*, 561 U.S. 742, 764 (2010); *Washington v. Glucksberg*, 521 U.S. 702, 721 (1997).
4. *Saenz v. Roe*, 526 U.S. 489 (1999).
5. *Troxel v. Granville*, 530 U.S. 57 (2000); *Santosky v. Kramer*, 455 U.S. 745 (1982) *Wisconsin v. Yoder*, 406 U.S. 205 (1972); *Pierce v. Soc'y of Sisters*, 268 U.S. 510 (1925); *Meyer v. Nebraska*, 262 U.S. 390 (1923).
6. *Loving v. Virginia*, 388 U.S. 1 (1967) (recognizing the right to marry a person of a different race); *Turner v. Safley*, 482 U.S. 78 (1987) (recognizing the right to marry while in prison); *Obergefell v. Hodges*, 576 U.S. 644 (2015) (recognizing the right to marry a person of the same sex). Compare, *Reynolds v. U.S.*, 98 U.S. 145 (1878) (holding that polygamy [having more than one wife] as a Mormon's religious duty was not a defense to a criminal indictment for bigamy [having two wives]).
7. *Skinner v. Oklahoma ex rel. Williamson*, 316 U.S. 535 (1942).
8. *Griswold v. Connecticut*, 381 U.S. 479 (1965).
9. *Stanley v. Georgia*, 394 U.S. 557 (1969); *Osborne v. Ohio*, 495 U.S. 103 (1990); *Paris Adult Theatre v. Slayton*, 413 U.S. 49 (1973). However, obscenity is "unprotected speech" under the Free Speech Clause. *Roth v. U.S.*, 354 U.S. 476 (1957).
10. *Moore v. E. Cleveland*, 431 U.S. 494 (1977).
11. *Cantwell v. Connecticut*, 310 U.S. 296, 303 (1940) (discussing the incorporation of these rights through the Due Process Clause of the Fourteenth Amendment).
12. *Barron ex rel. Tiernan v. Mayor of Baltimore*, 7 Pet. 243, 247-251 (1833).
13. *Gitlow v. New York*, 268 U.S. 652 (1925).
14. In other words, the federal constitution expressly restricts Congress. In some cases, the restriction on Congress has been implied to the states when the first eight amendments are involved. As a result, some cases involve an implied right and an implied restriction. Several U.S. Supreme Court justices and legal scholars have been critical of this method. Some argue that it compromises the separation of powers doctrine. Others say it gives the U.S. Supreme Court veto power on matters that were left to the states under the Tenth Amendment. Despite any shortcomings, we have had implied rights and implied restrictions for nearly 100 years. For a list of federal constitutional rights that have been made applicable to state and local governments, *see* Cornell Law School, LII Legal Information Institute at https://www.law.cornell.edu/wex/incorporation_doctrine.
15. *Wisconsin v. Yoder*, 406 U.S. 205, 232-233 (1972) (citing, *Meyer v. Nebraska*, 262 U.S. 390 (1923)).
16. *Wisconsin v. Yoder*, 406 U.S. 205, 232-233 (1972).
17. *Meyer v. Nebraska*, 262 U.S. 390, 401 (1923).
18. *Pierce v. Soc'y of Sisters*, 268 U.S. 510, 534 (1925).
19. *Santosky v. Kramer*, 455 U.S. 745, 753 (1982).
20. *Troxel v. Granville*, 530 U.S. 57, 60 (2000).
21. *Wisconsin v. Yoder*, 406 U.S. 205, 213-214 (1972).
22. *Wisconsin v. Yoder*, 406 U.S. 205, 213-214 (1972).
23. *Meyer v. Nebraska*, 262 U.S. 390 (1923); *Pierce v. Soc'y of Sisters*, 268 U.S. 510 (1925); *Wisconsin v. Yoder*, 406 U.S. 205 (1972); *Santosky v. Kramer*, 455 U.S. 745 (1982); *Troxel v. Granville*, 530 U.S. 57 (2000).
24. Incorporation by reference is "the method of making one document of any kind become part of another separate document by referring to the former in the latter, and declaring that the former shall be taken and considered as part of the latter the same as if it were fully set out therein." *Black's Law Dictionary, Sixth Edition*, West Publishing Co., St. Paul, Minnesota (1990), pp. 766-767.
25. *Cantwell v. Connecticut*, 310 U.S. 296, 303 (1940).
26. *Frazee v. Illinois Dep't of Emp't Sec.*, 489 U.S. 829 (1989).
27. *Torasco v. Watkins*, 367 U.S. 488 (1961).
28. *U.S. v. Seeger*, 380 U.S. 163 (1965).
29. *Emp't Div. v. Smith* 494 U.S. 872 (1990) (citing *U.S. v. Ballard*, 322 U.S. 78 (1944)).
30. *Kennedy v. Bremerton Sch. Dist.*, 597 U.S. ___, 142 S. Ct. 2407, fn. 1 (2022) (emphasis added) (citing *Emp't Div., Dept. of Hum. Res. of Oregon v. Smith*, 494 U.S. 872, 877 (1990)).
31. *Kennedy v. Bremerton Sch. Dist.*, 597 U.S. ___, 142 S. Ct. 2407, fn. 1 (2022) (citing *Emp't Div., Dept. of Hum. Resources of Ore. v. Smith*, 494 U.S. 872, 877 (1990)).
32. *Sherbert v. Verner*, 374 U.S. 398 (1963); *Wisconsin v. Yoder*, 406 U.S. 205 (1972).

33 *Emp't Div. v. Smith*, 494 U.S. 872 (1990). *See also, Kennedy v. Bremerton Sch. Dist.*, 597 U.S. __, 142 S. Ct. 2407, fn. 1 (2022); (stating that "[a] plaintiff may also prove a free exercise violation by showing that "official expressions of hostility" to religion accompany laws or policies burdening religious exercise; in cases like that we have "set aside" such policies without further inquiry. *Masterpiece Cakeshop, Ltd. v. Colorado Civil Rts. Comm'n*, 584 U.S. ___, ___ (2018) (slip op., at 18)").
34 Religious Freedom Restoration Act of 1993, Pub. L. No. 103-141, 107 Stat. 1488 (November 16, 1993), codified at 42 U.S.C. §§ 2000bb through 2000bb-4.
35 The House bill was introduced by Congressman Chuck Schumer (D-NY), and a companion Senate bill was introduced by Ted Kennedy (D-MA). Only three Senate members voted against the bill.
36 *City of Boerne v. Flores*, 521 U.S. 507 (1997).
37 *Wisconsin v. Yoder*, 406 U.S. 205 (1972); *Emp't Div. v. Smith*, 494 U.S. 872 (1990).
38 *Kennedy v. Bremerton Sch. Dist.*, 597 U.S. __, 142 S. Ct. 2407 (2022); *Widmar v. Vincent*, 454 U.S. 263, 269, n. 6 (1981); *Rosenberger v. Rector and Visitors of Univ. of Va.*, 515 U.S. 819, 841 (1995).
39 *Carson v. Makin*, 596 U.S. ___, 142 S. Ct. 1987 (2022); *Espinoza v. Montana Department of Revenue*, 591 U.S. ___ (2020) (holding that the state could not exclude religious schools from private aid programs "solely because of their religious character").
40 *Carson v. Makin*, 596 U.S. ___, 142 S. Ct. 1987 (2022) (citing Me. Rev. Stat. Ann., Tit. 20–A, §2951(2)).
41 These three situations apply in the federal courts and state courts that follow the decisions of the federal courts. *Fulton v. City of Philadelphia*, 141 S. Ct. 1868, 593 U.S. __ (2021).
42 *City of Boerne v. Flores*, 521 U.S. 507 (1997) (holding that the federal RFRA could not be applied to the states; rather, it only applied to federal laws and federal government infringements on the free exercise of religion guaranteed under the federal constitution). *See also, Gonzales v. O Centro Espírita Beneficente União do Vegetal*, 546 U.S. 418 (2006) (holding that under the federal RFRA, the government did not demonstrate a "compelling interest" in prosecuting a religious group for drinking a sacramental tea made from plants in the Amazon Rainforest that contain a Schedule 1 controlled substance); *Burwell v. Hobby Lobby Stores, Inc.*, 573 U.S. 682 (2014) (holding that under RFRA, a privately held for-profit corporations can be exempt from a regulation that its owners object to on religious grounds if there is a less restrictive means of furthering the government's interest).
43 The Becket website also tracks the state versions of the federal Religious Land Use and Institutionalized Persons Act of 2000, 42 U.S. Code §§ 2000cc, et seq., or http://www.justice.gov/crt/religious-land-use-and-institutionalized-persons-act, which protects individuals, houses of worship, and other religious institutions from certain types of discrimination.
44 For example, the Civil Rights Act of 1964 has at least two "Titles" that prevent religious discrimination. P.L. 88-352, 78 Stat. 241. Title VI prohibits discrimination based on "race, color, religion, sex, or national origin" and applies to any program or activity that receives federal financial assistance, which includes public schools. 42 U.S.C. § 2000d et seq. Title VII *prohibits employment discrimination based on a worker's race, color, gender, religion, or national origin.* 42 U.S.C. § 2000e et seq. Title VII can apply to federal, state, and private-sector employers. Both titles have a reporting process and are enforced by federal agencies. Title VI is enforced by the Office of Civil Rights ("OCR") when the discrimination is in a public school (i.e., because the federal assistance is from the U.S. Dept. of Education). Title VII is enforced by the Equal Employment Opportunity Commission ("EEOC"). Agency leadership often changes with each new President. Please note that all federal laws are open to constitutional challenges and, at the end of the day, they must not conflict with the rights protected under the U.S. Constitution.
45 Also, Congress can pass a bill to block an executive order. If the bill is vetoed by the President (which is likely), Congress can override it — if possible.
46 *Quick Bear v. Leupp*, 210 U.S. (1908) (upholding tuition grants for Sioux Indians attending Catholic school); *Bradfield v. Roberts*, 175 U.S. 291 (1899) (upholding federal funds given to Catholic hospitals); *Everson v. Board of Educ.*, 330 U.S. (1947) (upholding reimbursement plan for parents for the cost of transporting their children to and from religious schools).
47 *Lemon v. Kurtzman*, 403 U.S. 602 (1971).
48 *Kennedy v. Bremerton Sch. Dist.*, 597 U.S. __, 142 S. Ct. 2407 (2022) (stating that the Court "abandoned *Lemon* and its endorsement test offshoots [in] ... *Town of Greece v. Galloway*, 572 U.S. 565, 575-577 (2014)").
49 *Kennedy v. Bremerton Sch. Dist.*, 597 U.S. __, 142 S. Ct. 2407 (2022).
50 *Mozert v. Hawkins*, 827 F.2d 1058 (6th Cir. 1987) (the Sixth Circuit Court holding that public schools can teach religious material to students if they are not endorsing, condoning, or encouraging any aspect of a student's faith). The states within the Sixth Circuit include Kentucky, Michigan, Ohio, and Tennessee. *Wood v. Arnold*, 321 F. Supp. 3d 565, (4th Cir. 2018) (Fourth Circuit Court holding

that the context of public school instruction about Islam and the way it was presented did not violate the student's right to free exercise of religion). The states within the Fourth Circuit include Maryland, North Carolina, South Carolina, Virginia, and West Virginia.
51   20 U.S. Code § 4071. See also, *Westside Cmty. Bd. of Educ. v. Mergens*, 496 U.S. 226 (1990).
52   *Zorach v. Clauson*, 343 U.S. 306 (1952) (upholding the constitutionality of released time programs for religious instruction for public school students during the school day).
53   Alabama, New York, Ohio, South Dakota, Utah, Wisconsin, and others have laws permitting released time programs for religious instruction.
54   For example, *see* Released Time Jewish Hour (https://www.jewishhour.org/); and Lifewise Academy (https://www.lifewiseacademy.org/).
55   *Reynolds v. U.S.*, 98 U.S. 145, 164 (1878); *Everson v. Bd. of Educ.*, 330 U.S. 1 (1947).
56   *Wallace v. Jaffree*, 472 U.S. 38 (1985).
57   *Wallace v. Jaffree*, 472 U.S. 39, 92 (1985) (Rehnquist, J., dissenting).
58   *Wallace v. Jaffree*, 472 U.S. 39, 107 (1985) (Rehnquist, J., dissenting).
59   *Wallace v. Jaffree*, 472 U.S. 39, 107 (1985) (Rehnquist, J., dissenting) (emphasis added).
60   *Zorach v. Clauson*, 343 U.S. 306, 312 (1952).
61   *Zorach v. Clauson*, 343 U.S. 306, 312-313 (1952).
62   D. Elton Trueblood was an American author, theologian, and chaplain at Harvard and Stanford Universities.
63   *Cantwell v. Connecticut*, 310 U.S. 296, 303 (1940) (discussing the incorporation of these rights through the Due Process Clause of the Fourteenth Amendment).
64   *Tinker v. Des Moines Indep. Cmty. Sch. Dist.*, 393 U.S. 503 (1969) (holding that students wearing black armbands in school to protest government policies constituted protected speech).
65   *Texas v. Johnson*, 491 U.S. 397 (1989) (holding that a Texas law prohibiting flag desecration was unconstitutional).
66   *Kennedy v. Bremerton Sch. Dist.*, 597 U.S. ___, 142 S. Ct. 2407 (2022); *Widmar v. Vincent*, 454 U.S. 263, 269, n. 6 (1981); *Rosenberger v. Rector and Visitors of Univ. of Va.*, 515 U.S. 819, 841 (1995).
67   *W.Va. State Bd. of Educ. v. Barnett*, 319 U.S. 624 (1943) (holding that state law requiring public school students to salute the American flag is unconstitutional).
68   *Simon & Schuster, Inc. v. Members of the New York State Crime Victims Board*, 502 U.S. 105 (1991); *Brown v. Entertainment Merchants Ass'n*, 131 S. Ct. 2729 (2011).
69   *Roth v. U.S.*, 354 U.S. 476 (1957) (holding that obscenity is unprotected speech); *Ginsburg v. New York*, 390 U.S. 629 (1968) (holding that states may use a different definition of obscenity for material deemed harmful to minors than the definition of obscenity for adults).
70   *Bd. of Tr. of State Univ. of New York v. Fox*, 492 U.S. 469 (1989).
71   *Terminiello v. Chicago*, 337 U.S. 1 (1949).
72   *Terminiello v. Chicago*, 337 U.S. 1, 4-5 (1949) *See also, Reed v. Town of Gilbert*, 576 U.S. 155, 179 (2015) (stating that "whenever government disfavors one kind of speech, it places that speech at a disadvantage, potentially interfering with the free marketplace of ideas and with an individual's ability to express thoughts and ideas that can help that individual determine the kind of society in which he wishes to live, help shape that society, and help define his place within it").
73   *Virginia v. Black*, 538 U.S. 343 (2002).
74   In 2002, the U.S. Supreme Court held that "true threats" of imminent bodily harm are not protected speech. *Virginia v. Black*, 538 U.S. 343 (2002). In 1992, the Court held that hate crime ordinances that apply only to fighting words that provoke violence or insult others on the basis of race, religion, and gender are invalid. *R.A.V. v. City of St. Paul*, 505 U.S. 377 (1992). The U.S. Supreme Court further held that restrictions on "opprobrious words," "abusive language," and "annoying conduct" are unconstitutional because these are not fighting words. *Gooding v. Wilson*, 405 U.S. 518 (1972). Regarding comments from the crowd around a speaker, the U.S. Supreme Court stated that a heckler's response to constitutionally protected speech does not render the speech "unprotected." *Gregory v. Chicago*, 394 U.S. 111 (1969). The U.S. Supreme Court held that "the constitutional guarantees of free speech and free press do not permit a state to forbid or prosecute advocacy of the use of force or of law violation except where such advocacy is directed to inciting or producing imminent lawless action and is likely to incite or produce such action." *Brandenburg v. Ohio*, 395 U.S. 444 (1969). Advocating the violent overthrow of the government is not protected speech. *Dennis v. U.S.*, 341 U.S. 494 (1951).
75   This right is separate from the Fifth Amendment right to remain silent in a criminal case and not be "a witness against [one]self." U.S. CONST. amend. V.
76   *Pacific Gas & Elec. Co. v. Public Utils. Comm'n*, 475 U.S. 1, 11 (1986).

77 *Pacific Gas & Elec. Co. v. Public Utils. Comm'n*, 475 U.S. 1, 11 (1986) (emphasis in original); *Harper & Row Publishers, Inc. v. Nat'l Enters.*, 471 U.S. 539, 559 (1985); *Estate of Hemingway v. Random House, Inc.*, 244 N.E.2d 250, 255 (N.Y. 1968).
78 *Rumsfeld v. Forum for Acad. & Institutional Rts., Inc.*, 547 U.S. 47, 61 (2006).
79 *Knox v. SEIU, Local 1000*, 567 U.S. 298, 309 (2012).
80 *W.Va. State Bd. of Educ. v. Barnett*, 319 U.S. 624, 633-34 (1943).
81 *W.Va. State Bd. of Educ. v. Barnett*, 319 U.S. 624 (1943). *See also, Wooley v. Maynard*, 430 U.S. 705 (1977) (holding that the government could not punish a motorist for blocking the phrase "Live Free or Die" from his license plate if the identifying numbers and letters on the plate were visible).
82 *Kennedy v. Bremerton Sch. Dist.*, 597 U.S. ___, 142 S. Ct. 2407 (2022); *Widmar v. Vincent*, 454 U.S. 263, 269, n. 6 (1981); *Rosenberger v. Rector and Visitors of Univ. of Va.*, 515 U.S. 819, 841 (1995). *See also,* Taruschio, Anna M., *The First Amendment, The Right Not To Speak And The Problem of Government Access Statutes*, Fordham Urban Law Journal, Vol. 27, No. 3 (2000).
83 *Perry Educ. Ass'n v. Perry v. Educators' Ass'n*, 460 U.S. 37 (1983).
84 Terry, Marc L., *First Amendment at Board Meetings: Protect Your Citizens' Free Speech Rights at Your Meetings*, National School Board Association, October 1, 2019.
85 *Good News Club v. Milford Cent. Sch.*, 533 U.S. 98 (2001).
86 *Bethel Sch. Dist. v. Fraser*, 478 U.S. 675 (1986); *Morse v. Frederick*, 551 U.S. 393 (2007).
87 *U.S. v. Albertini*, 472 U.S. 675 (1985); *Flower v. U.S.*, 407 U.S. 197 (1972).
88 *U.S. v. Kokinda*, 497 U.S. 720 (1990).
89 *Bethel Sch. Dist. v. Fraser*, 478 U.S. 675 (1986).
90 *Bethel Sch. Dist. v. Fraser*, 478 U.S. 675 (1986).
91 *Morse v. Frederick*, 551 U.S. 393 (2007).
92 *Bethel Sch. Dist. v. Fraser*, 478 U.S. 675 (1986).
93 *Hazelwood Sch. Dist. v. Kuhlmeier*, 484 U.S. 260 (1988).
94 *Tinker v. Des Moines Indep. Cmty. Sch. Dist.*, 393 U.S. 503 (1969).
95 *Tinker v. Des Moines Indep. Cmty. Sch. Dist.*, 393 U.S. 503 (1969).

ACKNOWLEDGEMENTS

1 "*The Office*," Daniel's Deedle-Dee Productions and Reveille Productions, the American version, Season Five, Episode 23 (2009). For those who do not watch "The Office," the phrase is a comic misstatement of the phrase "how the tables have turned."

ABOUT THE AUTHOR

An attorney with over three decades of experience in law and education, **Kelly Himes Brolly** graduated with distinction from the University of North Carolina at Chapel Hill, with an undergraduate degree in early childhood education with a concentration in social studies. After three years of teaching in the public school system, she attended Seton Hall University School of Law, and graduated *cum laude*. While in law school, Kelly was a National Moot Court Competitor, the Director of the Moot Court Board, and a judicial intern for the Chief Judge of the United States District Court, District of New Jersey.

Kelly was admitted to the Pennsylvania and New Jersey bars in 1994 and began her litigation practice as a judicial clerk for a trial judge in Center City Philadelphia. Thereafter, she gained extensive litigation experience at Fox Rothschild, LLP, a large nationally-ranked law firm. After moving to Georgia, Kelly became involved in education legislation, full-time clinic coverage, public school funding, charter systems, charter schools, school system policy, and various federal programs for students such as 504 Plans and Individualized Education Plans. Kelly added to her bar admissions when she was admitted to practice in Georgia in 2016. Thereafter, she worked for a firm in Roswell, Georgia, representing clients in education law matters.

Well-versed in trial and appellate work, in 2019 Kelly co-authored an *amicus curiae* (friend of the court) brief submitted to the United States Supreme Court on a federal constitutional issue. In addition to three state bars, she is admitted to practice before several United States District Courts as well as the Court of Appeals of the Third Circuit and the Supreme Court of the United States.

HOW TO WORK WITH KELLY

Kelly Himes Brolly, of Double Umbrella Publications, LLC, offers writing, podcast, and consulting services.
For more information and to make quantity purchases, visit www.doubleumbrellapublications.com.

DOUBLE UMBRELLA PUBLICATIONS, LLC

Made in the USA
Middletown, DE
18 April 2023